Second Edition

TOP 10 RULES OF ETHICS FOR PARALEGALS

Deborah K. Orlik

Prentice Hall

Boston   Columbus   Indianapolis   New York   San Francisco   Upper Saddle River
Amsterdam   Cape Town   Dubai   London   Madrid   Milan   Munich   Paris   Montreal   Toronto
Delhi   Mexico City   Sao Paulo   Sydney   Hong Kong   Seoul   Singapore   Taipei   Tokyo

Editor in Chief: Vernon Anthony
Senior Acquisitions Editor: Gary Bauer
Editorial Assistant: Megan Heintz
Director of Marketing: David Gesell
Marketing Manager: Leigh Ann Sims
Marketing Assistant: Les Roberts
Production Manager: Kathy Sleys
Creative Director: Jayne Conte
Cover Designer: Margaret Kenselaar

Manager, Cover Visual Research & Permissions:
Karen Sanatar
Cover Art: Christine Balderas / IStock Exclusive /
Getty Images, Inc.
Full-Service Project Management: Integra
Composition: Integra Software Services
Printer/Binder/Cover Printer: Courier Companies
Text Font: 10/12, Minion

Library of Congress Cataloging-in-Publication Data

Orlik, Deborah K.
  Top 10 rules of ethics for paralegals / Deborah K. Orlik. — 2nd ed.
    p. cm.
  Originally published: Ethics : top ten rules for paralegals. c2006.
  Includes index.
  ISBN-13: 978-0-13-506393-4 (alk. paper)
  ISBN-10: 0-13-506393-0 (alk. paper)
  1. Legal ethics—United States.   2. Legal assistants—United States—Handbooks, manuals, etc.
I. Orlik, Deborah K. Ethics : top ten rules for paralegals.   II. Title.   III. Title: Top ten rules
of ethics for paralegals.
  KF306.O75 2011
  174'.30973—dc22

                                                                    2010000008

2 3 4 5 6 7 8 9 10   V088   14 13 12

Prentice Hall
is an imprint of

www.pearsonhighered.com

ISBN 10:   0-13-506393-0
ISBN 13: 978-0-13-506393-4

CONTENTS

RULE 3 GET AND STAY COMPETENT   33

RULE 4 CHARGE ONLY FAIR FEES   49

RULE 5   MAKE LEGAL SERVICES AVAILABLE   71

RULE 6   REPRESENT EACH CLIENT WITH DILIGENCE AND DEDICATION . . . WITHIN THE BOUNDS OF THE LAW   85

RULE 7 DON'T PRACTICE LAW WITHOUT A LICENSE   103

RULE 8 BE LOYAL TO EACH AND EVERY CLIENT   127

PREFACE

It is my fondest desire that you enjoy this book and the study of ethics it presents. To me, there is little more fascinating than a convoluted ethical issue. You're thinking: Get a life. Perhaps—but, ask any teacher: Ethics is one of the best subjects to teach, primarily because there are so many "right" answers. I think it is fun to learn for the same reason. As you are reading this book, you must be taking an ethics (or professional responsibility) course, an Introduction to Law or Introduction to Paralegal Studies course, or perhaps a course on law office practices. Good! You're going to enjoy ethics!

You'll enjoy this book, in particular, because it is written in a no-nonsense, low-fluff manner. There are some sensitive areas to discuss in ethics, and we discuss them here in a one-on-one (just you and me), up-front, and otherwise hyphenated manner. I try to use humor, or at least a light-hearted approach (which is also hyphenated) to make the subject, well, more fun to read. The discussions are still as important and as deep, but the approach is not weighted down with legalese (although there may be an excess of hyphens!). If you can, imagine you and I are having a conversation. Read what I have to say and then stop and respond to me—as if we were talking in real time. During this discussion, you and I will cover the ethics topics you need to be familiar with to succeed in the paralegal profession at a reasonable price. Can't ask for better than that.

In this second edition, I've moved some sections from one Rule to another and included several more sections. Most of these are in response to the comments I have received from teachers and students along the lines of, "Hey! Where's the section on ___?" Rather than respond, as I have been, "That's discussed in my other textbook: *Ethics for the Legal Professional*," I've included them in here, in the second edition. If there is something you think ought to be added, just google my name and send me an e-mail.

CHANGES IN THIS EDITION

In the second edition, as in *Ethics for the Legal Professional*, I've completely abandoned that general discussion of the ABA Model Rules that you'll find in all of the other ethics textbooks in favor of a targeted discussion of the Rules of Professional Conduct of *your* state. If you are in California, the table in Appendix A will help you get from the Rules of Professional Conduct numbers (adopted by 49 states) to the various rules of California professional responsibility law. (I firmly believe that California will change to the ABA Rule format sometime . . . in the next . . . well, sometime.) This book is just getting better and you're not going to find another like it. Here's a complete list of what else has been changed.

There is a huge change in the approach to researching answers throughout the book. Although this may make the course of study longer, these research assignments (using the Internet) are a crucial part of the promise we have made—that the student will know how to research the answers to ethical questions by the end of the course of study. These research assignments should be added to the ethics notebook you are going to make.

We have provided much more in the way of backup information on the publisher's Web site. These are cases and articles chosen to add substance to the course of study as well as to give the student some practice in reading cases without requiring more research.

Throughout the book, cases have been updated along with references in the What Do You Think? and Law Firm Spotlight boxes in the text. Many 2009 cases have been newly provided as examples.

Additionally, some parts of the book have been moved:

The discussion about intimate relations between clients and lawyers has been moved from Rule #1 on Integrity to Rule # 8 on Conflicts of Interest.

The discussion of Referral Fees has been relocated from Rule #4 to Rule #5.

The discussion of Courtesy to the Court has been moved from Rule #6 to Rule #10.

And here is a list of what has been added:

The discussion on reporting misconduct has been expanded in Rule #1 along with the section on stress and alcohol and drug abuse.

In Rule #3, we've expanded the section on Good Faith as a Defense to professional negligence.

In Rule #3, we've included a new section on Keeping Track of Time and "padded" the section on padding timesheets!

In Rule #5, you will find a new section on Runners and Cappers.

Rule #6 has a new section on Fairness to Opposing Counsel.

Rule #7 has a new section on Asking Questions under the general category of things that are *not* UPL.

Rule #8 has a new section on Family and Friends.

Although our study of "ethics" is the study of rules of law and not the study of "morals," everyone in the legal profession must be prepared to use your own morality, your own thresholds of right and wrong, to discuss the scenarios in this book. This is a good thing because it is your morality that you take with you into the workplace. This course of study will give you an opportunity to take out some feelings and opinions you may not have used in a while, dust them off, and get them ready to go to work.

No one book can provide the answers to all ethical issues. But this text will give you a starting place. By the end of your course of study, you should be able to (1) identify an ethical issue, (2) put it into a general category—one of the Top Ten Rules, and (3) know where to start researching the answer to your particular issue. This is our promise. In this second edition, we've included more Internet research assignments for the student so that our third promise (the one about researching) is addressed more thoroughly.

Your goal, then, is to engrave these 10 rules of ethics on your arm, or somewhere else where you won't lose or forget them. My goal is to make that something you really want to do because you enjoy the textbook and the discussions that it engenders. The goal of the paralegal profession is this: Protect the public.

This is very important: Before you begin, go get a copy of your state's Rules of Professional Conduct that you can keep and annotate. You can study the ABA Model Rules or Model Codes all you want, but in the final analysis, those models are not the law. They are only models, examples that your state used when it created and codified its own rules of professional responsibility (except, of course, unless you're in California where neither of those models applies). Get a copy of your state's Rules of Professional Conduct for lawyers and get all of that itty-bitty print enlarged. (If you need help finding this body of law in your state, look in Appendix B for a chart that will help you find it on the Internet.) Buy a 3-ring binder to create a notebook where you can divide your state's codes into the categories of your Top Ten Rules. Divide your notebook into 10 sections and add cases, articles, and your notes to each section as you study this book. Okay! Now you're ready. Good luck.

RESOURCES FOR STUDENTS

Companion Web site: www.pearsonhighered. com/orlik

The *Ethics for the Legal Professional 7e* companion Web site contains useful tools to help students learn and apply key concepts and extend their knowledge, including state-specific resources, links to online resources, and practice quizzes and the video case studies in the textbook.

RESOURCES FOR INSTRUCTORS

The following instructor supplements are available for download from the Pearson Instructor's Resource Center. To access supplementary materials online, instructors need to request an instructor access code. Go to *www.pearsonhighered.com/irc*, where you can register for an instructor access code. Within 48 hours of registering, you will receive a confirming e-mail including an instructor access code. Once you have received your code, locate your text in the online catalog and click on the Instructor Resources button on the left side of the catalog product page. Select a supplement and a log-in page will appear. Once you have logged in, you can access instructor material for all Prentice Hall textbooks

Instructor's Manual

The instructor's manual, written by the author, contains Sections with the author's general thoughts about teaching ethics, sample syllabi, lesson plans, notes on teaching methods and tools, and lesson lecture suggestions for each chapter of the text, including activities, assessment suggestions, and answers to end of chapter review questions.

Powerpoint Lecture Presentation

The PowerPoint Lecture Presentation includes key concept screens and exhibits from the textbook.

ACKNOWLEDGMENT

Thank you to the many people who read, reviewed and used this text (reviewers, stutents, program directors, book adopters and family members.) your comments, as always, have helped me write a better textbook.

INTRODUCTION

Why do we have to study ethics? Hmmmm . . . good question. The first reason is that it is required. In order to be accredited by various institutions, your paralegal education must include the study of ethics. The second reason is although it may seem like an intuitive subject, the study of *legal ethics* is not the same as the study of "ethics" that you might find in a philosophy program. The study of legal ethics is the study of rules of law. These are rules of law that you must know to be a successful paralegal. You must know them because others around you may not know them. You must know them for day-to-day survival in your new profession. And, you might find that learning them is kind of fun and leads to all sorts of interesting and exciting discussions.

Legal ethics is also known as "professional responsibility." Lawyers have been writing laws about professional responsibility—about their responsibilities to the judicial system, to the public, and to each other—for over a century. Luckily, we don't have to study the really old laws.

Our study necessarily includes the American Bar Association (ABA). The ABA is a voluntary organization of lawyers. You should take a look at its Web site—*www.abanet.org*—to see all of the things that it does. For our purposes, however, the ABA does two things: (1) It has written a document for lawyers regarding the proper use of paralegals, and (2) it has provided model laws dealing with professional responsibility applicable to both lawyers and paralegals.

The way this drafting works is this: Some members of the ABA who are knowledgeable in any particular subject get together and draft some sample laws, called Codes or Rules, and then they provide these samples (models) to the state legislatures for their consideration. This saves the states from having to spend the resources to draft their own rules, and it provides for some continuity in the rules from state to state. They do this on all sorts of subjects, but we're only concerned about the ones they have written about legal ethics.

The ABA produced its first rules of professional responsibility in 1908. We won't bother with them. The second group of Rules it drafted is called the Model Code of Professional Responsibility. The Model Code had nine **canons** and each canon had a set of Ethical Considerations and Disciplinary Rules. You will see them referred to as ECs and DRs. The ECs are aspirational. They set forth the reasons for the canons and contain guidelines that you may want to consider when making ethical choices. The DRs are exactly that. If a DR is violated, discipline by the appropriate authority is likely. The Model Code was written in the 1960s, and for many years, many of the states adopted Rules of Professional Conduct that were modeled after this format: the Canon, Ethical Consideration, and Disciplinary Rule. You need to know this because when you are researching the law in cases, if the case is prior to the time your state updated its ethical rules, the case will talk about Canons, ECs, and DRs. These cases, although old, may be just as valid as newer cases. All you have to be able to do is "translate" that EC or DR into the Rule number your state is using now. You'll be able to do that by categorizing the Canon, EC, or DR into one of the Top Ten Rules of ethics and then update to the Rule your state is using now.

Let's take an example of how that would work. Let's say you are researching attorney negligence (aka malpractice) and you locate a case from 1975 that talks about what it means to be "competent" (the opposite of negligent), but the code the opinion cites is EC 1-1. That's okay! Because you know that the rule on competence that your state currently uses is Rule 1.1. You can still use that case (assuming it hasn't been overruled or something) and make a note (or footnote) of the fact that EC 1-1 is the equivalent of the state's new Rule of Professional Conduct 1.1.

In the 1980s, the ABA wrote a revised model. This one is called the Model Rules of Professional Conduct. The format of this model is entirely different. The idea of the canons was abandoned. The Rule is stated in the form of an ordinary rule, and then Comments are provided that help you interpret and use the Rule in context. The Rule may be subject to many interpretations, but the Comments help to narrow them down. All of the states (except for California) have adopted the new format and most of the text of the Rules model. Some states adopted the Comments along with the Rules. Other states did not adopt the Comments. (It makes for a very long document, so when you are photocopying your state's Rules for your 3-ring binder, you may want to consider not copying all of the Comments. You can add some later if they are important.) California, ever the individual, never adopted either format. California has some of its rules in a document called Rules of Professional Conduct, some rules in its Business and Professions Code, and other rules scattered about in other codes. If you are using this book in California, you'll need to refer to Appendix A, where we have provided a translation table—it will you get from the ABA style Rule to the California Rule.

Although you will see the Models referred to in many writings, it is not the ABA's Model that has the force of law. *Only the rules actually adopted by your state have the force of law in your state.* You probably don't want to quote a Model Rule in your work. You always want to refer to your own state's Rules. If this looks a little confusing right now, don't worry. There are many examples in the text you are about to read that will help clarify this stuff.

Periodically, the ABA amends its Model Rules. After the amendments are written, they are offered up to the states for consideration. Your state may be in the process of amending its rules of professional responsibility to adopt some of the changes suggested by the ABA, so you should be on the lookout for changes in this law. You should always be on the lookout anyway because the law changes every day by statutory changes and case law changes. The law is a moving target. That's part of what makes it so much fun!

FINDING THE LAW IN YOUR STATE

Finding the law on ethics isn't always easy, but if you walk step by step through the Top Ten Rules and do the Internet and library exercises suggested, by the time you've reached Rule #10, you'll have all of the research tricks down cold. The first place you'd want to look (go look right now) is the table in Appendix B that tells you where to find your state's Rules of Professional Conduct and explains the numbering system to you. The ABA's numbering system begins with 1.1 and then goes to 1.2, and so on. Your state uses either the identical numbering system or something very close. If you are in Florida or Missouri, for example, your numbering system looks like the standard ABA except you need to put a 4- in front of the number. So, where I say "Look at Rule 1.1," you need to look at your Rule 4-1.1. Pretty easy, right? Texas has this thing about two-digit numbers, so where I say "Look at Rule 1.1," in Texas your rule will be 1.01. Go figure. Here's one more thing to keep in mind: Your state may have created an extra rule or two that the ABA did not include in its Model Rules. That would cause the numbering of the Rules in your state to be slightly different from the Rule you'll be given in this book. So, where I say "Look at Rule 7.3 on ***" and you look there and your state's 7.3 isn't about that subject, look at the next Rule (7.4) or the one before (7.2). It will be around there somewhere close. Also, remember, your state may not have adopted every single Rule that is in the ABA Model. We're going to talk about one of those right away in Chapter 1.

You need to concentrate on your state's rules of ethics. You can find your state's Rules online, and we've provided a link for you on the publisher's Web site as well as the URL in Appendix B. When you're reading this book, always keep a dictionary and your state rules 3-ring binder with you.

You probably want to see the ABA publication called *Model Guidelines for the Utilization of Legal Assistant Services.* It was last revised in February 2004. You can see it in pdf format on the ABA's Web site, *www.abanet.org.*

Have Integrity

WHY START HERE?

If you're wondering why Rule #1 is "have integrity," the answer is this: If we don't have integrity, the rest of the rules are useless. Integrity means steadfast adherence to an ethical code, and that's what you will be asked to have when you enter the legal profession. All of the Top Ten Rules require steadfast adherence. That's the beginning. Rule #1 includes our duty (if we actually have one) to report our own misconduct and that of others, the pervasive problems stemming from drug and alcohol abuse, and sexual harassment in the workplace. If all of these topics seem dark or depressing to you, here's the good news: For the most part, legal professionals are good people. They enter the field of law, just as you are, out of a desire to help people—to help the public. The topics we discuss in Rule #1 are things that you must know so that you can recognize the issue if it comes up and so that you know how to deal with it. That's the other good news: After reading about Rule #1, you'll be prepared to face these issues in the (we hope) rare instance that they occur.

WE'RE IN CHARGE OF OUR OWN PROFESSION

U.S. Supreme Court Chief Justice Cardozo, as early as 1928, recognized that every person who works in the legal profession has a duty to police the profession for traces of impropriety. In *People ex rel. Karlin v. Culkin*,[1] he wrote: "If the house is to be cleaned, it is for those who occupy and govern it, rather than for strangers, to do the noisome work." What he meant was this: If the legal profession does not want to be judged by laypeople, it will have to police itself. He also wrote that if the legal profession maintains a high standard, it will not be vulnerable to outside criticism.

Who's In Charge Here?

In this book, we're going to be talking about "the regulatory authority," so you have to know who that is in your state. There are three types of states in this regard: states that have an agency called "the state bar" that regulates lawyers, states that have a committee or commission under the supervision of the state supreme court that regulates lawyers, and states where the state bar that regulates lawyers is an agency of the state supreme court. You need to know what kind of state yours is, so go look that up right now. If you are in California, your "regulatory authority" is the State Bar of California. If you are in Ohio, the Supreme Court of Ohio has responsibility for overseeing the practice of law, and the Court has established three offices—Office of Disciplinary Counsel, Board of Commissioners on Grievances & Discipline, and the Client Security Fund; so one of those would most likely be your regulatory authority depending upon the circumstances of the ethical issue. In Florida, the Florida Bar is an official agency of the Supreme Court of Florida, and it is responsible for the lawyer disciplinary system. Go find out about your state. When we talk about "the regulatory authority" in your state, you need to know who we're talking about.

> To find out: Google [*who regulates lawyers in Georgia*]. The third choice down is gabar.org. In that Web site, click on "About the Bar" and learn all about it!

Which Rules Apply to Me?

You are entering the paralegal profession, not the practice of law, so you're asking yourself right now "What do lawyer-rules have to do with me?" Here's the answer: everything! The majority of rules that apply to lawyers also apply to the paralegal—so we're studying them here. Unfortunately, we're going to start out with an exception to that rule right now.

Report Violations—The Lawyer's Duty

We talk about your state's Rules of Professional Conduct in this chapter. If you don't have your own copy of these Rules, go get them right now.

You now have a copy of your state's Rules, so take a look at Rule 8.3. This rule requires lawyers to report violations of the rules of ethics to "the regulatory authority" in order to maintain the integrity of the profession. This is what Chief Justice Cardozo was talking about in *Karlin v. Culkin*, and it is called *self-policing*. Here's a sample of Rule 8.3:

"Shall" is mandatory.

> **Rule 8.3(a)** A lawyer having knowledge that another lawyer has committed a violation of the rules of professional conduct that raises a substantial question as to that lawyer's honesty, trustworthiness or fitness as a lawyer in other respects, **shall** inform the appropriate professional authority.

The rule is easy to understand. If you are a lawyer and you know another lawyer has violated the rules of professional conduct, you need to report that person to the appropriate authority. But the rule is difficult to apply because what looks like a "substantial" question to one person may look trivial to another. Likewise the words "honesty," "trustworthiness," and "fitness." These are words to which we will all apply our own thresholds of morality, so knowing what to report must be a very difficult decision for lawyers. Notice that in the sample Rule 8.3 mentioned earlier, the rule says "shall inform," which means that it is mandatory. You need to look at Rule 8.3 of your state and look for that "shall" because your state's rule may say "should," or "may," making the duty to report discretionary. Some states make reporting mandatory for some really bad things and discretionary for some violations of the rules that are not really bad things. Let's look at an example of that:

Texas Disciplinary Rules of Professional Conduct

Rule 8.03 Reporting Professional Misconduct

(a) Except as permitted in paragraphs (c) or (d), a lawyer having knowledge that another lawyer has committed a violation of applicable rules of professional conduct that raises a substantial question as to that lawyer's honesty, trustworthiness or fitness as a lawyer in other respects, _shall inform_ the appropriate disciplinary authority.

Note that this rule makes some reporting mandatory. It says "shall inform" in the first two sections but makes reporting drug/alcohol abuse discretionary.

(b) Except as permitted in paragraphs (c) or (d), a lawyer having knowledge that a judge has committed a violation of applicable rules of judicial conduct that raises a substantial question as to the judge's fitness for office _shall inform_ the appropriate authority.

(c) A lawyer having knowledge or suspecting that another lawyer or judge whose conduct the lawyer is required to report pursuant to paragraphs (a) or (b) of this Rule is impaired by chemical dependency on alcohol or drugs or by mental illness _may report_ *that person to an approved peer assistance program rather than to an appropriate disciplinary authority.* If a lawyer elects that option, the lawyer's report to the approved peer assistance program shall disclose any disciplinary violations that the reporting lawyer would otherwise have to disclose to the authorities referred to in paragraphs (a) and (b).

(d) This rule does not require disclosure of knowledge or information otherwise protected as confidential information.

And here's the part where confidential information is excluded.

In Texas, then, the duty to report bad acts is absolute, but if the lawyer believes that the bad acts are a result of a drug or alcohol addiction, the lawyer has the choice to report to a place that will help the other lawyer overcome the addiction.

The important thing here is what **your** state rule is, so take a look. If you are looking and looking and you cannot find Rule 8.3, your state may not have adopted a reporting rule. In California, for example, lawyers have a duty to "self-report" certain bad acts. (If you are in California, look at Appendix A right now. You will see that Rule 8.3 translates to Business & Professions Code 6068.) California lawyers have the duty to report themselves to the state bar, for example, if a court sanctions them over $5000. California has always believed in self-reporting, not reporting other lawyers. Interesting, huh?

Report Violations—The Paralegal's Duty

Okay. Let's get down to the important question: "Is there a duty under Rule 8.3 for me to report wrongdoing by anyone in my office?" Answer is: Not a legal duty, no. In other words, there is no case or statute that says that Rule 8.3 applies to paralegals. We started out agreeing that the rules of ethics that apply to lawyers also apply to paralegals and, for the most part, this is true. In this instance, however, because the repercussions of reporting a lawyer can be so devastating, most authorities agree that the paralegal is not bound by Rule 8.3.

However, some paralegal groups advocate applying the rule to you. Bearing in mind that the ethical codes of the paralegal associations do not carry the weight of law (are not enforceable), here is what they say: National Federation of Paralegal Association's Model Code includes two ethical considerations that require reporting misconduct. EC 1-2(f) <u>requires</u> the advising of the proper authority of any trust fund violations by a lawyer, and EC 1-3(d) <u>requires</u> reporting any action by a lawyer that demonstrates fraud, deceit, or dishonesty. You can see that the point of the reporting rule is to protect the public. If you are a paralegal working for a lawyer who is (to take an extreme example) stealing money from clients, do you have a legal duty to report? Or, a slightly different question, if you don't report, are you liable to those clients for their loss? These are such great questions because, truly, there just isn't any case law that holds an answer for us.

Let's change the question a bit to say that the wrongdoer is a paralegal in your firm. Do you have a legal duty to report that the paralegal has done something wrong or illegal? No. There is no legal duty. You may decide that there is a moral duty, but that is a different issue. Only you can answer your own moral questions.

WHAT DO YOU THINK?

What kind of wrongful act would you report? If you saw the file clerk stealing a wallet from a coworker's office, would you report it? Would you still report this theft if the thief was your supervising attorney? Why? Why not? Instead of reporting this conduct, would you confront the wrongdoing file clerk? How about the wrongdoing attorney?

Let's move on from the idea of reporting and go on to the idea of responding to authority's request for information. These reporting rules all exclude reporting any information that is confidential (a concept we tackle in Rule #2), but they otherwise require you to give the information to a *tribunal* that asks for it. So, Hypothetical 1: you are Lawyer A's paralegal, and you have knowledge that he was stealing from clients. When you are called as a witness in the case against A, you must tell the truth. You are not "reporting," you are responding to a lawful request for information. To not tell the truth is "perjury" (a felony in many states). Hypothetical 2: Lawyer A is a client of your law firm and, as part of that representation, he tells you that he was stealing from clients. When you are called as a witness in the case against A, you must . . . . . what? The answer is this: What you know is confidential and protected by the attorney/client privilege, so you cannot give testimony against A—but we tackle this whole issue in Rule #2, discussed in the next chapter.

Tribunal means a court of justice.

How Does This Apply in Real Life?

There is some authority for the proposition that if the lawyer does not report the ethical violations of opposing counsel, that misconduct cannot later be used as the basis for an appeal.[2] So, for example, if you have knowledge that opposing counsel is tampering with the jury or trying to influence jurors in some illegal way, and you don't tell your supervising attorney so that the misconduct can be brought to the attention of the judge, you can't wait for the trial to be over and then, presuming you have lost, use that jury tampering charge to ask for a new trial or an appeal.

WHAT DO YOU THINK?

Is there a flaw in that argument? What would be the likely outcome in your state?

The Threat of Disciplinary Action

It is improper to use the threat of disciplinary action to gain an advantage in a case.[3] In other words, it is improper for you or a lawyer to say to a lawyer, "If you don't agree to these terms, I'm going to report you to the state bar." If the client believes that a lawyer has committed a bad act, it is okay to explain to the client how to go about filing a disciplinary complaint, but it is not proper to encourage the filing of a disciplinary complaint as a tactic in winning. Further, in many states the lawyer "must" (it's mandatory) withdraw from the representation if the client insists on using such a threat.

One of the very few cases where an attorney was actually disciplined for not reporting a lawyer who did something unethical is *In re Himmel*, 533 N.E.2d 790 (Ill. 1988). Here are the facts: Attorney Himmel represented a woman who claimed that another attorney (Casey) had taken off with her money. Himmel agreed to get the money back from Casey in exchange for one-third of the recovery. Casey agreed to settle the case. The settlement agreement that Himmel drafted included the woman's agreement not to initiate any criminal, civil, or disciplinary action against Casey. Himmel was later disciplined for failing to notify the appropriate authorities of Casey's misappropriation of the client's money. The disciplining authority found that Himmel possessed **unprivileged information** of another attorney's misconduct. Himmel's argument that he did not report Casey because his client directed him not to do so was an unacceptable excuse. The opinion pointed out that Himmel's primary duty is to **protect the public** and **assist in maintaining the integrity of the legal profession.** The lawyer cannot get around the rules by saying that he or she was instructed not to tell.

The *Himmel* decision has been cited as authority in other Illinois cases standing for the proposition that the attorney's duty to report is "absolute."

If you don't know what privileged information is, you have to read Rule #2.

Who Are the Proper Authorities?

Once the decision is made to report, to whom should the report be made? Who is the "proper authority"? Some 8.3 rules require lawyers to report to the "regulatory authority." But let's say we're talking about you (the paralegal). In the case of the paralegal, the answer is this: It depends. If you know of something improper going on in your firm or corporation, the proper authority may be found inside the company. Perhaps there is a supervisor, office manager, or ethics committee in charge of allegations of improper conduct. If not, the state bar, district attorney, or attorney general may be the proper authority depending upon the severity of the wrongdoing and who the wrongdoer is. If you are in a state that is regulated by the Supreme Court, there may be a committee or commission there that receives this sort of reporting. The authority to which you should report, however, is not your best friend or the person standing next to you in the elevator. Treat evidence of wrongdoing as confidential information—only speak to the authority to whom you report and keep it to yourself. Taking a mature and responsible position will earn you respect and help you keep your job.

Although there is no authority for the proposition that reporting unethical conduct is mandatory for you as a paralegal, there may be times when you feel that reporting someone else's conduct is the right thing to do. When making a determination about reporting unethical or criminal behavior of another legal professional, consider the following (not exclusive) factors:

1. Do you have all of the facts?
2. Who is being harmed by the behavior? The public?
3. What are your motives for reporting the behavior?
4. Who is the "proper authority" in your law firm?
5. Who is the "proper law enforcement authority" in your state?
6. How much do you need your job? Can you risk retaliation?
7. In your state, is there an affirmative duty to report misconduct?
8. Are there laws in your state that protect "whistle-blowers"?
9. Is there someone else with whom you can discuss the problem to get another perspective? A member of the clergy, doctor, or teacher?
10. Does anyone else have knowledge of the wrong behavior who could support your position?

A case from Pennsylvania (*Brown v. Hammond* [E.D.Pa 1993] 810 F.Supp. 644) suggests that the client is definitely not the proper authority for purposes of reporting misconduct. In that case, the paralegal had evidence that another person in her firm was engaged in "fraudulent overbilling" of a client. The paralegal told the client about the billing fraud and was fired from her job for "blowing the whistle." In the paralegal's wrongful termination action against the employer, the Pennsylvania court said that the paralegal should not have made "gratuitous disclosures" of the alleged misconduct to the affected clients. The court mentioned that there were "proper authorities" and "persons responsible for reporting such conduct or for protecting the public interest" but did not elucidate on who those authorities might be.

The Pennsylvania court also drew a distinction between having evidence of others engaging in unethical billing practices and the paralegal being asked or required to engage in similar practices. The judge wrote that "no employee should be forced to choose between his or her livelihood and engaging in fraud or other criminal conduct." In other words, the Pennsylvania employment laws would offer some protection to the employee who is discharged for refusing to personally commit fraud but will not protect the employee discharged for blowing the whistle on the employer who is committing fraud. Does your state have whistle-blower protection?

We'll talk about this again in Rule #4

GENERAL AND MISCELLANEOUS MISCONDUCT PROHIBITED

The tradition of the legal profession requires us to maintain the highest standards of professional conduct and to encourage others to do so as well. We should be "temperate and dignified" and "refrain from all illegal and morally reprehensible conduct." This is because people who are engaged in the practice of law are held high in the public esteem.

If we want to know what conduct is considered professional misconduct, let's look at your state's Rules more closely to see if they define the specific conduct. Here's a sample:

> **Rule 8.4 Misconduct: It Is Professional Misconduct for a Lawyer to:**
>
> **(a)** violate or attempt to violate the Rules of Professional Conduct, knowingly assist or induce another to do so, or do so through the acts of another;
>
> **(b)** commit a criminal act that reflects adversely on the lawyer's honesty, trustworthiness or fitness as a lawyer in other respects;
>
> **(c)** engage in conduct involving dishonesty, fraud, deceit or misrepresentation;
>
> **(d)** engage in conduct that is prejudicial to the administration of justice;
>
> **(e)** state or imply an ability to influence improperly a government agency or official <u>or to achieve results by means that violate the Rules of Professional Conduct or other law</u>; or
>
> **(f)** knowingly assist a judge or judicial officer in conduct that is a violation of applicable rules of judicial conduct or other law.

General Misconduct and the Paralegal

Case law indicates that under the doctrine of *respondeat superior,* employer-attorneys will be liable for the criminal or other dishonest acts performed by their employee-nonlawyers (including paralegals) under the "course and scope" of the employee's employment. This seems so logical. If the paralegal steals money from the client trust account, it's the lawyer's fault for not properly supervising (or paying attention!). If the paralegal makes a mistake (completely innocently), this will be the lawyer's fault, too. How do we know? The doctrine

This would be a good time to look up your state's rule on "general misconduct," but the bigger question is what does this rule mean in the day-to-day life of a paralegal?

Respondeat superior is Latin for "let the master answer."

of *respondent superior* is just a time-honored rule. If that's not good enough for you, though, take a look at your state's Rule 5.3. Here's a sample:

5.3 Responsibilities Regarding Non-lawyer Assistants

With respect to a nonlawyer employed or retained by or associated with a lawyer:

(a) a partner, and a lawyer who individually or together with other lawyers possesses comparable managerial authority in a law firm, shall make reasonable efforts to ensure that the firm has in effect measures giving reasonable assurance that the person's conduct is compatible with the professional obligations of the lawyer;

(b) a lawyer having direct supervisory authority over the nonlawyer shall make reasonable efforts to ensure that the person's conduct is compatible with the professional obligations of the lawyer; and

(c) a lawyer shall be responsible for conduct of such a person that would be a violation of the Rules of Professional Conduct if engaged in by a lawyer if:

(1) the lawyer orders or, with the knowledge of the specific conduct, ratifies or ignores the conduct involved; or

(2) the lawyer is a partner or has comparable managerial authority in the law firm in which the person is employed, or has direct supervisory authority over the person, and knows of the conduct at a time when its consequences can be avoided or mitigated but fails to take reasonable remedial action.

How cool is that! Do you see how, in sections (a) and (b), the lawyer has the duty to make sure your conduct is compatible with "the professional obligations of the lawyer." That confirms that you are held to the same rules of ethics as the lawyer. And section (c) says that the lawyer is responsible if you (as a paralegal) violate a Rule of Professional Conduct if the lawyer knows or is involved in the conduct or fails to remediate (fix) it. This Rule may come in handy one day. Here's your hypothetical: A lawyer knows that it is a violation of the rules of ethics for him to do a certain action (let's say it's falsify a client's signature on a completely harmless document), but the lawyer thinks that if *you* do it, then it's not a violation of the Rules. (Lawyers can be silly that way.) At this point you whip out your handy-dandy 3-ring binder of Rules of Professional Conduct of the State of [*yourstate*] and point to Rule 5.3. If it would be improper for the lawyer to do it, it's just as improper for you to do it. You are so off the hook!

Be aware, though, that, although traditionally courts punish the lawyer instead of the paralegal for wrongdoing committed while working for a lawyer, this is not always the case. Courts have jurisdiction over you, too. As we will see in Rule #3 on the unauthorized practice of law, a paralegal who practices law without the supervising lawyers knowledge can (and will!) be enjoined, sanctioned by the court, and may face criminal penalties.

Remember: The dishonesty or level of wrongdoing should be viewed not from the vantage point of the attorney or paralegal, but from the viewpoint of the public. "Protect the public" is the legal professional's foremost duty.

Here's an example of how the general misconduct rule works: A lawyer who told the small claims court that money she owed to her landlord had been paid when the lawyer knew that there were insufficient funds in her bank account to cover the check engaged in conduct involving dishonesty, fraud, deceit, or misrepresentation as set forth in Rule 8.4.[4] This was true even though the improper conduct had to do with the lawyer's personal life as opposed to her representation of a client.

"Conduct that is prejudicial to the administration of justice" is so broad that it acts as a backup charge for almost every other instance of wrongdoing (as committing fraud, for example, is prejudicial to the administration of justice) and serves as a catchall for improper conduct that doesn't fit under any other category. In Maryland, a lawyer was suspended indefinitely under this "prejudicial to the administration of justice" category for emailing sexually explicit material to a client.[5]

Stress and Alcohol/Drug Abuse

Let's face it. The legal profession is extremely stressful. And here's another truism: People who are stressed often turn to alcohol and/or drugs. The rules that govern us have provisions designed to protect the public from legal professionals who are physically or mentally incapable of doing their job. Go right now and read your Rule 8.4 (or thereabouts). Find the part that says that it is professional misconduct for a lawyer to "engage in conduct that is prejudicial to the administration of justice." The disciplinary authority of your state can use this clause to discipline an attorney for drug or alcohol addiction. You might want to see if your state's laws include a rule (somewhere in 1.16) that requires the lawyer to withdraw from representation when "the lawyer's physical or mental condition materially impairs the lawyer's ability to represent the client."

The ABA established the Commission on Impaired Attorneys all the way back in 1988.[6] The commission works as an informational bureau for lawyer-impairment issues and programs. The commission has published surveys of lawyer assistance programs, including each state's opinions on confidentiality and immunity rules and case law. These surveys make it clear that the states differ widely on these issues. For example, New York has held that drug addiction may be considered a mitigating factor in attorney discipline.[7] Simultaneously, another state court refused to recognize drug and alcohol addiction as a mitigating factor.[8]

In the 1990s, there was a movement among legal professionals to treat alcoholism and drug dependency as diseases that need to be medically treated. Many states created diversion programs that take the lawyer off the disciplinary track and into a program for counseling, treatment, and monitoring.[9] (See *www.otherbar.org*.) The Utah State Bar Association's Web site reports surveys showing 20% of lawyers and judges suffer from alcohol dependence. Its program "Lawyers Helping Lawyers" is designed as a support mechanism for lawyers suffering from mental illness, substance abuse, or any other disabling condition. You can find out more about this program on the Utah Bar Web site: *www.utahbar.org*. Your state has an organization that assists people in the legal profession with addictions, and you need to know where it is. Often they are called "Lawyer Assistance Program" or "LAP," so log on to your favorite Internet search engine and do a search that looks like this "lawyer assistance program" + [*yourstate*].

There is no doubt that drug and alcohol abuse impairs a person's ability to do competent work. The pervasiveness of the problem is staggering. A survey of managing partners of law firms based in one large U.S. city showed that 82% of the partners polled had worked with a partner with "personal problems" that affected job performance; 39% said that the "personal problem" was alcoholism.[10] In 2002, 120 million Americans 12 years and older reported drinking within 30 days of the survey. That's 51% of our population. Fifty-four million reported binge drinking. If that didn't scare you, this should: About 1 in 7 Americans 12 years or older in 2002 (14.2 percent, or 33.5 million, persons) drove under the influence of alcohol at least once in the 12 months prior to the survey interview.

An estimated 20 million Americans are current users of illicit drugs, meaning they used an illicit drug at least once during the 30 days prior to the interview.[11] That's 8.3% of our population. When we're talking about drugs here, we're not just talking about marijuana or cocaine, although marijuana is the most commonly used illicit drug. "Of the 1.4 million emergency room visits associated with drug misuse in 2005, 31 percent involved illicit drugs only and 27 percent involved pharmaceuticals only. An additional 36 percent involved combinations of illicit drugs, alcohol, and/or pharmaceuticals."[12] Overdose-related emergency room visits are increasing each year. In 2005, there were over 100 million of these emergency room visits. For updated statistics on all sorts of drug- and alcohol-related statistics, go to the Web site of the U.S. Health Department's Substance Abuse and Mental Health Services Administration: *www.samhsa.gov*. For information about drug and alcohol abuse in your state, use this

search: "drug and alcohol abuse" + "*yourstate*" to find the government branch that keeps these statistics.

Nonlawyers who work in the highly stressful legal world are not immune from these pressures. "Paralegal burnout" is as likely to occur as attorney burnout.[13] As a paralegal, you want to be aware of the potential for abuses of drugs and alcohol among our ranks, as well as other signs of mental and emotional deterioration. Help is available if we know where to look for it. Now would be a good time to investigate the various support groups and help lines in your state or city so that you can make this information available to those who need it.

WHAT DO YOU THINK?

You are a paralegal for a sole practitioner. You are fond of your boss and want the firm to be successful both for the boss and for you. Then you discover that your boss has a serious addiction to cocaine. You have a lot of options. What would you do? What are the possible outcomes of your action or inaction?

Sexual Harassment

Why do we talk about sexual harassment here in a chapter on integrity? Because sexual harassment is another one of those uncategorized "general misconduct" behaviors. It is illegal. It is unethical. But it is also something that happens, and you ought to know what to do about it if and when you see it or if you are a victim.

Here's the law: Title VII of the Civil Rights Act of 1964 makes it "an unlawful employment practice for an employer . . . to discriminate against any individual with respect to his compensation, terms, conditions, or privileges of employment, because of such individual's race, color, religion, sex, or national origin."[14] Without question, when a supervisor harasses a subordinate because of the subordinate's sex, that supervisor "discriminates" on the basis of sex.[15] Sexual harassment is, among other things, "unwelcome sexual advances, requests for sexual favors, and other verbal or physical conduct of a sexual nature."[16] The victim as well as the harasser may be a woman or a man. The victim does not have to be of the opposite sex.

Here's an example: In *Weeks v. Baker & McKenzie*[17] a high-powered senior partner continually lambasted legal secretary Weeks, dropped candies in the pocket of her blouse, groped her breasts and rear end, and made sexual remarks to her and about her. When Weeks sued for sexual harassment, it became apparent that the partner's conduct was not an isolated incident but a pattern of behavior. Six other female employees who had worked for that partner came forward to testify that he had also touched them, made inappropriate remarks, and pressured them for sex. Most of the women had told the law firm management or their immediate supervisors about the sexual harassment, but the firm either ignored the complaints or simply transferred the complainants to work for other people. One woman was fired after she complained. To make matters worse, the firm concealed the partner's conduct by keeping the written complaints in the women's personnel files instead of in his. Net result: The law firm was popped for $3.5 million for failure to protect these female employees from the unlawful misconduct of a senior partner.

The EEOC reports that from 1997 to 2008, the number of sexual harassment complaints have dropped (from 15,800 to 13,900), but the percentage of claims filed by men has increased from 11.6% to 16%. About half of the claims were found to be without reasonable merit. About $50 million was paid out on the meritorious claims through the EEOC, but that number does not include money paid through litigation. Sexual harassment claims are difficult to prove unless, as in the case mentioned earlier, there is a pattern of behavior over a period of time including several witnesses. Reporting sexual harassment is a puzzle that was exemplified on national television during Supreme Court justice Clarence Thomas's confirmation hearings. Many people believed that the justice's accuser was trying only to make a name for herself. Many believed that she had been sexually harassed by a man who was about to become a Supreme Court justice. For a case against a judge where the complaints of women were believed, see *Office of Disciplinary Counsel v. Campbell*[18] where a judge used his powerful position to harass inexperienced women attorneys engaged in new jobs early in their careers. The disciplining court found that the judge's unwelcome and offensive sexual remarks and physical contact were grounds for suspension in spite of his complete denial, his dozen character witnesses, and over 40 reference letters lauding his exemplary life.

In 2009, for the first time, a federal judge was accused of sexual harassment of court employees. He lied to FBI investigators and the Special Committee appointed by the 5th Circuit about his conduct and eventually pled guilty to obstruction of justice based on his lies. He was impeached by the U.S. House of Representatives and sentenced to prison.[19]

There's a "How to" section on the publisher's Web site just for you. Take some time now and go read "How to Deal With Supervisors" (*http://www.prenhall. com/orlik*).

PROOF OF UNFIT CHARACTER

Whatever authority in your state that licenses attorneys has the burden to prove an attorney's unfitness by a ***preponderance of the evidence***. Once this charge is proven against a member of the bar, the burden of proof shifts to the attorney to show if and when he or she is able to resume professional duties. The attorney must show the same moral fitness as an applicant for original admission.

*A **preponderance of the evidence** is a legal term that means that there is slightly more evidence that tends to proves the point than evidence that tends to disprove it. It is like a 51% standard.*

It is likely that paralegals will be held to the same standards and burden of proof as attorneys where paralegals are held responsible for their own actions (such as in the unauthorized practice of law). Thus far, however, it appears that in most instances it will be the employing and supervising attorneys who are held liable for the acts of their paralegals and other assistants. Misconduct in the areas covered by Rule #1 may cost paralegals their jobs, and a court could impose sanctions against them including restitution to the client. Although paralegals are not licensed by the state, the state could impose sanctions such as a temporary or permanent suspension from working as a paralegal.

RULE #1 WRAP-UP

We've finished the first Rule. How do you feel? There is some stuff in this Rule that's hard to talk about. The bad news is that there are some scary things in the practice of law. The good news is that we've covered the scariest of them. In Rule #1 we covered the concept of our duty to report our own misconduct and the misconduct of others, the pervasive problems stemming from drug and alcohol abuse, and sexual harassment in the workplace. Take a deep breath. It gets better from here.

RULE #1 REVIEW QUESTIONS

1. What is "integrity"? Why is it an important concept for study for people entering the legal profession?
2. Describe the concept of "self-policing."
3. Is there a statutory duty (a law) that says that paralegals must report the improper conduct of attorneys? or of other paralegals? What are some possible consequences of enacting such a law?
4. If you have the duty to report misconduct, what kinds of things would you have to report (mandatory), and what kinds of things should you report (discretionary)?
5. If you had absolute proof that a fellow paralegal was not working all of the hours he is reporting on his time sheets, what would you do about it, if anything?
6. If you are asked out for lunch by a client of the firm, would you go? Why or why not?
7. What are some signs that you are overly stressed from work? What are some options available to you to help remedy the problem in the short term? and long term?
8. If you witnessed a person in your firm being sexually harassed by another person, what are some of the options available to you?

9. What if you saw someone being discriminated against as a result of race or sexual preference? Is this against the law? If it is, what are some of the things you might do?

10. What is the burden of proof in a discipline case against an attorney for misconduct? How does this burden of proof compare to the burden of proof in a criminal case (proof beyond a reasonable doubt)?

---

[1] 162 N.E. 487 (N.Y. 1928).

[2] See *Magness v. Magness*, 558 A.2d 807, 815 (Md. App. 1988), where the court found that the failure to report the alleged misconduct of opposing counsel was a "concession" that the alleged conduct was not a violation of any ethical standards.

[3] See Maine Ethics Op. 100 (October 4, 1989) opining that when the legal professional is representing someone in a malpractice case against another lawyer, it is improper to use the threat of a disciplinary complaint to gain advantage in the civil matter.

[4] *Matter of Redding*, 672 N.E.2d 76 (Ind. 1996).

[5] http://www.courts.state.md.us/attygrievance/sanctions08.html

[6] The commission can be contacted at (312) 988–5359; 541 N. Fairbanks Court, Chicago, Illinois 60611.

[7] *In re Winston*, 528 N.Y.S.2d 843 (1989).

[8] *Twohy v. State Bar*, 769 P.2d 976 (Cal. 1989).

[9] Stephanie Goldberg, *Drawing the Line; When is an Ex-Coke Addict. Fit to Practice Law?* A.B.A. J. 49 (February 1990).

[10] *Id.*

[11] Substance Abuse and Mental Health Services Administration, *1999 National Household Survey on Drug Abuse.*

[12] Emergency Room Visits Climb for Misuse of Prescription and Over-the-Counter Drugs, SAMHSA Press Release (March 13, 2007).

[13] *Paralegal Burnout*, 70 A.B.A. J. 30 (1984).

[14] 42 USC §2000e—2(a)(1).

[15] *Meritor Savings Bank FSB v. Vinson*, 477 U.S. 57, 106 S.Ct. 2399 (1986); *Burlington Industries Ellerton* (1998).

[16] 29 CFR §1604.11(a) (1985).

[17] 63 Cal. App. 4th 1128 (1998).

[18] 623 N.E.2d 24 (Ohio 1993).

[19] House Resolution 520, 111th Congress, Session 1 (2009).

Preserve the Confidences and Secrets of the Client

Most of us know that it is improper (and probably illegal) for a lawyer to divulge the secrets of a client to other people. But! Most people don't know the strange and interesting ways this rule is broken. In fact, most lawyers, even well-educated, experienced lawyers, do not fully understand this rule or the differences between the confidentiality rule and evidentiary privileges. This chapter is designed to provide some clear explanations of confidentiality and privilege and how the two are different. The possession of confidential information leads to conflicts of interest, but we discuss conflicts in Rule #8 on loyalty.

KEEP THE CLIENT'S SECRETS

The first thing we have to know is that confidentiality is a "duty." It is a "must do." The duty of confidentiality is made of two separate but dependent concepts: (1) the clients' need to feel secure that the information they give their attorneys (and everyone in the law firm) will remain confidential, based on (2) the attorneys' need to have *all* relevant information from the clients.

Think about this for a moment. If you were asked to defend a man in a criminal matter, to do your job competently, you need to know all of the facts. You need to know *all* of the facts, even the ones that seem insignificant and perhaps especially the incriminating ones. But your client is afraid to tell you the facts. Your client is afraid that you will use the facts against him, or that if you know all of the facts, you won't want to defend him, or that you will tell the authorities or other people his secrets. So, you tell your client: "It's alright. You can tell me everything. I'll keep your secrets confidential." But what does that mean exactly?

What Is "Confidential"?

It is commonly said that it is improper to divulge "confidential information." Without knowing what information is "confidential," however, we do not know what it is we should not divulge.

Your state's Rule of Professional Conduct 1.6 gives you the formula for determining our definition:

> A [legal professional] shall not reveal information *relating to representation of a client* unless the client consents after consultation, except for disclosures that are impliedly authorized in order to carry out the representation, and except as stated in paragraph (b).

Paragraph (b) gives us two exceptions to this rule. We'll talk about them later in this chapter.

Check out Rule 1.8(b) [relating to conflicts of interest] because it probably uses the same expression: "a [legal professional] shall not use information *relating to representation of a client* to the disadvantage of the client unless the client consents after consultation."

This information that "relates to the representation" doesn't have to be information learned from the client. For example, if the client's spouse, coworker, or friend gives you information about the client's case, that is confidential, too. Think of the situation where the friend tells you that although the client is using him as an alibi, the client was not really with him at the time of the crime. Is that information that the client would want you to divulge to anyone? No. What about other information that you find out about the client on your own by reading his documents, his notes, his diary? Yes, that's confidential, too, so long as it relates to the representation of the client. Confidential information can be any information relating to the representation without regard to the source. The confidential information relating to the representation need not be personal secrets of the client, either.

Confidential information, then, is **all information relating to the representation of a client**, regardless of the source.

WHAT DO YOU THINK?

Okay. I can't tell anyone the confidential information I have, but can I "use" that information? To start your research for an answer, see *U.S. v. O'Hagan*, 521 U.S. 642 (1997).

Let's contrast the duty of confidentiality with the attorney/client privilege because this is the concept that confuses many people.

First, the attorney/client privilege is a rule of evidence that protects the client from having his or her legal team divulge client secrets **while under oath.** An example of the use of the attorney/client privilege is this: The client has confessed to a lawyer that he did the crime, but the grand jury cannot subpoena the lawyer (or paralegal!) to testify as to what the client said because of the privilege. Similarly, because of the privilege, the lawyer or paralegal cannot be called upon to testify in court about this confession.

In a civil court, the opposing side that serves an interrogatory requesting all information that the client told the lawyer, will receive only "Objection. Attorney/client privilege" as a response. This is because interrogatories are questions that must be answered under oath. (Interrogatories are just like questions asked in a deposition, but they are in writing.) When you are part of a legal team representing a client, the opposing side cannot take your deposition and ask questions about what you know about the case (doesn't this seem obvious?) because the attorney/client privilege protects the client from having you answer those questions.

Second, there are many differences between what is confidential and what is protected by the attorney/client privilege; for example, the attorney/client privilege does not protect information that is freely available to the public. However, the obligation (the duty) to keep information confidential does encompass information that is public.

Consider this scenario: The district attorney announces to the news media that your client was found in possession of the murder weapon. The news media reports that information, and it appears in the newspaper and the television news. Your client has told you that he was found with the murder weapon. You do not violate the attorney/client privilege by repeating to your roommate that the press is reporting that your client was found with the murder weapon. You do not violate the attorney/client privilege by telling your roommate that you happen to know that your client was <u>in fact</u> found in possession of the murder weapon. This is because the attorney/client privilege only applies to situations where you are under oath. You do not violate your duty of confidentiality when you tell your roommate that the press is reporting that your client was found with the murder weapon because what the press is reporting, really, has nothing to do with your client or your representation of your client. However, to tell your roommate that your client <u>was in fact</u> found with the murder weapon is a violation of your duty of confidentiality because this is information relating to the representation of your client. You gained that information through your representation of the client. It is confidential. Your client told you this information in confidence. It may seem illogical that you have to keep information confidential that is already reported in the press, but the duty of confidentiality is a duty that is personal to you. It does not matter what others are doing or saying. By accepting the representation of the client, you have given your word that you will not discuss the client's confidences. **Confidentiality is a duty you have promised to your client.** Attorney/client privilege is an evidentiary privilege.

Third, the attorney/client privilege encompasses information that the lawyer (and all of the lawyer's agents) obtains from the client only. Confidentiality encompasses all information "relating to representation of a client," regardless of its source.

Fourth, the attorney/client privilege prevents disclosure only inside the judicial process. Confidentiality prevents disclosure anywhere at any time to anyone.

Fifth, as we discussed in Rule #1, Rule 8.3 says that if a lawyer knows that another lawyer has committed a violation of the Rules of Professional Conduct, the lawyer with knowledge must tell an appropriate authority, but the Rule does not require disclosure of information otherwise protected by the rules regarding confidential information (Rule 1.6). For example, if a lawyer is a client of your law firm and tells you the facts of the crime he has committed, this is not reportable under Rule 8.3 because it is confidential under 1.6. (It is information relating to the representation of the client.) It is not discoverable by the court (as in put the lawyer on the witness stand and ask: What did your client tell you about the crime?) because it is protected by the attorney/client privilege.

In brief, the duty of confidentiality is a *duty*—a personal responsibility. The attorney/client privilege is an evidentiary *privilege*—a protection against disclosure.

The concept of confidentiality is always of concern to people in the legal profession, especially because of the increasing number of freelancers and contract employees. It must also be of prime concern when changing jobs (discussed in Rule #8). The most difficult aspect of this concept, however, may be the vigilance required in ordinary conversation. For example: You and your friend are talking about Client X as you leave the office and get into the elevator. Someone else in the elevator might know someone involved in Client X's case or X's adversary. You walk to a restaurant. Someone there overhears your conversation. You go home and innocently tell your spouse about your day, including information about X, and the next day your spouse repeats X's information to an acquaintance who, unbeknownst to you or your spouse, has some connection to X's adversary.

Any one of these examples illustrates how easy it is to violate your duty of confidentiality. Law firm employees as well as corporate employees should not discuss confidential information about clients with their spouses or other relatives, with friends, or with strangers. (BTW: An exception to this rule may be when a legal professional is undergoing psychiatric care and feels the need to discuss a case with regard to his or her feelings about it. In this instance, although the duty of confidentiality has technically been violated, the mental health professional is also bound to keep the confidences from being revealed.)

Confidentiality rules differ slightly from state to state. As with all of the rules of ethics, it is important to read and understand the authority on confidentiality in your jurisdiction. Now is a good time to go find your state's rule. It probably looks something like this:

Rule 1.6. Confidentiality of Information

(a) Consent Required to Reveal Information. A lawyer shall not reveal information relating to representation of a client except as stated in subdivisions (b), (c), and (d), unless the client gives informed consent.

(b) When Lawyer Must Reveal Information. A lawyer shall reveal such information to the extent the lawyer reasonably believes necessary:

(1) to prevent a client from committing a crime; or

(2) to prevent a death or substantial bodily harm to another.

(c) When Lawyer May Reveal Information. A lawyer may reveal such information to the extent the lawyer reasonably believes necessary:

(1) to serve the client's interest unless it is information the client specifically requires not to be disclosed;

(2) to establish a claim or defense on behalf of the lawyer in a controversy between the lawyer and client;

(3) to establish a defense to a criminal charge or civil claim against the lawyer based upon conduct in which the client was involved;

(4) to respond to allegations in any proceeding concerning the lawyer's representation of the client; or

(5) to comply with the Rules of Professional Conduct.

From the Florida Rules of Professional Conduct

NPFA's EC 1-5(a) says that the paralegal should familiarize himself or herself with the legal authority in his or her jurisdiction as to confidential information and abide by that authority. EC 1-5(b) says that the confidential information shall not be used to the disadvantage of the client.

The NFPA Model Code: Canon 5. A paralegal shall preserve all confidential information provided by the client or acquired from other sources before, during, and after the course of the professional relations.

The NALA Model Standards simply state that "Legal Assistants should preserve the confidences and secrets of all clients."

When Is It Okay to Disclose Confidential Information?

Quite obviously, some confidential information must be disclosed. As you can see, Rule 1.6 specifically exempts from the nondisclosure rules any disclosures that the client authorizes after the client has been advised about any possible adverse effects from the disclosure ("unless the client gives informed consent"). Also exempted are disclosures that are impliedly authorized in order to carry out the representation ("to serve the client's interests"). This allows the disclosure of information as necessary to answer interrogatories or to respond to other discovery.

Even though all of the information relating to the representation of the client is confidential, the law firm may use some confidential information to defend itself against a criminal or malpractice claim by the client or to collect its fees from the client. Care should be taken not to reveal more than is necessary to accomplish the task. Using the threat of release of confidential information as a weapon against the client is prohibited.[1]

> (2) to establish a claim or defense on behalf of the lawyer in a controversy between the lawyer and the client, to establish a defense to a criminal charge or civil claim against the lawyer based upon conduct in which the client was involved, or to respond to allegations in any proceeding concerning the lawyer's representation of the client.

The most interesting part of this rule is the subsection (b) part that exempts from confidentiality information that the legal professional may have to reveal "to prevent the client from committing a serious criminal act," as in your client shows up with a gun and tells you she is going to use it to kill someone. You believe that she will actually try to kill. What do you do? What she told you is technically confidential. But your state's Rule 1.6 may say that you don't have to keep this knowledge secret. Various states adopted this part of the rule in different forms. Some states made revealing a future or ongoing crime mandatory (like Florida), while others leave it to the discretion of the legal professional (like Alaska). Some states limit "the crime" to a crime of death or serious bodily harm, and others enlarge it to include fraud. This is worth looking up so that you are aware of the standard in your state. When the emergency arises, you may not have time to conduct in-depth legal research.

California's exemption is found in B&P Code 6068.

> **(b)** A lawyer **may** reveal a confidence or secret to the extent the lawyer reasonably believes necessary:
>
> **(1)** to prevent the client from committing a criminal or fraudulent act that the lawyer believes is likely to result in death or substantial bodily harm, or substantial injury to the financial interest or property of another . . . .
>
> From the Alaska Rules of Professional Conduct

When is your duty of confidentiality over? Not at the conclusion of the matter. Not when you don't work for that law firm anymore. Not when your client moves away or dies. The duty is personal to you. It never ends. You must carry the confidential information of your client with you to your grave. The same is also true of the attorney client privilege[2]—but you should check your state statute as this might change because of the recent case of two attorneys who released their former client's secret after he died. The attorneys knew that Former Client committed the crime for which another man was in prison. After Former Client died they publicly told their story so that the wrongly convicted man would be released from prison. They claimed that it was the attorney/client privilege that prevented them from coming forward earlier, but it was the duty of confidentiality that applied, not the privilege. (The privilege would only apply if they were forced to give the information under oath.) Regardless, both the duty and the privilege last forever. There is no exception for the commission of a past crime or righting an old wrong, but since this case, states are considering a change.

WHAT DO YOU THINK?

You don't work in a vacuum. You have lawyers around you. If a client is telling you that she's going to take "this here gun" (which she pulls from her handbag) and shoot her *&^%#!! boyfriend, you first have to decide if you believe her. Then you can decide which people in your firm you should talk to about it. Who's on your list? What's your approach?

To start your research, see *Rocca v. Southern Hills Counseling Center*, 671 N.E.2d 913 (Ind.App.1996).

Some Stuff That Happens in the Law Office Is Not Confidential

So, you walk into the law office on the first day of your new job. You meet with the office manager, a very busy person. She says to you: "Just remember that everything that goes on here in the law office is confidential." Well, that's not exactly true. The facts surrounding the smoking gun brought in by the firm's criminal defendant are confidential and therefore

must not be disclosed by law firm personnel. The client's false income tax reports are also protected. The documents that show that your client breached the contract willfully and maliciously are confidences, as well. However, the lawyer standing over the paper shredder destroying those documents is not covered by the confidentiality duty. It happened in the law office, but it is not confidential. This is because: (1) The shredding is not "information gained in the representation of the client" (although you may be engaged in the representation of your client while you are standing in the doorway watching the destruction of the client's documents); (2) The shredding is criminal activity constituting the lawyer's intent to commit a fraud upon the court. Therefore, the activity of the papers being shredded is not confidential under Rule 1.6 or Rule 3.3. This shredding is a violation of some of the other rules of professional conduct, is probably a crime, as well, and should be reported to the "appropriate professional authority" under Rule 8.3 if, of course, you are in a state that has adopted Rule 8.3. So, whereas the client's documents may not be disclosed because they are covered by the duty of confidentiality, evidence of criminal activity such as the destruction of evidence should be disclosed to the appropriate authority if that's what your state law requires.

WHAT DO YOU THINK?

Lawyer A gets permission from Client to confer with other lawyers, lawyers not in the same law firm, about Client's case. Lawyer A speaks with Lawyer B, who works for a different law firm. Does Lawyer B owe Client a duty of confidentiality?

When you are finished with your discussion, check out D.C. Bar Association Ethics Opinion 346 (2009)

Of course, all of Rule #2 applies to you just as it applies to lawyers. In *U.S. v. Kovel*, 296 F.2d 918 (2d Cir. 1961), one of the first cases that extended the attorney/client privilege to a nonattorney employed by a law firm, the court used the analogy of the employment of an interpreter in order to extend the privilege to an accountant. The court said that, just as attorneys may have to employ an interpreter through whom to speak to a foreign client, they may employ an accountant to interpret complex financial matters for them. The court reasoned that both the interpreter and the accountant should be protected by the privilege because they were conduits of information between attorney and client. As a result, the accountant in *Kovel* could not be made to testify as to information given to him in confidence by a client of the attorney who employed him.

One More Time: The Attorney/Client Privilege Is Different from the Duty of Confidentiality

The attorney/client privilege will be found in your state's rules of evidence. It will say something like this: The lawyer cannot be called upon to testify as to information the client has given to the lawyer. This is true of the attorney and all nonlawyer personnel to whom the client may have divulged information. You have to go find that rule now and you can do that on the Internet pretty easily. Try "attorney client privilege" + [*yourstate*]. Make a copy of the statute and put it in your Professional Responsibility 3-ring binder because it applies to you.

Wigmore, in his treatise on evidence, claimed that "it has never been questioned that the privilege protects communications to the attorney's clerks and other agents."[3] It was the 1974 U.S. Supreme Court case of *Procunier v. Martinez*[4] that extended the attorney/client privilege to the paralegal for the first time. The Supreme Court in that case held that the assistance of paralegals, secretaries, outside investigators, and the like is "indispensable" to the work of an attorney, and, because communications to the attorney from the client must often be made through such assistants, the privilege must apply to them. Further, the Court also said that an unjustifiable restriction on the use of such assistants by attorneys representing prisoners was held to be an unconstitutional restriction on the right of access to the courts.

The client who discloses to you that he killed his wife and buried her in the backyard has given you two things: confidential information <u>and</u> information that is protected by the attorney/client privilege. The first means that you cannot tell anyone (aside from your employing lawyer) what that client has said to you (even if you change the names, dates, places, or other identifying information), and the second means that you cannot be called upon to testify as to what the client said to you. If you were asked to testify, you should refuse to answer the question on the ground of attorney/client privilege.

Need to know circle: Other people in the law office may be told client confidences, but only those people who "need to know." In other words, just because your friend works for the same law office, it doesn't mean that you can tell client confidences to that person. If your friend isn't working on the same case (doesn't need to know), then confidences should not be shared.

> Federal Rules of Civil Procedure Rule 26(b)(3): Work product doctrine protects from disclosure material prepared in anticipation of litigation by or for a party or by or for that party's attorney acting for his client.

Work Product Is Confidential and Privileged at the Same Time

Work product is simply the work produced by a legal professional. Some examples are research memoranda, witness interviews, and notes resulting from other investigation. A legal professional's work product is given almost absolute protection from discovery. Historically, this is because

any slight factual content that such items may have is generally out-weighed by the judicial system's interest in maintaining privacy of the legal professional's thought processes and in ensuring that each side relies on its own wit in preparing its respective cases. This is true of lawyers and nonlawyers alike. You can find your work product privilege statute hanging around somewhere near the place where you found your attorney/client privilege. Go see if you can find it, and put a copy in your notebook.

TECHNOLOGY AND CONFIDENTIALITY

What has technology done to the concepts we have just studied? Nothing, really. The fax machine became the fastest way to deliver a letter in the 1970s. It delivered the attorney letter to the client faster than the postal system, but with speed and convenience, it brought with it the possibility that the correspondence could go to the wrong person. If we think about it, the same thing could happen with a regular U.S. postal system letter. If the envelope is inadvertently addressed to opposing counsel instead of the client, some confidential or privileged information would be released. What is opposing counsel's duty regarding receipt of privileged and confidential information? The answer depends on the jurisdiction, not how fast the information reached the wrong person. Those jurisdictions that say the receiving attorney has a duty to return the correspondence without reading it say the same thing whether the correspondence went by mail carrier, messenger, e-mail, or fax. Take a minute and check out your Rule of Professional Conduct 4.4. It probably says that if you receive something that you know was sent to you by mistake, you should notify the sender right away.

Did you know?

Title III of the Omnibus Crime Control and Safe Streets Act of 1968, as amended, prohibits the interception of wire, electronic, and oral communications.

What has e-mail done to confidentiality? Nothing, really. Although there was a great deal of discussion about it when e-mail was new, most jurisdictions have found that breaking into your computer isn't much different from breaking into your mailbox. Stolen information is the same today as it was yesterday, only faster. The inaccurately addressed letter might be rescued out of the mailroom. The inaccurately addressed email is gone in an instant. Well, perhaps it could be recovered out of your Outbox, but probably not. The rules remain the same for theft or inadvertence.

Likewise the cell phone. Again, there was a lot of discussion about cell communications not being "secure" and conversations being "stolen" out of the air. There could well be people who will use hi-tech equipment to eavesdrop on your cell communication. But these are no doubt the same people who used hi-tech equipment to bug your landline or otherwise listen in on your telephone conversations. However, when we had to make phone calls from our office, there was less likelihood of the wrong person overhearing our conversation. Now that we can carry a phone around in our ear, the likelihood of inadvertent release of confidential information has increased.

Should you encrypt the information on your laptop or PDA just in case they fall into enemy hands? We don't have that standard for the old-fashioned box of documents that may inadvertently be left or lost, so why would we have it for our technologically superior equipment? Until a court rules, or a state passes a law, that says that we have to write our legal documents, memos, and other confidential information in code, we should not have to worry about encryption.

What's the takeaway here? Has technology changed the laws of confidentiality, attorney/client privilege, or work product? No. Should we be more vigilant? Absolutely. Technology has given us more ways to communicate, and the communication is faster and more frequent, so there are more opportunities for mishandling or theft of information. Has the standard changed? No, but perhaps we have. We are more casual in our conversations and more open with our personal information. We publish our secrets on MySpace and Facebook. We blog and we twitter. Our lives are open books. As legal professionals, we need to keep our duties and our privileges firmly in mind and take care of our secrets and those of our clients.

ABA Standing Committee on Ethics and Professional Responsibility, Formal Opinion No. 99-413 (March 10, 1999): "The Committee believes that e-mail communications, including those sent unencrypted over the Internet, pose no greater risk of interception or disclosure than other modes of communication commonly relied upon as having a reasonable expectation of privacy."

For an article about Wi-Fi and potential confidentiality issues, go here: *http://www.abanet.org/lpm/ lpt/articles/nosearch/ tch05041_print.html.*

At least one court has ruled that misdirected e-mail do not lose their privileged status. In *City of Reno v. Reno Police Protective Assn.*, one side came into possession of a hard copy of the other side's privileged e-mail message. The receiving party attempted to use the e-mail, claiming that the privilege had been waived by the fact that the message had been e-mailed. The Nevada Supreme Court held that the e-mail retained its privileged status and should not have been used by the other side. The court relied, in part, on ABA Formal Opinion 99-413 (1999). The court also noted that both federal and California statutes say that unlawfully intercepted electronic communications do not lose their privileged status. Here's your cite: 59 P.3d 1212 (Nev. 2002), modified, 2003 Nev. LEXIS 25 (Nev. May 14, 2003). And in California, a lawyer who made copies of opposing counsel's documents (accidentally left in a conference room) was disqualified from the case.

WHAT DO YOU THINK?

Does a conversation with an attorney lose its privileged status if it is accidentally recorded? What a great case! *Jasmine Networks, Inc. v. Marvell Semiconductor, Inc.*, 117 Cal. App. 4th 794 (Cal. Ct. App. 2004).

CLIENT FILES AND CONFIDENTIALITY

Just think of all of the confidential information being stored in the file room! And what do we do with all of that stuff after the case has concluded?

We know we have a responsibility to take care of things that belong to the client that we have in our possession. The Restatement (3d) of Law Governing Lawyers requires that a lawyer "take reasonable steps to safeguard documents in the lawyer's possession relating to the representation of a client or former client."[5] This means that we can't just toss the client files in the trash or recycle bin when the case or matter has concluded. In general, we can give the files back to the client. If your firm's fee agreement specifies that the client is responsible for the files at the conclusion of the representation, with a few exceptions, we can box up the files and ship them out to the now-former client. Exceptions to this rule are certain documents that are subject to a confidentiality agreement that, by agreement, the client cannot see; certain original documents that are subject to probate or criminal code restrictions or might have to be filed with the court later; and documents that for some other reason the client should not see.

If the policy is to return all of the files to the client, the firm should consider keeping a copy for future use. If you photocopy the files so the firm can have a copy, you cannot charge the client for the copying. The files belong to the client. Any copies the firm wants to make for its own records must be done at its own expense.

If the policy is to destroy the files, you should know that most states have record retention requirements that are somewhere between five and ten years, so you should definitely find your state's requirement first. And you should check with the firm's professional liability insurance carrier. The carrier will probably tell you that you should keep the files at least for the time during which a malpractice action or breach of contract action could be filed—usually between five and ten years.

You can store the files in any secure place, although your basement probably isn't a very good idea. There are lots of inexpensive document storage facilities. And you can store files electronically.

No matter what you do, store or destroy, a comprehensive index of what the file contains should be created and kept. And, naturally, you should never destroy any document that has some intrinsic value such as money orders, travelers' checks, stocks, bonds, wills, original deeds, original notes, judgments, and the like. Also, you should never destroy documents that create or extinguish legal rights or obligations.

The ABA offered an Informal Opinion that recognized the continuing economic burden of storing retired and inactive files.[6] Sympathetically, the ABA opined that the issue of how to deal with this burden is primarily a question of business management and not of ethics or professional responsibility. However, dealing with client files is always a question of confidentiality from the file you have open on your desk to the client document carelessly put in the trash.

There is no general duty to preserve all files permanently. The public interest is not served by unnecessary additions to the costs of legal services that would be incurred by substantial storage costs. However, the ABA also concluded that clients (and former clients) reasonably expect that valuable and useful information in the lawyer's files will not be prematurely and carelessly destroyed. Now would be a good time to look at your state's Rules. Is there something in Rule 1.15 about "safekeeping" the client's property for a certain amount of time? If there is no specific time in your state's Rules, there are some "good commonsense" considerations provided in an old ABA Informal Opinion. If you are put in charge of file retention, you can read the ABA Informal Opinion 1384 (1977) (*http://www.prenhall.com/orlik*).

Maine has an April 2004 opinion on storing client files. You can find it here: *http://www.mebaroverseers. org/.*

Here's an article about Delaware's position on file retention: *http://www.dsba.org/Assoc Pubs/InRe/mar01et.htm.*

> A lawyer may comply with the mandatory record retention provision by storing certain records as computer-generated images. The lawyer must ensure that the electronic storage technique will safeguard the records from inadvertent destruction at least as effectively as the paper record, and that it will permit prompt reproduction of accurate, unaltered copies upon proper request. Before disposing any of the paper records, the lawyer must ensure that all required copies have in fact, been transferred. Certain records must be retained in their original form: check books, check stubs, bank statements, prenumbered and canceled checks, duplicative deposit slips, and other documents that are not referred to as "copies."
>
> New York State Bar Association Opinion 680 (October 1, 1996)

If there is no clause in your firm's fee agreement about retention of client files, which there probably isn't, and there is a need or desire to destroy these old files, which there probably is, many states require that you at least attempt to notify the client about the destruction of the files and the client's right to claim them. There will be technical requirements about how and when to give notice and how long you have to wait after you have not gotten a response from the former client. If the client is dead by the time you think to return his files, there will be even more requirements designed to protect the client's confidentiality requirement (which continues beyond the client's death) and any value the estate might find in the file such as continuing legal rights.

You don't have to do this the old-fashioned way. There are a number of readily available software programs to help you organize open and closed files and to put together a storage and destruction schedule.

As you have an obligation to protect the confidentiality of the client files, destruction of the files should be as complete as possible, such as by confetti shredding or burning. There is no obligation to hire a professional to destroy the documents, and destruction of the documents is not billable time. So long as the information cannot be retrieved, the confidentiality has been protected.

Here's an article about West Virginia's position on file retention from 1997:
http://www.wvbar.org/barinfo/lawyer/APRIL97.HTM.

And here's one from Minnesota:
http://www.courts.state.mn.us/lprb/fc022299.html.

RULE #2 WRAP-UP

Confidentiality is a bear. If you don't believe that most lawyers don't understand the difference between confidentiality and attorney/client privilege, run an Internet search on the term "duty of confidentiality" and take a look at the numerous Web sites where some lawyer, trying to sell the public on his/her knowledge of the law, completely confuses the two concepts. Famous, brilliant lawyers who worked on the O.J. Simpson case consistently got their confidentiality confused with their attorney/client privilege. If you didn't get it the first time around on this chapter, then, don't feel bad. Just let it soak in. If you want to read some cases on this topic, some are provided for you on the publisher's Web site.

Don't forget about the importance of confidentiality when using technology. Although the standards have not changed, the speed at which we can now communicate with each other makes it important to be more vigilant, more watchful.

And we learned about the confidential nature of client files in Rule #2. We have duties regarding these files that stem from our duty to protect the client's confidences.

RULE #2 REVIEW QUESTIONS

1. What is a short definition of "confidential information"? What are your duties under your state's law about keeping client information confidential? What client information is confidential? When does the duty begin? When does it end?

2. Compare and contrast the attorney/client privilege with the duty of confidentiality.

3. Your firm has a written fee agreement with your client. Is that fee agreement confidential? Is the fact that the client is your firm's client confidential?

4. You want to teach a class for your local paralegal program. Good! Can you use a closed file from a former firm client for your sample pleadings? How about if you black out the names and other identifying information? Why? Why not?

5. What is the "work product privilege"? What does it do for you that the attorney/client privilege does not do?

6. If you keep notes on your PDA, do you have to encrypt them?

7. What should you do with a fax transmission that is obviously confidential information and obviously not intended for you or your firm—in other words, it was accidentally sent to the wrong place?

8. How long must client files be kept after the client's case is concluded?

9. To whom do client files belong? What is the public policy reason for this rule?

10. What are the advantages to scanning all of the documents in client files and keeping them in electronic format? What are the disadvantages?

WHAT DO YOU THINK?

The client discloses the whereabouts of the dead bodies of his victims. What do you do with that information? Check out this case: *McClure v. Thompson*, 323 F.3d 1233 (9th Cir. April 2, 2003).

[1] *Elkind v. Bennett,* 958 So.2d 1088 (Fla. 2007).

[2] The attorney/client privilege continues after the client's death so long as there is an heir or personal representative who holds the deceased client's privilege.

[3] *Wigmore on Evidence*, 3d ed. (1961, Section 2290).

[4] 416 U.S. 396, 94 S.Ct. 1800 (1974).

[5] Rest.3d Law Governing Lawyers §46(1) 9(1).

[6] ABA Informal Opinion 1384 (1977).

Get and Stay Competent

The public has a right to competent professionals. This is especially true in the legal field because lawyers have traditionally been viewed in a "paternalistic" way. That is to say, members of the public traditionally did not question the lawyer's word, similar to the way they reacted to the word of doctors. Rule #3 explains what competence is in the eyes of the law and how to get and stay that way. This Rule also touches on professional negligence, even though there are no reported cases where a paralegal has been held liable for professional negligence.

WHAT YOUR STATE'S RULES SAY ABOUT COMPETENCE

As a testament to the importance we place on competence, it is the first section of your state's Rules of Professional Conduct. Here's a sample:

> **Rule 1.1:** A lawyer shall provide competent representation to a client. Competent representation requires the legal knowledge, skill, thoroughness and preparation reasonably necessary for the representation.

So, we have a clear definition of competence from this Rule. Competence is having the knowledge and skill necessary for this particular representation, plus putting in the time to thoroughly prepare. The definition of competence is the same for each person who works in the field of law. The NALS, NALA, and NFPA Codes also cover competence.

NALS Code of Ethics says:

Canon 1 Members of this association shall maintain a high degree of competency and integrity through continuing education to better assist the legal profession in fulfilling its duty to provide quality legal services to the public.

> NALA Code of Ethics and Professional Responsibility says at Canon 6: "A paralegal must strive to maintain integrity and a high degree of competency through education and training with respect to professional responsibility, local rules and practice, and through continuing education in substantive areas of law to better assist the legal profession in fulfilling its duty to provide legal service."

> NFPA's Model Code says:
>
> CANON 1. A paralegal shall achieve and maintain a high level of competence.
>
> **Ethical Considerations**
>
> EC 1.1(a) A paralegal shall achieve competency through education, training, and work experience.
>
> EC 1.1(b) A paralegal shall aspire to participate in a minimum of twelve (12) hours of continuing education, to include one (1) hour of ethics education, every two (2) years in order to remain current on developments in the law.
>
> EC 1.1(c) A paralegal shall perform all assignments promptly and efficiently.

All of these Codes make continuing education an affirmative duty for paralegals. It was already your duty under your state's Rule 1.1, because that rule logically makes continuing legal education an affirmative duty for the lawyer.

No doubt, your state's Rules also devote an entire rule to the lawyer's responsibilities regarding nonlawyer assistants. (Here is one of the few rules that applies exclusively to lawyers.) The ABA's position is that the employing lawyer is directly responsible for the competence of the employee paralegal. Go look at your state's Rule 5.3. It says something like this:

Rule 5.3. Responsibilities Regarding Nonlawyer Assistants

With respect to a nonlawyer employed or retained by or associated with a lawyer:

(a) a partner, and a lawyer who individually or together with other lawyers possesses comparable managerial authority in a law firm, shall make reasonable efforts to ensure that the firm has in effect measures giving reasonable assurance that the person's conduct is compatible with the professional obligations of the lawyer;

Did your state adopt the ABA Model Comments along with the Rules? If it did, read the Comment that follows Rule 5.3. It reaffirms that a lawyer should give appropriate training and supervision to nonlawyer assistants. Notice that the Comment doesn't seem to address substantive or procedural law matters so much as it addresses ethical issues. Here's a sample:

> Lawyers generally employ assistants in their practice, including secretaries, investigators, law student interns, and paraprofessionals. Such assistants, whether employees or independent contractors, act for the lawyer in rendition of the lawyer's professional services. <u>A lawyer must give such assistants appropriate instruction and supervision concerning the ethical aspects of their employment</u>, particularly regarding the obligation not to disclose information relating to representation of the client, and <u>should be responsible for their work product</u>. The measures employed in supervising nonlawyers should take account of the fact that they do not have legal training and are not subject to professional discipline.

The last sentence of the Comment, that nonlawyers do not have legal training, is not true. The second part of the sentence, that nonlawyers are not subject to professional discipline, is not necessarily true either. NFPA has a model disciplinary code in place, and several local paralegal associations are taking responsibility for disciplining their members. Moreover, there is nothing to say that a court could not sanction a nonlawyer.

Nevertheless, the Comment says that the lawyer "should be" responsible for the paralegal's work product. Rule 5.3 makes the lawyer responsible for everything the paralegal does as part of his or her employment with the lawyer.

Protection of the Public Is the Goal

The rules of legal ethics are aimed at protecting the attorney/client relationship, maintaining public confidence in the legal profession, and ensuring the integrity of judicial proceedings.[1] In short, the rules are meant to protect the public.

Minimum Standards

How can we know if we are competent? The NALA Model Standards provide a list of qualifications regarding paralegal education and training. Among the listed items are graduation from an ABA-approved paralegal program or a program that is accredited and requires not fewer than 60 semester hours of classroom study. In other words, the NALA standards look for graduation from a paralegal program of substance. Alternatively, graduation from a short course of study or holding a baccalaureate degree, plus in-house training as a paralegal, is accepted.

> In 2004, more than 35,000 victims initiated claims against lawyers who had legal malpractice insurance. Of those victims, 12,000 people successfully recovered money.

Of course, there are many long-term paralegals who never went to college, and they are competent, too. The NALA Standards use two years of paralegal work as a minimum.[2]

Does education by itself make you competent? No. But it's a good place to start when we have to draw some minimum qualification lines. We are all competent to some degree. The trick is being confident that we have the required *knowledge* and *skill* to do *this particular task* and, when we're not confident, we know when to ask for help. The problem many of us get into is when we're working alone, we feel we have no one to ask, and don't realize we're in over our head.

PROFESSIONAL NEGLIGENCE

The modern trend has been to use the expression "professional negligence" rather than "malpractice" because malpractice implies a bad intent. The legal standard is really negligence, not intentional wrongdoing.

Historically, the plaintiff in a professional negligence case had to establish that the attorney had acted in a "grossly negligent" manner toward the client.[3] More recently, however, the plaintiff in a professional negligence case needs to establish only *simple negligence* as in any other tort/negligence action. The elements of the action are these: (1) the existence of the attorney/client relationship (which gives rise to a duty); (2) acts that constitute negligence or the lack of use of reasonable skill and care; (3) the acts or omissions are the proximate cause of the damage to the client, or "but for" such negligence, the client would have been successful in his or her action; and (4) actual damages.[4]

Competence in General

A paralegal's general competence comes from education and training. Paralegals, as you have no doubt been told, are educated and trained in the "how to" of law as opposed to lawyers who learn primarily legal theory in school.

Lawyers, as members of a profession, have a bad reputation for honesty and competence. We've all heard the lawyer jokes. These jokes stem from the small minority of incompetent and dishonest lawyers. Each person's reputation reflects upon the reputation of the profession in the eyes of the public. Each negligent or dishonest act reflects badly on the individual, the supervising lawyer, the law firm, and the profession as a whole. That's why paralegals must be extra-attentive to integrity (Rule #1) and competence (Rule #3)—so that we don't see paralegal jokes making the rounds on the Internet. (How many paralegals does it take to screw in a lightbulb?)

Most Professional Negligence falls in the following classes of errors:

(1) **Administrative Errors:** Failure to Calendar, Failure to File/No Deadline, Clerical error, Procrastination.

(2) **Substantive Errors:** Failure to Know Deadline, Inadequate Investigation, Failure to Know the Law, Conflict of Interest.

(3) **Client Relations:** Failure to Communicate, Failure to Follow Client Instructions, Failure to Obtain Client's Consent, Improper Withdrawal.

(4) **Intentional Wrongdoing:** Libel, Malicious Prosecution, Civil Rights, Fraud, Theft.

Kentucky Bench and Bar, January 2007

Of the insured negligence claims, the most prevalent professional negligence occurred in the area of personal injury—Plaintiffs (25% of all insured claims). Then came Real Estate law (20%). Probate and estate claims along with business start-ups (approximately 10% each).

Competence in a Specific Area

Law is becoming increasingly specialized. As the law becomes more complex, it becomes harder to keep up with it. Gone are the days of the "general practitioner." Taken to an extreme, of course, the trend toward specialization would mean that the new practitioner could practice nothing, and the user of legal services would have to go to a different lawyer for each different need. But some of the most important skills for the legal practitioner don't have anything to do with specialization or knowing any law in particular. These important skills are the ability to find the law, analysis of the law, evaluation of facts, and legal writing. To be competent, then, does not mean memorization of great bodies of law, but it does require those fundamental skills such as being able to determine what kinds of legal problems a situation may involve and to think analytically and critically about them. Once the problems are analyzed, all of the answers are in the library. Diligence and thoroughness, coupled with the ability to think and communicate, are the key to competence in the field of law.

To be competent in a specific area, more training and preparation are necessary. To maintain that higher level of competence, continuing

---

1,900 of the 35,000 plaintiffs were paid over $100,000 in damages.

---

education is a must. Continuing education should be more than reading in your chosen area; it should include sharing ideas with others.

In order to become competent in a specific area, we all have to start with that first case, some extra reading and studying, and talking to others who specialize in that field, even if we have to spend more time that is not billable to the client. Some sage advice: Never be afraid to ask a question; never take a project unless you are qualified, or unless you can get qualified or get assistance. When something is assigned to you, don't be ashamed to say: "I don't have any experience in this area."

How do we know an act (or failure to act) constitutes negligence? There is a lot of case law to guide us. The most obvious negligence is the failure to follow the law. Lack of knowledge or nonobservance of local statutes, rules, and case law can in itself justify a finding by the court of professional negligence.[5] In *Stewart v. Sbarro*,[6] the court held that while an attorney "is not an insurer, nor is he answerable to client for every error in judgment or mistake, <u>he contracts to use the reasonable knowledge and skill in the transaction of business which lawyers of ordinary ability and skill possess and exercise</u>." Although *Stewart v. Sbarro* speaks of "contracts," the client's action will ordinarily be in tort . . . . as an ordinary negligence action. Punitive damages are not ordinarily available in contract actions, so the wise plaintiff includes the tort cause of action and tries to prove "gross negligence."

Although failure to follow the law seems like a clear path to a professional negligence action, if the law is new or uncertain, there is perhaps no liability.[7] Laws that are clear, however, such as simple court filings, are easy pickings for a professional negligence action. For example, in *DeBakey v. Staggs*,[8] the lawyer was hired to have the clients' daughter's name changed. The attorney filed the necessary papers only after being badgered by the clients, and his papers were not signed by the court because of several defects. After seven months of urging the attorney to complete the job (for which he had been partially paid), the clients hired another attorney to perform the name change. In the lawsuit against the original attorney, the clients were awarded treble damages[9] under the state Deceptive Trade Practices Act and $1,000 attorney's fees for the professional negligence action. This is a classic example of two of the most common competence problems: failure to communicate and procrastination— a deadly combination.

Examples of Negligence

Legal professionals will be liable for any loss sustained by their client as a result of their negligent failure to prepare, file, or serve the appropriate pleadings.[10] In fact, failure to file an action accounts for 25% of

If you google "case within a case" + negligence + [*yourstate*], you will find out. (Internet research is not an exact science, so you might try putting the search terms in a different order.)

professional negligence claims. But, if the underlying case is never filed, and the *statute of limitations* runs, how can the injured client prove losses? In *Gyler v. Mission Insurance Co.*,[11] the court held that the attorney's failure to file a suit before the statute of limitations has run on the action is "<u>plainly malpractice</u> where the attorney can show no reasonable justification for his inaction." But, the Illinois Appellate Court held that the plaintiff has to show that "but for" the attorneys' negligence in allowing the statute to run, the plaintiff would have won his or her case.[12] In essence, this rule forces the plaintiff not only to show negligence on the part of the attorney but also to sustain the burden of proof on the underlying action. In other words, the plaintiff has to litigate the case that the lawyer failed to litigate *inside* the professional negligence case. Because the underlying action was never litigated and therefore no discovery was ever gathered, this burden is a difficult one.

In instances where the underlying action was never filed, your state is either a "plainly malpractice" state or a "case within a case" state. Wouldn't you like to know which one it is?

> **Statute of limitations** is the length of time between the bad thing happening and the filing of the lawsuit that the law allows. Most states have statutes of limitations that allow one year for negligence actions and up to four years on contract actions.

WHAT DO YOU THINK?

Should an attorney be found negligent for not taking a case? If the attorney fails to do the minimum research before telling the client that there is no cause of action in her complaints, should he be liable for her failure to seek out another opinion? What if he also fails to tell her about the running of the statute of limitations? Has an attorney/client relationship been established if the lawyer never officially "takes the case?" You can start your research with *Dogstad v. Veseley, Otto, Miller & Keefe*, 291 N.W.2d 686 (Minn. 1980).

Negligent Disregard for the Client

Lack of communication with clients is a problem of growing concern to the state bars. Polls consistently show that among the top three client complaints is this: "My attorney doesn't communicate with me." An increasing number of attorneys accept the representation of more clients than they can conceivably represent competently, and that often means neglecting some clients in favor of others. Paralegals can assist their lawyer-employers, help the clients, and promote good public relations by keeping clients informed. Clients need to know the important developments in

Let's look at a real estate legal matter. They account for 20% or so of professional negligence cases. In *Kotzur v. Kelly*,[13] purchasers in a real estate transaction brought a professional negligence action against the seller's attorney after they were forced to pay off a judgment lien against the seller following the closing. The attorney argued that because he was never employed to represent the purchasers, no attorney/client relationship existed, and no cause of action for professional negligence could be brought. The attorney testified that he didn't feel that he was dealing with two different parties and that he knew that the purchasers did not have a separate attorney. He prepared all the documents relating to the sale transaction for the purchasers on a "family-type basis." The purchasers thought that the attorney was handling the documents and that he was representing them. Purchasers' testimony was that the attorney did not tell them that he was not representing them nor did he tell them that it would be better if they hired a separate lawyer. The court found the existence of an attorney/client relationship for purposes of the professional negligence action. (Wait until you get to Rule #8 and you study conflicts of interest. Then think about this case again.) What should have the attorney done to protect himself against this action?

their cases. They need the procedural steps explained to them. They are entitled to explanations for delays. Their telephone calls and letters should be responded to in a timely fashion. With proper supervision and direction, paralegals and other nonlawyer assistants can and should do all of these tasks and assist the lawyer in avoiding professional negligence claims and action by the disciplinary authority.

Drug and Alcohol Abuse

We covered this topic under Rule #1, but it is important enough to repeat here. A person who is addicted to drugs or alcohol is not "competent." The addicted lawyer fails to communicate with the client; does not file pleadings on time; forgets to make appearances at depositions, hearings, and meetings. You can see that all of the types of negligence we are discussing can be the result of addiction.

The Legal Profession Assistance Conference reports that 1 in 5 lawyers is addicted to alcohol and 90% of serious disciplinary matters are the result of alcohol addiction.[14] A person can be a social drinker for many years before crossing the line into alcoholism. The LPAC reports that lawyers aged between 40 and 50 years are at the greatest risk of crossing that line. Don't think that addiction is limited to lawyers. Addiction does not discriminate on the basis of age, race, religion, color, national origin, or job title. If you or someone you know shows the signs of drug or alcohol addiction or severe depression, you know where to get help because you did that research for Rule #1.

The Simple Miscalendaring Issue

About 25% of claims brought against attorneys have to do with missing a deadline. Deadlines are typically missed because: (1) the firm doesn't have an adequate calendaring system; or (2) the deadline was calendared, but on the wrong date. It is typical, then, for the lawyer to blame the paralegal (or the calendar clerk, or the secretary, or whomever) for the miscalendaring. But you and I know that the doctrine of *respondeat superior* means that the lawyer has the ultimate responsibility. And we know that Rule 5.3 protects the nonlawyer from liability.

Respondeat superior is Latin for "let the master answer".

In an interesting twist on simple miscalendaring, take a look at *Hu v. Fang*.[15] Under California law, a party can seek forgiveness from a default if the party can prove that the lawyer made an error. This default turned on a calendaring error that caused the plaintiff's attorney to miss a status conference, but, naturally, it was not the lawyer who miscalendared—it was the paralegal. The trial court refused to grant the plaintiff's attorney relief from the default because the statute requires "attorney error." Using the doctrine of *respondeat superior*, the appellate court did not hesitate to reverse the lower court and hold the lawyer responsible for the paralegal's calendaring error and, ultimately, grant relief from the default judgment.

Calendaring may seem like a simple task, but it is not. Every element of a lawsuit has different deadlines: 10 days for this, 30 days for that. And which day is the "first" day when we are counting days? Is it the 30th day when it must be filed or the 29th day from the day the notice was received? Each rule is different and, as if that weren't bad enough, there are state statutes with one set of deadlines and court rules with a different set. In a large law firm, being the calendar clerk looks a lot like being in air traffic control. To avoid disasters, every calendaring system should be checked and double-checked, including by the lawyer who will be ultimately responsible for any errors.

Good Faith as a Defense

Where the legal professional acts in good faith with an honest belief that his or her acts and advice are in the client's best interest and that they are based on accurate information and adequate research, the legal professional will not be liable for "mere errors in judgment." *Biomet Inc. v. Finnegan* is a 2009 case that discusses this issue very well. Finnegan was Biomet's defense law firm in a case brought against Biomet for patent infringement. The trial court's judgment against Biomet was enormous in both actual damages and punitive damages, but Biomet stuck with

Finnegan for the appeal. After Finnegan's appeal reduced the actual damages to about $500, the $20 million punitive damages award was too disproportionate to be upheld. However, the appellate court held that punitive damages could not be reargued because they were not part of the original appeal. Here's Finnegan's conundrum: They are writing the appeal from the trial court's judgment. They do not include an appeal to the $20 million punitive damages award because, at the time of the appeal, the $20 million was not unconstitutionally disproportionate to the actual damages. Further, Finnegan argued in defense of the professional negligence claim that it was a tactical decision to not appeal the punitive damages award because that would lead to reargument of the horrible stuff that Biomet did that gave rise to that big punitive damages award. Biomet is stuck with paying $500 in actual damages and $20 million punitives. Well, the court said the following about the case—It's a two-part test: (1) Was the alleged error an error of professional judgment, and (2) did the attorney exercise reasonable care in making that professional judgment?

> **WHAT DO YOU THINK?**
> What do you think? Was Finnegan negligent?

Standard of Care

Generally, the standard of care is "such skill, prudence, and diligence as lawyers of ordinary skill and capacity commonly possess and exercise in the performance of tasks which they undertake."[16] However, where attorneys hold themselves out to the public as specialists in areas of law, they will be held to the same standard of care and skill as that of other specialists of ordinary ability who specialize in the same fields.[17] In *Wright v. Williams*,[18] the court held that attorneys who held themselves out to the public as specialists in maritime law should be held to the standard of care of a "reasonably prudent specialist" in that field. The court allowed expert testimony of other maritime law specialists in order to determine if the defendant/attorney breached the duty he owed to his clients.

Statute of Limitations in Negligence Actions

Now would be a good time to know something about the statute of limitations in negligence actions in your state. Believe it or not, there's a Web site just for this moment: www.statutes-of-limitations.com. When you are researching, remember to look specifically for "legal malpractice" or "professional negligence" because that's what we're talking about.

The statute of limitations on ordinary negligence cases begins to run at the time of the negligent act. That's because in a typical negligence case (such as a automobile collision) the damage happens right after the negligence act. With professional negligence, however, it is possible that the injured party will not become aware of the problem until many years after the attorney's representation has ended. For that reason, some courts have held that the statute of limitations doesn't begin to run until a reasonable person would have noticed the harm. For example, in cases of negligent drawing of a will, the statute should begin to run at the time of the testator's death when the will is probated.[19]

This is often called "the discovery rule."

In *Neel v. Magana, Olney, Levy, Cathart & Gelfand*,[20] the court held that the "discovery" theory for beginning the statute of limitations in attorney negligence cases is most appropriate. In other words, the statute of limitations on the action does not begin to run until the client has discovered, or a reasonable person should have discovered, the negligence, error, or omission. In *Johnson v. Simonelli*,[21] the client brought an action against his former attorney for professional negligence claiming that the attorney did not ensure that adequate security existed for a debt owed to the client arising out of the sale of the client's business. The court held that the statute of limitations began to run at the time of the buyer's default. Citing *Neel*, the court said:

> The statute of limitations in a legal malpractice action does not begin to run until the client <u>discovers, or should have discovered</u>, the attorney's negligence and the client has sustained actual and appreciable harm.

To get around the statute of limitations for negligence, plaintiffs will often file a negligence lawsuit but label it something else. Breach of fiduciary duty, fraud, and breach of contracts all have longer statutes of limitations and are likely candidates, but if the court recognizes any of these longer-statute of limitations causes of action as disguised negligence claims, it will typically dismiss them.[22]

Another problem in this area is that of privity of contract. Where the negligence claimant has actually employed the attorney or has consulted with the attorney in contemplation of retaining the attorney, the privity of contract is clear. The problem arises where the heirs of a client allege that the attorney performed legal services for the testator in a negligent manner. In that case, the person in privity of contract is dead, and it is this person's heirs who want to sue the attorney. Where the plaintiff is an heir of the decedent, the plaintiff is not the one who hired the attorney and has no *fiduciary relationship* with the attorney. The law in this area varies from state to state and is different for unmentioned heirs and heirs that are mentioned in the will. If you want to research it in your state, you need terms like "estate planning" and "liability to third parties" and the name of your state.

A *"fiduciary relationship"* is one founded on trust or confidence placed by one person in the integrity and fidelity of another.

Bottom line: In order to sue a lawyer for professional negligence, the plaintiff must be in privity of contract with the lawyer. The attorney/client relationship and all of the duties involved in that relationship are key to a professional negligence action. There are a few exceptions that create "hidden parties" such as the will situation, limited instances where a professional negligence action can be passed along to someone who "steps into the shoes" of the client, and some hypertechnical exceptions we won't worry about.

PROFESSIONAL NEGLIGENCE LIABILITY INSURANCE

Lawyers' professional liability insurance (also known as errors and omissions or E&O insurance) became available after World War II. Before that time, only Lloyds of London would underwrite a policy for any professional other than a doctor. Because of the increasingly complex nature of the law and legal practice, compounded by the fact that cases handled by lawyers involve increasingly large amounts of money, professional liability insurance has become a standard expense of the practicing lawyer. Some states require that a lawyer disclose his or her liability insurance (or lack thereof) in each retainer agreement so that the client can make an informed choice.

Professional liability insurance is now available to paralegals. Policies look very much like policies for attorneys and have similar coverage. The rates, however, are substantially less. This may be because the potential liability of a paralegal, who primarily works for a lawyer, is lower than the potential liability of the lawyer. If, indeed, the doctrine of *respondeat superior* still protects the negligent paralegal, what is the need for insurance? Here's the need: Many lawyers don't have professional liability insurance. There is no law that requires them to have it (except in Oregon) although most states require a disclosure to clients if they do not have insurance. Whether or not the paralegal is negligent, he or she may well be sued. Even if the paralegal is not found liable, professional liability insurance will protect the paralegal from prohibitively high defense costs. As there have been instances of paralegals being named as defendants in professional negligence lawsuits in the 1990s, this type of insurance is something to think about.

Freelance paralegals may more likely have potential liability, as they may not be covered by an attorney's policy, and the attorney-employer may not have liability insurance. Those who walk the dangerous line between typing services and practicing law without a license should also think seriously about this kind of insurance. Legal technicians, authorized to practice in limited areas, should look at professional liability insurance.

Paralegal/Law Errors and Omissions

Coverage is arranged for errors and omissions for paralegals and law clerks, either as part of an attorney's professional liability package or as a separate E&O form under various programs. E&O limits range from $100,000 per claim and $300,000 aggregate on claims-made forms to $1 million/$1 million. Premiums and limits are lower for paralegals who work under the supervision of an attorney.

You can be held liable for legal professional negligence even if you are not licensed to practice law,[23] although it is unlikely that you can be insured for negligence if you are not authorized to engage in the activity in which the negligence was committed.

Additionally, independent insurance coverage may make you more desirable when you are looking for a job. In any case, it is a good idea to find out if your employer has liability insurance and look into your own if you are not otherwise covered.

Ordinarily, professional liability insurance covers direct monetary loss and expense to the legal professional or a firm that arise from claims of neglect, omissions, or errors. This type of insurance does not cover bodily injury or property damage and will compensate only for loss that actually "arises from" the conduct of professional legal services. Professional liability insurance usually does not compensate for intentional torts, only negligence.

Look at your state's Rule 1.8. Does it say that lawyers must not attempt to limit their liability for professional negligence by contract with their client? Doesn't that make sense? How would it be if lawyers could just include a clause in every contract that says that the client promises not to sue for professional negligence or that the lawyer is not liable for negligence?

LIABILITY FOR OTHERS

A law partnership, as well as all its members, is liable for the negligent acts of the individual members of the firm performed within the scope of their authority,[24] but not for acts committed outside of the course of business.[25] The firm will not be held liable for the negligent acts of a partner that are committed outside of his or her position with the firm. Limited liability partnerships (LLPs) have proliferated in the 1990s in an attempt to narrow the scope of law firm liability. Limited partners are typically not responsible for the negligent acts of their partners.

> We've put a case on the publisher's Web site for you to illustrate what can happen to a lawyer who does not properly supervise employees.

Somewhere in your state's Rule 5.3, it says that the attorney should exercise due care in the <u>selection</u> of competent and trustworthy people to conduct the affairs of the attorney's clients. As we discussed before, under the doctrine of *respondeat superior*, attorneys will be held liable for the negligent acts of their nonattorney employees if those acts occur during the course and within the scope of their employment. Further, attorneys will be held negligent themselves for improperly supervising all of their nonattorney personnel. Although a lawyer will not be held to have knowledge of "every small detail" of his office, he must accept responsibility for the supervision of the work of his staff.

Although a paralegal may draft all the pleadings and papers necessary to be drawn for the attorney's practice, the attorney is responsible for examining those papers, approving them, or altering them to meet the standards of due care and diligence of an ordinary attorney of like skill and knowledge.

The standard of care used to determine negligence on the part of a paralegal will probably be that of a "reasonable paralegal under the circumstances." When people represent themselves as having even greater skill than that of the ordinary person, they will be held to that higher standard. Since paralegals are engaged in a specific profession, they will be held to the standard higher than that of the ordinary person: that of a person of their training and abilities and of the type of professional they hold themselves out to be. There is no case law on this at this time. The best guess, then, would be that paralegals will be held to a standard lower than that of an attorney, but higher than that of the layperson.

Whereas attorneys may not be held liable for a "mere error of judgment" to avoid liability under a negligence theory,[26] since paralegals are not supposed to use legal judgment, this theory may not be available to them. As yet, it is difficult to determine what "customary practice" may be for paralegals; thus, that professional negligence defense is eliminated as well. It may be that once they step outside of their limited realm of practice, paralegals will be held to the standard of the full professional, in spite of their inability to utilize that standard in their daily interaction with clients and the courts.

To clarify this problem, take the example of the person who is engaging in the unauthorized practice of law (UPL). There are many cases of UPL but none that hold that the UPL makes the work product "*per se* negligent." If you think about it this means, all of the mortgage documents drafted by companies that should not be drafting them, and all of the corporate documents created by people who should not be creating them,[27] and all of the wills![28] If all of those things were found to be *per se* incompetently drafted, it would invalidate thousands of home sales and incorporations, not to mention the hundreds of thousands of wills. So what we see instead is civil or criminal penalties against the UPL-er, and an injunction against further unauthorized practice, but not the invalidation of the work that was performed. These people, then, are probably held to the same standard as the lawyer who has the authority to draft these documents.

Technically, a lawyer who practices law in a state where he or she is not licensed to practice is engaging in UPL. Even so, that lawyer will be held to the same standard of competence. The UPL, then, appears to make no difference in a negligence action. One is not more or less negligent as a result of the UPL.

Per se
is a Latin expression
meaning "by itself."

RULE #3 WRAP-UP

Some rules of thumb on competence are:

1. Keep abreast of changes in the law. Take continuing education classes. Read legal journals and periodicals.
2. Hold yourself out as a specialist in a field only if you have worked in that field for a substantial length of time or have a specialist certificate in that field.
3. Be completely honest about what you know how to do and what you do not know how to do. If you are unsure of your skills, be sure that you are working in a place where you will get training and supervision.
4. Keep in mind that your loyalties must be to your firm, supervising attorney, paralegal supervisor, and your firm's clients. Don't let outside influences affect the quality of your work.
5. As soon as you notice a problem, such as a missed statute of limitations or other serious error, bring it to the attention of your supervisor.
6. Never, under any circumstances, try to hide a potential ethical or legal problem from your employing firm or company.

RULE #3 REVIEW QUESTIONS

1. What is "competence"? Why is it important to the legal profession to be competent?
2. What duties does a lawyer have regarding the duty of the paralegal to be competent?
3. What is the primary goal of the competence requirements?

4. List some of the requirements for paralegal competence provided by the paralegal associations.

5. Why do we use the expression "professional negligence" rather than the expression "malpractice"?

6. What does the Latin expression "*respondeat superior*" mean?

7. Who is responsible for the errors of one lawyer or paralegal in a firm of many lawyers?

8. What is the ordinary standard of care? When is a higher standard of care used?

9. What does it mean that "good faith" is a defense to a claim of attorney negligence?

10. What are some of the things each paralegal can do to ensure competence?

1 *SK Handtool Corp. v. Dresser Industries*, 619 N.E.2d 1282 (Ill.App. 1993).

2 NALA Model Standards and Guidelines. This is taken from the NALA Web site at *http://www. nala.org.*

3 *Pearson v. Darrington*, 32 Ala. 227 (1858).

4 *Christy v. Saliterman*, 179 N.W.2d 288 (Minn. 1970).

5 *George v. Caton*, 600 P.2d 822 (N.M. 1979), *cert. quashed*, 98 P.2d 215.

6 At 586, quoted from *McCullough v. Sullivan*, 132 A. 102 (N.J. 1925) [362 A.2d 581 (N.J. 1976)]

7 *Medrano v. Miller*, 608 S.W.2d 81 (Tex. 1980).

8 605 S.W.2d 631 (Tex. Civ. App.—Houston [1st Dist.] 1980).

9 The difference between DeBakey's fee and the fee they paid the other attorney tripled.

10 *Goebel v. Lauderdale*, 214 Cal.App.3d 1502, 263 Cal.Rptr. 275 (1989); *Smith v. Lewis*, 530 P.2d 589 (Cal. 1975).

11 514 P.2d 1219 (Cal. 1973).

12 *Connaughton v. Gertz*, 418 N.E.2d 858 (Ill. App. 1981).

13 791 S.W.2d 254 (Tex.1990).

14 Drug and Alcohol Addiction in the Legal Profession, Legal Profession Assistance Conference, The Benchmark Institute publication

15 *Hu v. Fang*, 127 Cal.Rptr.2d 756, 104 Cal. App., 4th 61 (Cal. App., 2002)

16 *Ishmael v. Millington* (3rd Dist. 1966) 241 Cal.App.2d 520, at 523.

17 *Rodriguez v. Horton*, 622 P.2d 261 (N.M. 1980).

18 47 Cal.App.3d 802, 121 Cal.Rptr. 194 (1975).

19 *Millright v. Romer*, 322 N.W.2d 30 (Iowa 1982).

20 491 P.2d 421 (Cal. 1971).

21 231 Cal.App.3d 105, 282 Cal.Rptr. 205 (1991).

22 *Murphy v. Gruber*, 241 S.W.3d 689 (Tex. App., 2007).

23 *Busch v. Flangas*, 837 P.2d 438 (Nev. 1992).

24 *Allen v. Frawley*, 82 N.W. 593 (Wis. 1900).

25 *Blackmon v. Hale*, 463 P.2d 418 (Cal. 1970).

26 *Hodges v. Carter*, 80 S.E.2d 144 (N.C. 1954).

27 *Dayton Bar Assn. v. Stewart,* 116 Ohio St.3d 289, 2007-Ohio-6461 (2007).

28 *In the Matter of Kingsley, No. 138,* 2008 (Del. June 4, 2008) (Del. 2008).

Charge Only Fair Fees

Even though we typically refer to law as a "profession," it is also a business. Just as with any other business, one objective is to make a profit. The fee agreement with a client, then, is the place where we balance the cost of that client's case and the amount of money that can be generated by that case so that the firm makes a profit. It may be lore that fee agreements have nothing to do with paralegals. You have likely been told that paralegals cannot "make fee agreements" or "negotiate fee agreements" with clients. However, as a billable employee, you are part of the fee chain and have the ethical obligation to be fair. Here we go.

FEE AGREEMENTS WITH CLIENTS

Fee agreements are typically not negotiated between the client and the lawyer, but they should be. In the vast majority of instances, the law firm has a standard fee agreement that the client just signs without reading. It's not unlike buying a car. Did we read all of those documents? No, of course not. The sales agent explained the big points of the deal (cost of the car, the interest rate, and penalties) and showed us where to sign. And we signed. It's only after there's a problem that we read the fine print. But the car dealership is not under a duty to explain the contract to the consumer. The lawyer is. Furthermore, the more open communication there is between the law firm and the client at the inception of the case, the less likely there will be disputes later about the bills. The legal fee must not only be fully explained to the client but also must be *objectively reasonable.* If it is not a

Objectively reasonable: Reasonable in the minds of all people, not distorted by personal feelings or interpretation.

What's the law in your state on fee agreements? Do they have to be in writing? To begin your research, read your state's Rule of Professional Conduct Rule 1.5. To find cases and commentary on the Rule, try this search: [*yourstate*] + "Rules of Professional Conduct" + "Rule 1.5" + "fee agreement" + writing

reasonable agreement, the court will not enforce it. Your state's Rule 1.5 lists factors to be considered in determining the reasonableness of a fee. Included in this list are variables like the time and number of employees required, the novelty, complexity and difficulty of the issues, and the fee customarily charged for this work in your community. Your state has adopted (either by statute or case law) a list of factors for determining reasonableness of fees. Now would be a good time to locate that law.

UPL is Rule #7.

Paralegals are not permitted to "negotiate" fee agreements with clients on behalf of a lawyer.[1] The rationale for this rule is that the **negotiation** (i.e., bargaining) of a fee agreement necessarily involves the practice of law. If a paralegal did it, it would be the unauthorized practice of law (UPL). However, just as there are exceptions to UPL standards, there is an exception to this rule: that is where the paralegal is explaining a routine fee agreement to a client. In other words, if the agreement is not "negotiated," that is, if the client agrees to the contract as it is written, there is arguably nothing UPL-ish with having the contract explained by the paralegal or having the client sign the agreement without discussing it with an attorney. If the paralegal has been given instruction in the various elements of the contract and told to explain it to the client, this cannot constitute "the unauthorized practice of law," as the paralegal is doing nothing more than repeating what the lawyer said. (See Rule #7 for a discussion of "conduit of information.") We are balancing the need for the client to thoroughly understand the fee agreement against society's concerns regarding UPL and the need to have an efficient, cost-effective law practice.

Live in Florida? Check out *www.sunethics.com* for up-to-date ethics information in that state.

WHAT DO YOU THINK?

Should the client have to pay the lawyer's hourly rate for the time it takes to explain the fee agreement to the client?

Paralegals in most firms are viewed as **billable**; that is, the time they spend on a legal matter is billed to the client. It is helpful to be aware of the fee agreement that the law firm has with each client so that you can bill in accordance with the agreement. However, some law firms keep these fee agreements as closely held secrets. Additionally, the agreement with the client is a **confidential communication**, so it should not be discussed with anyone outside of the law firm.

In fact, that a particular person is the client of the firm is confidential.

Contingency Fees

There are many different kinds of fee agreements: contingency, hourly, mixed billing, and value billing are just some of them. The plaintiff's side of most personal injury cases is taken on a **contingency fee** basis.

This means that the law firm's recovery of legal fees is *contingent* upon the outcome of the case. The law firm may advance the costs of the lawsuit as well as dedicate hours to it. At the end of the lawsuit, if the judgment (or settlement) is in favor of the plaintiff, the law firm and the client will split the money. The expenses must be paid, as well. Expenses can include costs of litigation (such as filing fees, deposition costs, and expert witness fees) as well as costs pertaining to medical treatment of the plaintiff. Who pays these expenses and out of what money are two of the contract details that should be negotiated between the firm and the client.

Contingent *means dependent on conditions or occurrences not yet established.*

Let's take some examples:

Suppose that the client and the defendant have agreed to a $100,000 settlement amount.

Assuming the lawyer has a 40% contingency fee, spent $10,000 in costs, and the client's hospital bills total $30,000, the $100,000 could be apportioned like this:

> $40,000 to the lawyer.
>
> $60,000 to the client, but out of the client's portion, subtract $10,000 in costs (paid back to the lawyer) and hospital bills (paid to the hospital) of $30,000. Now the client has $20,000 remaining.

The $100,000 could be divided like this:

> $10,000 in costs (paid back to the lawyer).
>
> $36,000 (40% of $90,000) to the lawyer, leaving $54,000 for the client from which he must pay $30,000 to the hospital. Now the client ultimately gets $26,000.

The $100,000 could be divided like this:

> $30,000 to the hospital.
>
> $10,000 in costs (paid back to the lawyer), leaving $60,000; the lawyer gets 40% ($24,000), and the client gets the remaining $36,000.

As you can see, the method of calculating the fees can make a big difference in the amount the client will ultimately get from the lawsuit. This is why a careful and complete explanation of the fee agreement is important. The more the client understood and agreed to, the more likely the contract will be affirmed.[2]

Lawyers have been known to "overreach" in contingency fee agreements so that they are getting more than their fair share. For example, a contingency fee agreement allocating 20% to the client and 80% to the lawyer is overreaching. Even if the fee agreement is completely and carefully explained to the client, a fee that is *objectively unfair* will not be permitted (assuming the client contests it to a court or other tribunal). In determining the fairness of the contract, a court will look at the sophistication of the client, how well the contract was explained to the client by the law firm, and how acceptable the fee agreement would seem to the average person.

An infamous California civil rights attorney, after winning $44,000 in punitive damages for his clients, asked for and received $378,000 in attorney's fees under the federal civil rights statute 42 USC§ 1988 which allows the prevailing party to an award of attorney's fees from the losing side. But the attorney did not tell the U.S. district court that he had a fee agreement with his clients that entitled him to 45 percent of their damage award. The fee agreement also provided that the costs of the litigation would be deducted from the clients' 55 percent. This left the clients, who had suffered a substantial loss, about $800 each. The State Bar of California found that the attorney had taken an *unconscionable fee*. The double fee was "objectively unreasonable and unfair."

Rule 1.5 requires contingent fee agreements to be in writing and to fully set forth who gets what money and in what order of priority under the agreement. Most states have similar rules. The law in most states also provides that a contingency agreement is not permitted in some family law matters and all criminal matters. Rule 1.5 also discusses the rules for dividing fees among lawyers who are not in the same law firm.

Hourly Billing

Another method of billing, and probably the most widely used in personal injury defense and every other kind of legal representation, is **hourly billing**. When you begin working at a law firm, you will be assigned a certain **billing rate**. You should ask what your billing rate is just so that you will have an idea of what an hour of your time is worth (and so that you know, if you have an urge to cheat on your time sheets, how much you are cheating the client).

If your firm uses hourly billing, all billable employees (attorneys, law clerks, and paralegals, usually) will be asked to keep an account of the time spent on each task and for what client. For purposes of illustration, the smallest billable amount is 1/10 of an hour, or six minutes. In this illustration, the paralegal's billing rate is $100 per hour, and the attorney's billing rate is $250 per hour.

As a paralegal, you may be asked to keep a daily time log like this one that accounts for all of your time for each of the clients or cases you work on.

DAILY TIME SHEET

Date 06/24/05

Employee Renee A. Marcus—Paralegal

TIME	MATTER	DESCRIPTION
.3	Jones	telephone call to Secretary of State for corporate status check
.5	Dolan	draft letter to Dept. of Motor Vehicles regarding Mr. Dolan's driving record
.75	Dolan	research case law on driving/negligence
1.5	Jones	research client's employment record
2	Smith	track down previous students to provide information/references of Mr. Smith's teaching method
5.05	**TOTAL**	

DAILY TIME SHEET

Date _____06/25/05_____

Employee _____John B. Davis—attorney_____

TIME	MATTER	DESCRIPTION
.1	Dolan	telephone call to Dept of Defense to verify Mr. Dolan's release from the Army
.5	Smith	draft letter to Board of Education regarding Mr. Smith's work record and job performance
.7	Black	review file to look for copy of client's birth certificate
3.5	Dolan	review deposition summary of Accident Witness #1
.6	Dolan	review RAMs mark-up of draft letter and make appropriate revisions; put in final form
2.2	White	deposition summary/ Mr. Witness
7.6	**TOTAL**	

WHAT DO YOU THINK?

An attorney catches you in the hallway and says, "Quick! I need to know where the state's legal rate of interest is." You run on down the hall to the library. Unfortunately, you look and look and can't find the darned thing . . . but eventually you do. It took you five hours, and there it was, all along, in the state constitution. You have to account for your time. What do you do? What's fair to the client? Should the client be charged for 5 hours if it should have taken 30 minutes to find the answer? The answer is: It's not your decision. Your job is to keep accurate time records. If the time should be written down, the responsible lawyer will do that.

Over a period of one month, your time records and the time records of all billers on this client's matter will be put together on one account statement.

These time records are compiled by an accounting staff member, bookkeeper, or an outside service and sent to the client in a form that looks like this:

Law Office of John B. Davis

1234 Oak Avenue
Anytown, OH
404/555-1212

July 1, 2005
Mr. Charles J. Dolan
50 Tower Road
Anytown, OH

Re: Dolan v. State of Ohio—services through June 30, 2005

DATE	DESCRIPTION	INIT	TIME	RATE	TOTAL
06/24	draft letter to DMV	RAM	.5	$75	$37.50
06/24	research case law	RAM	.75	$75	$56.25
06/24	review files and arrest record	RAM	1.5	$75	$112.50
06/25	telephone call	JBD	.1	$150	$15.00
06/25	review of deposition summaries	JBD	3.5	$150	$525.00
06/25	draft letter to DMV	JBD	.6	$150	$90.00
06/30	depostion summary	JBD	1.5	$150	$225.00

TOTAL NOW DUE   **$1061.25**

If you have any questions or concerns about this bill, please call
immediately and ask to speak with Janice in Accounting.

This itemized bill above allows the client to see who is working on his
case, what each person is doing, and how much time is being spent. Years
ago, the client would be sent a bill that looked like this:

Law Office of John B. Davis
1234 Oak Avenue
Anytown, OH
404/555-1212

July 1, 2005
Mr. Charles J. Dolan
50 Tower Road
Anytown, OH

Re: Dolan v. State of Ohio—services through June 30, 2005

FOR SERVICES RENDERED   **$10,625.75**

But those days are over. State laws across the country now require enough detail to keep the client reasonably informed about who is working on the client's matter, what is being done, and how much time is spent doing it. Even if the law did not require this information, clients, who have gotten more sophisticated over the years, would demand it.

There are lots of software programs that make this time and billing accounting happen in the modern law office. Your daily time records may well be kept on a computer program so that they can be automatically integrated into the time records of the other billers.

Before any bill gets sent to the client, however, an attorney responsible for that client reviews the bill. At this point, the responsible attorney has an opportunity to see if the bill looks too high considering the work that was performed, if any discounts should be given, or if someone spent too much time doing some task. At this point, that responsible attorney will "write down" time or, in some instances, "write up" time.

Law Office of John B. Davis

MONTHLY TIME SHEET

Date 06/01/05–06/30/05
Client Charles J. Dolan

TIME	DATE	INIT	DESCRIPTION
.5	06/24/05	RAM	draft letter to Dept. of Motor Vehicles regarding Mr. Dolan's driving record
.75	06/24/05	RAM	research case law on driving/negligence
.1	06/25/05	JBD	telephone call to Dept. of Defense
3.5	06/25/05	JBD	review deposition summary of Accident Witness #1
.6	06/25/05	JBD	reviewed RAMs mark-up draft letter and made revisions; put in final form
~~.25~~	~~06/28/05~~	~~RAM~~	~~set up appointment to meet with arresting officer~~ *JBD*
1.5	06/30/05	JBD	review deposition summary/officer

| **6.95** | **TOTAL** | | |

Other Billing Methods

Another approach to billing is **value billing**. This describes an agreement with the client whereby the client will be charged a flat rate for certain tasks. For example, if your fee agreement says that Client will be billed $150 for each complaint that is drafted on Client's behalf, this is value billing. It is a favorite of corporate clients that require repetitive, routine legal assistance. If Client knows that interrogatories are $200 and court appearances are $500, it has a better idea of how much each matter will cost because the value billing cost is not dependent on the time it takes each individual to accomplish a task.

In some places, value billing refers to the contract under which the law firm gets paid a small amount for the work done and a bonus for a good result. In other words, the client is willing to pay more when he or she wins. Some people also refer to this kind of arrangement as **bonus billing**.

> ### WHAT DO YOU THINK?
>
> Morris Green died on March 3, 2004, allegedly as the result of a beating by Detroit police officers. His widow filed a wrongful death action and was very quickly offered $5.25 million to settle. Even though her attorney did very little work, his fee agreement entitled him to $1.7 million. Should he get that amount of money for filing a complaint? Is that objectively fair?

A cousin to value billing is **fixed fee billing**. This is an arrangement with the client whereby the client is charged one flat rate for the representation regardless of how long it takes or how much work is involved. In representations that are mass produced, such as some bankruptcy or consumer collection matters, fixed fee billing is very popular. It allows the client to budget legal fees from the beginning of the representation, it encourages efficiency, it encourages delegation of work to employees who are more suited to the tasks, and it provides training for new staff members in an atmosphere where "hours billed" is not the primary focus. In essence, the client is paying for a product.

> ### WHAT DO YOU THINK?
>
> The state of New York filed a class action lawsuit against the tobacco industry in 1997. In 2002, the case had ended, and the six law firms representing the state filed a motion for their unprecedented $625 million fee. The judge in charge of the case said that the fee didn't pass the "smell test." Does it? What factors would you consider if you were the judge?

A variation of the typical hourly billing system is **blended rate billing**. In this arrangement, rather than paying $250 an hour for the partner, $180 an hour for the associate, and $75 an hour for the paralegal, the client agrees to pay one hourly rate, a blended rate of, for example, $150 an hour, for all billing employees. This encourages the firm to utilize the lower rate billers and to use the expensive partners sparingly.

KEEPING TRACK OF TIME

Most paralegals keep track of their time as part of their job. Most of those paralegals work for law firms that have annual hourly expectations for all billing employees. That means that you will be told that you are expected to bill X number of hours per year. Keeping track of time may seem an easy task right now, but it can be difficult to do. Your duty is to keep time records that are **thorough, accurate, and contemporaneous**. Clear enough. There are so many questions, though, once you actually go to work as a paralegal.

The pressure to bill more hours appears to be ever increasing. A 1960 ABA study reported that associates billed 1400 to 1600 hours per year, and that partners billed 1200 to 1400 hours per year.[1] Since the 1990s, firms ask associates to bill 2300 or 2400 hours per year, and many use even higher "target hours" to award bonuses. It makes sense that law firms and lawyers want to make more money. The cost of education is higher. The interest on student loans is higher. Everything is more expensive, so we need to make more money. But what are people involved in the legal profession, people who are fiduciaries, doing to make more money? The good news is that most of them are honest, hardworking people. The bad news is that time sheet padding (and otherwise defrauding clients) is on the rise. According to a study on lawyers and professional responsibility, between 1989 and 1996, there were 36 cases of disbarred and/or imprisoned lawyers sanctioned for stealing over $100,000 apiece from their partners and their clients through billing or expense fraud.[2] Before 1989, there were none. Now it seems that the legal journals and newspapers are littered with stories of attorney fraud and time record padding. According to a survey from the early 1990s, 50.2% of attorneys surveyed admitted to either rarely, occasionally, or frequently double billing clients.[3]

Even when there is no criminal or disciplinary action taken, time sheet padding turns up in fee applications filed with courts. And courts love to make fun of lawyers who overbill. Here's an example:

> The time sheets contain numerous examples of excessive and unreasonable entries. As the trial judge herself noted, in one entry on July 7th, Martin Haines charged 35 hours, which he describes as essentially for reviewing files. Apart from the obvious rewriting of the laws of physics so that it took the earth 25% longer to rotate on its axis that day, there is nothing in the context to suggest the

necessity for such an extraordinary expenditure of time. Haines argues that the 35-hour entry actually encapsulated all the time he had spent on that holiday weekend working on the file. Some other time sheet entries, however, suggest a different conclusion. On June 30th, he claims to have spent 10 hours reviewing the file. On July 3rd, he claims 9 hours preparing for and attending a "bifurcation" hearing. On July 4th (which is apparently part of the same long holiday weekend), he claims to have spent 2.5 hours reviewing records and preparing an order.

There are many other questionable entries on these time sheets. For example, on July 2nd, one associate billed 6.9 hours, while another billed 4.8, essentially for reviewing and organizing the file. On that same day, an associate billed 4.8 hours for research, while a paralegal billed 3 hours for research on retaining liens and substitution of counsel and 2 hours for other research. On July 10th, the same associate and law clerk spent 4.2 and 4.5 hours researching the same legal issue. Two days later the law clerk charged 11 hours drafting a position paper, which the same associate charged 3.4 hours to redraft, while still another associate charged 3 hours to continue reorganizing papers from the client. On July 15th, Haines charged 6 hours preparing for a hearing. Later in the month, Haines, the associate, and the paralegal all charged for working on a petition for certiorari. Indeed in the month of July alone the firm's attorneys and paralegal racked up more than 194 hours![4]

WHAT DO YOU THINK?

You are called into the senior partner's office and told to increase your billable hours, even if it means inflating your actual billable hours. You need this job. You decide to pad your hours on contingency fee cases because in those cases the firm gets paid a portion of the client's settlement or award. That way, no client will be actually harmed. Have you made the right decision? To aid you in your answer, read *In re Lawrence*, 884 So. 2d 561 (La. October 19, 2004).

BILLING PRACTICES

When you go to work, someone will explain the firm's billing practices to you. Someone will explain how to keep your time sheets or what software the firm uses, the smallest amount of billable time, what you should bill and what should be left out, and how much detail should be included.

If the smallest billable amount in your firm is 0.25 (15 minutes), what do you do with the tasks that you do that take 5 or 10 minutes each? What do you do with the task that takes you 4 hours that should have taken 15 minutes? What do you do if, at the end of the day, you have not written down each task and time and cannot clearly remember? (Your duty is to keep "contemporaneous" time records, but does that mean minute by minute or is every few hours often enough to record your time?) Can you lump all of your tasks together (e.g., researched statute of limitations, wrote two-page memo to Partner, made requested revisions, and forwarded to client with cover letter) or should each task have its own time entry? If your law firm offers a bonus for reaching a certain number of billable hours, does your written down time count toward that amount? Is there a relationship between your billable hours and your salary, bonuses, and benefits? Should you record clerical tasks? If you don't get an explanation up front, you should ask the questions.

Each employer will be different and will have different expectations of you. What will you do if those expectations are offensive to you? For example, it is a common practice for insurance companies to offer a large number of cases to a law firm in exchange for a discounted rate. It was also a common practice for firms to accept these cases at a discounted rate but inflate their hours to compensate for the discount. To see how this worked out for one attorney, read *Maryland Grievance Committee v. Hess.*[5]

Another popular billing strategy is to charge the client a set amount for court appearances (or other task) regardless of how long the task actually takes. Remember: Fee agreements are negotiable. If the client has agreed to this type of billing (fixed fee), then there is nothing wrong with it. To see what happened to an attorney who did not have a fixed fee billing contract with his client, see *Disciplinary Counsel v. Holland.*[6]

It is said that 90% of all legal fees is generated by hourly billing. Seventy percent of paralegals work for law firms. It is likely, then, that these questions will come your way.

Now's a good time to ask the gnarly question: What will I do when I'm asked to cheat a client. To aid you in your answer, we have provided some cases on the publisher's Web site. Have a discussion with your classmates, then read the cases, and then have the discussion again.

In the Matter of Kellogg, 50 P.3d 57 (Kan., 2002)

In re Lawrence, 884 So. 2d 561 (La. October 19, 2004)

Bohatch v. Butler & Binion, 977 S.W.2d 543, 544 (Tex. 1998).

Check list for keeping your time records:

(1) Keep your time records contemporaneously.

(2) Keep accurate and detailed time records.

(3) Keep honest time records.

RETAINER AGREEMENTS

To ensure that it is paid, the law firm will often require a **retainer** from the client. Retainers can be confusing, but it is vital that the client understand what kind of agreement is being made, so you must understand it, too.

The **classic retainer** insures the attorney's availability over time; it is considered earned upon receipt, whether or not services are actually provided. For example, if you are O.J. Simpson, you might call your friend Robert Shapiro from Chicago and say, "I'm coming home soon. I need you to clear your calendar for me. Don't take any cases in the next few days." Bob says to him, "Well, okay, but I need to take cases so that I can make a living, so if you want me to keep my calendar clear, you need to pay me for that." O.J. wires him $10,000 to keep him "on retainer," or available.

Another type of retainer that is earned upon receipt regardless of services actually rendered is sometimes called a **nonrefundable retainer**. Some courts have declared nonrefundable retainers *per se* unreasonable because the client has an absolute right to fire the lawyer for any reason at any time. A nonrefundable retainer impairs that right. A nonrefundable retainer has also been condemned as an unearned fee.

WHAT DO YOU THINK?

Your friend is accused of cheating and is dismissed from school. She hires a lawyer who asks for a nonrefundable retainer. The agreement states that the lawyer will try to get your friend back into school because, of course, no one can guarantee a positive result. After the agreement is signed and the money is paid, the lawyer calls the dean of the school, explains your friend's innocence, and asks the dean to reinstate her. The dean says no. "Okay," says the lawyer, "I tried but can't get you back in." Has the fee been earned? Is it fair for the lawyer to keep the entire fee?

An **advance payment retainer** is present payment compensating the attorney for services to be performed in the future; it is considered earned upon receipt and may be a "flat fee." In other words, an advance payment retainer may be paid without expectation that the attorney will ask for more compensation once the amount of the retainer is exhausted.

The more common type of retainer is a **security retainer.** Its purpose is also to secure payment for future services. Technically, the security retainer remains the property of the client until it is applied to charges for services actually rendered, and any unused portion is refundable to the client at the end of the representation. This is the most typical kind of retainer used in hourly billing situations. When you hear your office coworkers talking about a retainer, this is probably what they are talking about.

It works like this: The client may give the law firm a $10,000 retainer by way of a check. This money is deposited into the Client

Trust Account (as opposed to a general operating account of the law firm), and is drawn against as the firm bills the client. So, at the end of the month, the firm sends the client a bill for $2,300. If the client does not object to any parts of the bill, the firm may take that $2,300 out of the $10,000 sitting in the Client Trust Account. When the $10,000 is nearly depleted, the firm may ask the client to replenish it. Alternatively, the firm may look to the client to actually pay (write a new check for) the $2,300. The $10,000 stays on deposit in the Client Trust Account just in case the client does not pay that bill and some future bills. The $10,000, then, is a cushion so that the firm can be sure that its bills will be paid.

The firm, of course, has many clients, so the money in the Client Trust Account is a compilation of the retainers from all of these different clients. It is one account, but it has the retainer money from all of the firm's clients in it. Each client's money can be used to pay the expenses of each client's case, but must never be used to pay for another client's case, the operating expenses of the law firm, or the personal expenses of any of the lawyers or employees. The sanctity of the Client Trust Account is discussed under Rule #10.

Law Firm Spotlight

Lindquist & Vennum, a firm of 200 lawyers and 25 paralegals, has two offices: one in Denver and another in Minneapolis. L&V boasts 100 percent of its lawyers and paralegals meet or exceed the ABA's pro bono hours challenge (donating an amount of time equal to three percent of the firm's total billable hours to pro bono work). Proving that law firms can help in the community in more ways than one, L&V formed the Winter Closet Foundation in 2002. The Foundation provides warm clothes for children in the Denver and Minneapolis regions. All the clothes are new and purchased by employees of the firm. The Winter Closet initiative was the key reason L&V was a recipient of the Minneapolis Regional Chamber of Commerce's 2003 Quality of Life Award. You can find L&V at http://www.lindquist.com.

PRO BONO WORK

Pro bono
is Latin for "for free."
Literally it means "for the good."

While we're talking about fees, we should talk about working for no fee. This is called **pro bono work**. Pro bono work is a big part of making legal services available to the public. Rule 1.5 says that reasonable fees should be charged to the client in appropriate cases in which the clients are able to pay them. Nevertheless, under Rule 6.1, persons who are unable to pay reasonable fees should be able to obtain necessary legal services. To ensure that all people can get legal assistance when they need it, legal professionals should support and participate in ethical activities designed to achieve that objective. This is covered in depth under Rule #5.

RECOVERY OF FEES FROM THE CLIENT

Years ago, the ABA took a strong position against lawsuits between attorney and client over fees. Based on a 1943 ABA Opinion (No. 250), the ABA's position was that an attorney "should be zealous in his efforts to avoid controversies over fees with clients." Further, "[h]e should not sue a client for a fee unless necessary to prevent fraud or gross imposition by the client." In the 1980s, however, the ABA's standards on "gross imposition" slackened. In reality, very few attorneys will ignore the unpaid client bill. In fact, many law firms employ paralegals to handle the collection of delinquent bills for the firm.

> If you think that $625 million was bad, the fee in the Florida tobacco cases was $2.8 **billion**. The lawyers went to court to fight for their fee. In his decision against the lawyers, the Florida judge estimated that the fees amounted to $7,716 an hour for each of the 12 private attorneys billing 24 hours a day for the 42 months that the case went on. "Perhaps tens of millions or hundreds of millions of dollars might be reasonable," Cohen wrote, "but 2.8 billion dollars simply shocks the conscience of the court." What do you think? Does it shock your conscience? Is it fair?

California and other states mandate fee arbitration between attorneys and clients who question the attorney's fees. California's Business & Professions Code §§6200–6206 require that the attorney give notice to the client of the client's right to elect to arbitrate any fee dispute. This is true in New York, as well. Can you find it in your state's law? Giving the client the opportunity to arbitrate the fee makes sense from a time and effort point of view. These arbitrations are informal; the client does not need to hire an attorney, so the arbitration often turns out more like a mediated conversation between the attorney and the client. This leads to agreements, rather than more litigation.

To recover the fee, of course, the attorney must show that the client retained him or her and that the services performed were with the client's informed consent. A thorough explanation of the fees before beginning the representation and an honest discussion about the anticipated costs will go a long way in avoiding fee disputes. Anyone involved in collecting fees from clients should also be aware that the Fair Debt Collection Practices Act[7] applies to your activities. Last, you need to review the rules on conflicts of interest and collecting fees from clients. Once the law firm sues the client for fees, the law firm is in an adverse position to the client and cannot continue representation.

RECOVERY OF FEES FROM THE OTHER SIDE IN LITIGATION

prevailing
means winning

A *prevailing* party may recover attorneys' fees from the other party in only limited circumstances: where attorneys' fees are provided for in a statute and where they are provided for in the contract. This is called the American Rule of attorneys' fees.[8] For example, at the conclusion of the lawsuit, the prevailing party can ask the court to award attorneys' fees under the Federal Rehabilitation Act[9] because the statute specifically provides that in cases of discrimination against individuals with disabilities, the prevailing party is entitled to "reasonable attorneys' fees." The prevailing party prepares a memorandum or declaration setting forth all of the time spent, hourly billing rates, tasks, and costs of the litigation. Ordinarily a separate motion will be heard on the issue of the reasonableness of the fees requested. The hourly rate requested will be reviewed by the court to ensure that it is reasonable and "the market rate" for that kind of attorney in that locale. Specialized attorneys, such as those who specialize in civil rights cases, are often awarded higher hourly fees.[10]

Interestingly, statutes and contracts provide for "attorneys' fees." Taken literally, that would mean that other legal professionals would not be included, that the cost of having such an assistant must be "overhead" and taken into account in determining the attorneys' hourly rates. The interpretation of the term "attorneys' fees" has been as far as the U.S. Supreme Court.

Missouri v. Jenkins[11] was a major school desegregation case in Kansas City, Missouri. The second issue tackled by the U.S. Supreme Court was "should the fee award compensate the work of paralegals and law clerks by applying the market rate for their work?" The Court:

> Clearly, a "reasonable attorney's fee" under [42 USC § 1988] cannot have meant to compensate only work performed personally by members of the bar. Rather, the term must refer to a reasonable fee for the work product of an attorney . . . [including] . . .

secretaries, messengers, librarians, janitors and others whose labor contributes to the work product for which an attorney bills her client; and it must also take into account of other expenses and profit. (p. 285)

The Court's footnote ten on page 288 points out: "Of course, purely clerical or secretarial tasks should not be billed at a paralegal rate regardless of who performs them."[12] In 2008, the U.S. Supreme Court cited its own decision in *Missouri v. Jenkins* and awarded paralegal fees in *Richlin Security Serv Co. v. Chertoff.*[13]

In spite of what appears to be a clear message from the Supreme Court, the issue is still far from settled among the state courts. The only way to know for sure is to research your state's law. Bear in mind, also, that where paralegal fees may be awardable under one statute, they may not be under another.

If you research the case law in your state, you will find cases that discuss whether paralegal fees should be awarded when the statute says "attorneys fees" and the appropriate billing rate for paralegals.

There are also cases where the court has reduced the amount of attorney's fees requested because the attorney was performing tasks more properly performed by a paralegal.[14] For the most part, the courts agree that it is the task, not the title of the billing employee, which is determinative of recoverability. Clerical tasks are not billable and will not be recoverable. Tasks that are nonclerical are billable and are usually recoverable at an hourly rate that is appropriate for the task.

From *Multi-Moto v. ITT Commercial Finance*, 806 S.W.2d 560 (Tex.App. 1990), here's a list of things you'll need if you're going to apply to the court for paralegal fees.

A party may separately assess and include in the award of attorneys' fees compensation for a legal assistant's work, if that assistant performs work traditionally done by an attorney. In order to recover such amounts, the evidence must establish: (1) the qualifications of the legal assistant to perform substantive legal work; (2) that the legal assistant performed substantive legal work under the direction and supervision of an attorney; (3) the nature of the legal work performed; (4) the legal assistant's hourly rate; and (5) the number of hours expended by the legal assistant.

Whenever applying for fees, these factors are essential for any declaration or motion filed with the court. Don't worry about this case being from Texas. This is a good list.

Here are some cases to help you begin your research. You'll find them on the publisher's Web site:

> *Information Sciences Corp. v. U.S.*, 86 Fed.Cl. 269 (2009), the Court of Federal Claims awarded paralegal fees at $102 per hour.
>
> *Nadarajah v. Holder,* — F.3d, —, 2009 WL 1588678 (9th Cir. June 9, 2009), the Ninth Circuit affirmed an hourly rate of $100 per hour for paralegals.
>
> *Precision Pine & Timber, Inc. v. United States*, 83 Fed.Cl. 544, 553 (2008), the court awarded paralegal time at upwards of $125 per hour.
>
> *Teresa R. v. Madison Metropolitan School Dist.,* — F.Supp.2d —, 2009 WL 1425192 (W.D. Wis. May 20, 2009), the court reduced the paralegal rate to $50 per hour.

To research the law on recoverability of nonlawyer fees in your state, try this search: [*yourstate*] + recover + "paralegal fees"

WHAT DO YOU THINK?

You are sent to Japan on a case for Client X. On the very long plane ride to Japan, you work on some other matters for Client M. Should you bill the time you spend on the plane twice, once to Client X and another time to Client M?

CLIENT FILES AND FEES

Repeat after me: "Client files belong to the client." Client files belong to the client. They cannot be "held hostage" to insure the payment of legal fees. This is true even if the contractual agreement between the law firm and the client specifically says that the law firm is entitled to a **retaining lien** on the files.

Several cases have discussed the common law **retaining lien**, or the idea that the attorney has an equitable right to keep all papers, money, and

---

Do you work in Illinois? If you do, this rule does not apply to you. If you look at Illinois' Rule 1.15, you'll see that it says that a lawyer can keep "disputed property" that the client claims until the dispute has been resolved, and Rule 1.16, which says that at termination of representation, the law should deliver to the client all papers and property to which the client is entitled. For more on this subject, see the article "More Than You Ever Wanted to Know about Retaining Liens" on the publisher's Web site.

other property of the client that the attorney has in his or her possession in order to secure payment of legal fees. Most courts have rejected the common law retaining lien theory in favor of a more important goal of not prejudicing the client's case.[15] Even though the law seems very clear that the client's files must be turned over, in reality, many lawyers still try to hold the files hostage until the client pays the fees.

WHAT DO YOU THINK?

Does absolutely *everything* in the file belong to the client? What about secret attorney thoughts? What about notes about impressions or unprovable facts. Give it some thought. Look up this case for some recent guidance: *Swift, Currie, McGhee & Hiers v. Henry*, 276 Ga. 571 (Ga. May 19, 2003).

A retaining lien is not the same as a **charging lien**. A charging lien secures the legal fees by attaching a lien to a future judgment or settlement in the case. For instance, if a law firm is hired on a contingency fee basis and does work for the client and then the client discharges that firm and hires a second firm, the first firm may file a charging lien in the lawsuit. When the case is settled or a judgment is rendered by the court, the first law firm has a lien on the amount awarded to the client. There may well be a fight about how much the first law firm is entitled to, but money should not be disbursed to the client or the second law firm before the percentages are all decided upon.[16]

Your Rule 1.16 says something like this: Upon termination of representation, a lawyer. extent reasonably practicable to protect a client's interests, such as giving reasonable notice to the client, allowing time for employment of other counsel, surrendering documents and property to which the client is entitled and refunding any advance payment of a fee that has not been earned. Upon the client's request, the lawyer shall provide the client with all of the client's documents, and all documents reflecting work performed for the client.

Rule 3-700(D)(1) of the California State Bar Rules of Professional Conduct requires that once an attorney's representation has been terminated, the attorney *shall* promptly release to the client all the client's papers and property. "Client papers and property" includes "correspondence, pleadings, deposition transcripts, exhibits, physical evidence, expert's reports and other items reasonably necessary to the client's representation."

What's the law in your state?

RULE #4 WRAP-UP

The overriding consideration in client billing is that the fee must be objectively fair. Profit margin on employees is not the barometer to use in determining fairness, but the sophistication and relative bargaining power of the attorney and client are proper considerations. The requirement that the fee be reasonable will override the terms of the contract in appropriate cases. Again, the more you can prove that the client understood the terms of the agreement, the more likely it will be that the agreement will be found to be fair.

RULE #4 REVIEW QUESTIONS

1. What is a billable task? Give some examples of billable and non-billable tasks.
2. Why should fee agreements with the client be in writing?
3. What is the rationale behind the rule prohibiting paralegals from negotiating fee agreements with clients?
4. What is a contingency fee agreement? When is a contingency fee agreement used?
5. Define "value billing" and "fixed fee billing." How are they different? How are they the same?
6. List five questions you should ask about your responsibilities as a time biller in a law firm.
7. What are the different kinds of retainer agreements? Are some more fair than others? Why or why not?
8. Can paralegal hourly fees be recovered from the losing side in litigation? How would you go about convincing a court that your client is entitled to recovery of those fees?
9. What is a referral fee? Can you accept a referral fee?
10. What is a retaining lien? A charging lien? How are they different?

---

[1] See William G. Ross, *The Honest Hour: The Ethics of Time-Based Billing by Attorneys* 20 (1996) (citing Eugene C. Gerhart, *The Art of Billing Clients*, 1 LAW OFF. ECON. & MGMT. 29, 34).

[2] Lisa Lerman, *The Slippery Slope from Ambition to Greed to Dishonest: Lawyers, Money, and Professional Responsibility*, 878 HOFSTRA LAW JOURNAL (2002).

[3] See William G. Ross, *The Ethics of Hourly Billing by Attorneys*, 44 RUTGERS L. REV. 1 app. A at 92 (1991).

[4] *Haines v. Sophia*, 711 So. 2d 209 (Fla. 1998).

[5] *Attorney Grievance Comm'n v. Hess*, 352 Md. 438, 453, 722 A.2d 905, 913 (1999).

[6] *Disciplinary Counsel v. Holland*, 106 Ohio St.3d 372, 2005-Ohio-5322.

[7] 15 USC Section 1692 et. seq.

[8] In England (the English Rule), the prevailing party always gets fees from the other side.

[9] 29 USC Section 794 et. seq.

[10] *Barker v. City of West Lafayette*, 894 N.E.2d 1004 (Ind. App. 2008).

11   491 U.S. 274 (1989).

12   See also footnote seven of the Court's opinion for a rundown on the various federal courts' handling of paralegal time.

13   *Richlin Security Service v. Chertoff*, 553 U.S. ___ (2008).

14   *Smith v. Roher*, 1997 U.S. Dist. Lexis 1411 (1997).

15   *Home Savings of America v. Malart*, 632 A.2d 827 (N.J.Super. 1993). But see *Matter of Estate of Benney*, 790 P.2d 319 (Colo. 1990) where the Colorado Supreme Court seems to say that Colorado's retaining lien statute is valid. If, for example, the lawyer has been hired to draft a will, in some states the lawyer may be allowed to keep the will and the notes, research, etc., until the client has paid. See also *In re Century Cleaning Services, Inc.*, 202 B.R. 149 (Bkrtcy.D.Or. 1996).

16   See *Rhodes v. Martinez*, 925 P.2d 1201 (N.M.App. 1996). For a case where the law firm was entitled to a charging lien, see *Kiernan v. Kiernan*, 649 N.Y.S.2d 612 (1996).

Make Legal Services Available

ACCESS TO JUSTICE

There is a gap between the need for legal assistance and the satisfaction of that need. This gap is getting larger and larger. The primary reason for this problem is the cost, real or perceived, of legal services. The secondary reason is that many people are unaware of their rights under the law, so they don't see that they have a need for legal assistance. The law appears complex and frightening to most people. There is a perception that only the rich are entitled to justice. Lawyers, even those portrayed on television, do not appear to be honest or caring. As a result, the uneducated and the poor are those who are the least likely to receive legal help, although it is these people who need help the most. This is why there is an affirmative duty placed on all of us to provide better access to the judicial system. We call it access to justice.

To see how one state is helping meet the need, see Kentucky's Access to Justice Foundation at *http://www.accesstojustice.org.*

Access to justice includes informing people about their legal rights, showing them how the law can help them, and making legal services affordable—even if affordable means free.

INFORMATION

Our justice system is based on ensuring that people understand their legal rights. The constitution guarantees us the right to a lawyer in criminal matters charged against us, and *Miranda v. Arizona*[1] makes it mandatory that we be informed of that right (as not many of us have the Constitution memorized). Our other legal rights are not necessarily obvious to us; for example, a public school education for our children might be obvious, but how many of us know that we have a legal right to that education? And there are many legal issues to which we do not have a right but would make life so much easier for us and for our loved ones. An example of this is a will. There is no constitutional

Now would be a good
time to find your state's
Rule 6.1.

guarantee to a will, but with just a little bit of assistance, we can all have a will and our heirs will be thankful that we have one. Because the legal solutions to problems are not always obvious, Rule 6.1 says that members of the legal profession should assist people in recognizing their legal problems. One way of doing this is to participate in educational programs for laypeople. Another way of assisting people in recognizing their legal problems is advertising.

WHAT DO YOU THINK?

Should everyone have access to legal representation for noncriminal defense matters? Should the government provide representation just as it provides education?

Advertising

Some form of "advertising," that is, letting the public know the attorney's name, telephone number, and address, has always been permitted. If this were not true, members of the public would not be able to find a lawyer when they needed one. Before the 1980s, however, the legal profession was very strict about the kind of advertising that was allowed. The law did not allow attorneys to advertise on television, for example. It did not allow billboards or using the side of a municipal bus as an ad. However, *Bates v. Arizona* changed the laws prohibiting lawyers from advertising more than just their names and whereabouts. Now, since *Bates*, attorneys advertise all over the place; use paid actors, scripts, and explanations about the legal services offered; and even invite people to think about a simple headache as a cause of action against employers.

Although the Supreme Court's decision in *Bates* should have ended the controversy about attorney advertising, it did not. In 1984, Attorney Zauderer was publicly reprimanded by the Ohio Supreme Court after

---

Bates & O'Steen v. Arizona, 433 U.S. 350, 97 S.Ct. 2691 (1977). The U.S. Supreme Court held that prohibiting advertising by attorneys was a violation of their First Amendment right to free speech. The Court ruled that because the speech can be regulated by the integrated bar and because such advertising serves to reduce the cost of legal services to the public, it benefits the administration of justice. The advertising in question was a newspaper advertisement that announced the legal work and prices of a legal clinic. It was not improper because it could not be classified as "in-person solicitation."

In a concurring and dissenting opinion in *Bates*, Chief Justice Burger wrote, **"To be sure, the public needs information concerning attorneys, their work, and their fees. At the same time, the public needs protection from the unscrupulous or the incompetent practitioner anxious to prey on the uninformed."** What do you think about his warning? Has his fear come true?

running an advertisement entitled "Did You Use This IUD?" which depicted a larger-than-life Dalkon Shield. The ad ran in 36 Ohio newspapers. It mentioned that the shield had led to infertility and spontaneous abortions and invited readers to telephone Zauderer with regard to his representation in a class action against the manufacturer and other parties. The U.S. Supreme Court reviewed the restrictions on lawyer advertising in *Zauderer v. Disciplinary Counsel.*[2] Zauderer's defense argued that the Ohio regulation violates his First Amendment right to free speech, an argument which may be worth trying in those states that prohibit legal assistant advertising. The Supreme Court upheld the reprimand on the basis that the advertisement was misleading, but affirmed the attorney's right to advertise in what many 1980s legal professionals thought was a less-than-tasteful manner. Even the Supreme Court cannot regulate good taste.

Advertising and the Paralegal

As a general rule, paralegals and other nonlawyers cannot give legal advice directly to the public. For that reason, paralegals cannot advertise their services directly to the public such as taking out a page in the telephone directory. The exception to the general rule (which we will cover in Rule #7) is where there is a statutory authority that allows nonlawyers to practice law. For example, the National Labor Relations Board allows nonlawyers to represent clients in their claims of unfair labor practices. They are called "non-attorney representatives" in the statute and they are held to the same standards of practice and professional responsibility as attorneys. Presuming, then, that you make your living representing people in this fashion, you would be allowed to advertise your practice in the telephone directory. As the object is to be found by people who need your services, it makes sense to list yourself under "paralegal" as opposed to "non-attorney representative," where you might never attract any clients.

With the exception of those administrative agencies that allow lay practice, the more useful rule is that paralegals may advertise their services to attorneys and law firms through letters, advertisements in legal directories, and legal periodical publications. Paralegals and other

The Martindale Hubbell directory is a very large listing of law firms and lawyers. You can find it in your law library and at *http://www.martindale.com.*

nonlawyers may be listed with the other legal professionals of firms in the Martindale Hubbell directory.

Of course, paralegals have business cards, which are a sort of advertising. Paralegal business cards must not be deceptive in any way. For example, it is wise not to include the designation "notary" on your business card with your "paralegal" designation. This is because some cultures and languages associate "notario" with a person who can practice law.

There are some cases of paralegals practicing law without a license (see Rule #7) and using deceptive business cards. In one case, where the paralegal argued that his business card was covered by his First Amendment right to commercial speech, the South Carolina court ruled that deceptive or false speech is not protected by the First Amendment, and the words "If your civil rights have been violated— call me" were unlawful because they were deceptive.[3] Such words would lead the average person to believe that he was licensed to practice law.

The internet has added another dimension to paralegal advertising. On counsel.net, a website designed to help people find an attorney (Attorney Classified), you will find classified ads posted by nonlawyers such as this one:

Divorce Paralegal Services
Posted by United States on October 27, 2009

For cases with no minor children my fee is $125.
For cases with minor children my fees are $175.

As a practicing Paralegal, I understand just how expensive attorneys can get in divorce cases. I know that a divorce can be a difficult, painful and confusing process. If you are unsure where to turn or find out that you could use a little bit help, that is where I come in. I am here to prepare all the paperwork you need and help you file for a divorce. I am not an attorney and offer a nonattorney service and do not give legal advice. But my service, when you compare it to the price of a divorce lawyer is a much cheaper option. I prepare divorce documents for all 50 states.

WHAT DO YOU THINK?

Does this advertisement violate any advertising regulations? Or does it suggest the ability to practice law without a license?

Solicitation

Although advertising is now permitted, solicitation is not. In your state's Rules of Professional Conduct, Rule 7.3 most likely prohibits in-person "soliciting":

> (a) A lawyer shall not engage in solicitation:
>
> > (1) by in-person or telephone contact, or by real-time or interactive computer-access communication unless the recipient is a close friend, relative, former client or existing client . . . . .
>
> (b) For purposes of this Rule, "solicitation" means any advertisement initiated by or on behalf of a lawyer or law firm that is directed to, or targeted at, a specific recipient or group of recipients, or their family members or legal representatives, the primary purpose of which is the retention of the lawyer or law firm, and a significant motive for which is pecuniary gain.
>
> From the New York Rules of Professional Conduct

Simply put, the difference between solicitation and advertising is that solicitation is in-person, by telephone, or by written communication that is directed to a specific individual or group. Advertising, on the other hand, is directed to the public at large.

Attorneys cannot solicit individuals as clients and cannot allow their employees to solicit them. The lawyers you see portrayed on television, hanging out in hospitals and mortuaries, trolling for clients, are fictional.

In *Idaho State Bar v. Jenkins*,[4] the court discussed the incidents involving contact of prospective clients by Paralegal Landeros for the purpose of soliciting them for her employer. In one case, Landeros contacted the parents of a young man who had been killed in an automobile accident. She went to their home and told the Martinez family that Jenkins "was the best lawyer in the firm" and that he had sent her out to their home to see what she could do "to help the family." Holding that it was not the attorney's fault that the paralegal was engaging in unlawful in-person solicitation, the court said:

> While one might characterize Francis Landeros as a loose cannon rolling around the deck of Jenkins' law office, the overwhelming evidence established a firm policy, supported by frequent staff meetings, aimed at educating Mr. Jenkins' non-lawyer staff about impermissible in-person solicitations. This program is precisely the kind of action a lawyer must take to assure himself that the impermissible conduct itself, as well as the consequences of an in-person solicitation, can be avoided or mitigated.

What Paralegal Landeros was doing was clearly solicitation because it was in-person, initiated by her, for the purpose of securing a client for her employer for profit. Note that it was the lawyer who was on the hook for the improper conduct of his employee because there was no penalty that the court could impose on the paralegal. The court has the authority to issue an injunction to prohibit her from similar conduct in the future, but, as there is no regulatory body that licenses or regulates her, no penalty could be imposed on her.

Take a look at your state's Rule 7.3 for the exceptions listed there. Talking to former or current clients about getting more legal work from them is not improper solicitation. Convincing friends and family members to bring their legal work to your law firm is also not improper solicitation even though it may be in-person and for the purpose of making a profit. However, attorneys who are leaving their current law firm for a new one probably should not "solicit" clients (current or former) of their firm in order to steal them away. Called "pre-termination solicitation," this is often considered a breach of the fiduciary duty each of us owes to our employer, an inappropriate use of confidential information and tortious interference with prospective business advantage. For a complete discussion of these theories and a paralegal as a central figure, take a look at *Dowd and Dowd, Ltd. v. Gleason*, 816 N.E.2d 754, 352 Ill. App.3d 365 (2004).

Corporate Clients

In-person solicitation prohibitions do not apply to corporate clients, however. For example, there is no law that says you cannot take the president of the bank out to lunch and ask her or him to use your law firm's services. The solicitation rules are designed to protect the unsophisticated user of legal services, not companies.

REFERRAL FEES

In 2001, the state of Louisiana made paying people to solicit or refer clients (typically called "runners and cappers") a cause for disbarment. It is also a felony in that state, so knowing that it is going on and not reporting that person is "misprision of felony"—also a felony. From 2001 to 2006, five attorneys have been disbarred (and one resigned with charges pending) for violating this law.[5] The runner is looking at a $5000 penalty and up to five years at hard labor for a first offense. The Supreme Court of Louisiana was reacting to what they saw as a new industry: runner-based solicitation. Take a look at Rule 7.2. It says, "A lawyer shall not give anything of value to a person for recommending the lawyer's services."

Here's the bottom line: No matter what state you live or work in, you cannot take a referral fee from a lawyer. This is because the ABA and most states agree that a referral fee looks like "buying a claim." Yes, of course, people get paid for their work on a case. Even freelancers or contract lawyers and paralegals get paid. But they may not be paid any more than the responsibility assumed or work performed is worth.

If this is the law, why is it that we hear so much about attorneys and nonattorneys alike being paid referral fees? What is a referral fee, and when is it permissible?

Let's look at your Rule 1.5—at the end of the rule—where it sets forth the rules for dividing a fee with an outside lawyer. It says that the lawyers who do the work or assume responsibility for the case should get paid accordingly. But this is not a "referral fee" in the traditional sense. A referral fee is a fee paid for doing nothing other than bringing the client to the lawyer. It is *champerty*—the purchasing of a claim or a client.

Champerty is a term that comes to us from the common-law rule prohibiting the *assignment* or sale of a "chose in action" (a cause of action). Champerty dates back to ancient Rome and Greece, but we won't go that far back. Feudal lords in medieval England would fund litigation, meritorious or not, for any of their important underlings. They did this to promote loyalty. It became common practice for a solicitor to purchase a cause of action from an injured party. It would work like this: A poor person is injured by someone else's negligent or intentional act. The poor person does not have the ability or resources to sue that wrongdoer, so he simply "sells" the case to someone who has those resources. The injured person gets some small amount of money, and the purchaser has the right to sue the wrongdoer. Between 1275 and 1540, the English Parliament enacted various statutes prohibiting maintenance. This was finally held to be an unlawful "upholding of quarrels leading to the disturbance of society and the hindrance of common right."[6] and was in line with a general distaste for litigation and litigiousness. Eventually, all contracts for the sale of a claim at law were held to be invalid. Some states have statutory laws that prohibit champerty, and some rely on the common law going all the way back to England. Some states have statutes that void champertous contracts.

You would think that the book on champerty is closed but it is not. The modern equivalent of champerty is the syndicated lawsuit—that is, selling interests in the potential proceeds of a lawsuit to raise money to support the costs of the lawsuit. The Supreme Judicial Court of Massachusetts allowed this sort of agreement in a 1997 case saying that they were not convinced that prohibiting champerty protected the public from the evils of frivolous lawsuits or overreaching people with more money and power.[6]

In California, referral fees to other lawyers are allowed under the Rules of Professional Conduct only so long as the client has consented in writing, the total fee charged to the client is not increased, and the money is a "gift" for making a recommendation that later results in employment. It cannot be a fee or a reward, and it cannot be made with the understanding that more such "gifts" will be made in the future for future referrals. The rationale in California is this: We don't want lawyers taking cases they are not qualified to take. We want them to refer, for example, criminal defense cases to criminal defense lawyers. But lawyers need to make money just as does everyone else. The state believes that if we let the lawyer make some amount of money instead of nothing from referring the case to a more skilled lawyer, it is more likely to happen. The public is better served that way. Referral fees are only from one lawyer to another. **Paralegals cannot accept referral fees**. This concept overlaps with improper division of fees covered in Rule #7.

Law Firm Spotlight

Jenner & Block has offices in New York, Chicago, Los Angeles, and Washington, DC. For the second year in a row, this firm was number 1 on the *American Lawyer*'s annual pro bono honor roll in 2009. Its 470 lawyers put in an average of 170 volunteer hours in 2008, and 90% of their lawyers clocked over 20 volunteer hours. The total hours: 47,000. Over 6,000 hours were volunteered helping people displaced by Hurrican Katrina in 2007. Additionally, Jenner & Block worked to gain asylum for people who have been persecuted in their own countries and to combat human trafficking in the United States. In addition, more than 200 lawyers devoted over 22,000 pro bono hours representing indigents accused of felony crimes and those on death row. Jenner & Block has been ranked in the top ten pro bono firms by *American Lawyer* since 1990—a true commitment to the tradition of pro bono work.

Good Solicitation

The American Civil Liberties Union can be found at www.aclu.org.

Just as the Supreme Court has determined that advertising can be good for society, it has decided that some in-person solicitation is good for society. For example, in one Supreme Court case, a woman solicited clients for the ACLU to file a case against the state of South Carolina when it was discovered that South Carolina was requiring women to undergo sterilization in order to qualify for Medicaid benefits. The State Bar of South Carolina filed an action against the attorney for unlawful solicitation after she met with some women and wrote them letters offering the free services of the ACLU. On appeal, the Supreme Court found that her actions were not improper writing:

> This was not in-person solicitation for pecuniary gain. Appellant was communicating an offer of free assistance by attorneys associated with the ACLU, not an offer predicated on

entitlement to a share of any monetary recovery. And her actions were undertaken to express personal political beliefs and to advance the civil-liberties objectives of the ACLU, rather than to derive financial gain.[7]

So, solicitation that is not for personal gain, informs members of the public of legal rights they might otherwise not have known about, and furthers some civil liberty objective is "good" solicitation.

WHAT DO YOU THINK?

Robin Ficker, an attorney, gets a list of people who have been issued traffic tickets. He writes letters to those people who could do jail time as a penalty and offers to represent them in court. The letter is addressed to each individual, reciting the traffic offense and all possible penalties. Is this solicitation or direct mail advertising? To help you with your answer, look at *Ficker v. Curran* (1996) 950 F. Supp. 123, affirmed 119 F.3d 1150.

Technology

Some states have specifically opined that lawyers and their paralegal employees cannot solicit clients via the Internet. For example, Florida, West Virginia, Virginia, Michigan, and Utah all have rules prohibiting solicitation of clients through Internet chat rooms. Chat rooms are defined as "real-time communications between computer users."[8]

However, Web sites as a form of advertising have generally been found harmless, so long as they do not include false or deceptive information. Because Web sites are advertising, they will have to conform to the regulations of the law firm's state regarding advertising.[9] Some states require a hard copy of the home page to be on file with the regulating agency[10] or have a copy of the entire Web site in some retrievable format.[11]

Law Firm Spotlight

American Lawyer magazine's A-List 2009 has Los Angeles law firm Munger, Tolls & Olson at number 1 with a diversity score of 195 (out of 200), an RPL (revenue per lawyer) score of 194, and a pro bono score of 185. If you're looking for associate satisfaction, though, Latham & Watkins with 194 is the place to go, ranked #3 overall. Irell & Manella, another Los Angeles–based firm, made to the Top 20 list for the first time this year. One of the associates there attributed this step up to this: "There are two rules at the firm: Do good work and don't be a jerk." Sound advice.

Direct Mail

Somewhere between traditional advertising and solicitation is direct mail. Sometimes referred to as "direct mail advertising," sometimes "direct mail solicitation," direct mail is legal.[12] Direct mail is often used in mass disaster cases and in many types of legal matters where a list of prospective clients can be obtained. For instance, many courts make the list of upcoming residential foreclosures available. A law firm gets a copy of this list from the court and sends out a mass mailing to everyone on the list touting that firm's ability to relieve the homeowner from the foreclosure.

WHAT DO YOU THINK?

Should a Web site have to comply with the advertising requirements of *every* state (because the Web site touches every state) or just the states where the law firm has offices?

Whereas advertising to the general public is permitted because it is subject to scrutiny by the public, these direct and private communications to a prospective client are not subject to the same kind of review. The fear that these private statements are misleading is balanced against the public's need to be informed about legal services and the attorney's right to free speech. By keeping the communications public, states hope to satisfy the public's need and the attorneys' rights while regulating the truth and accuracy of the advertising.

As a general rule, paralegals, or those who pretend to be paralegals, do not have the legal right to use direct mail advertising to the general public.[13] Again, this is because to advertise paralegal services to the public would be to offer to practice law without a license. In one such case in Illinois, a "paralegal" company called National Legal Professional Associates (NLPA)[14] used direct mail to contact prison inmates with the intent of convincing them to use its services in addition to their criminal defense attorney.[15] The marketing campaign was designed to convince inmates that their lawyers were not looking out for their best interests or were, perhaps, incompetent and lazy. The effect of the marketing was that inmates began to respect the advice of NLPA over that of their attorneys, effectively turning the attorney–paralegal relationship on its head. One judge took exception to this practice and issued a summons for the owner of NLPA. After finding that the company engaged in the unauthorized practice of law, he ordered the disgorgement of all fees paid and restitution made to the families of inmates who had wasted their money on NLPA's services. An injunction was issued restricting NLPA's activities. The judge made particular note of NLPA's "unsolicited marketing activities."

To disgorge means to give up.

In-person solicitation is still improper, whether by an attorney or nonattorney. The line between solicitation and helping a member of the public understand a legal problem is not a clear one, but the motivation of the legal professional is a guide: If the in-person communication is motivated by the desire to make money, it is probably improper solicitation. If it is motivated by a desire to assist a member of the public in recognizing a legal problem, it is more likely proper.

WHAT DO YOU THINK?

Is direct mail advertising more like solicitation or advertising? Should it be allowed?

Mass Disasters

Several states have enacted statutes that prohibit any contact for a certain amount of time with people who have been charged with crimes or people who are related to victims of mass disasters. These statutes are designed to protect people from making choices about legal representation while they are especially vulnerable. Although these statutes have been challenged, they have been upheld.

If you are in the New England area, take a look at *Alexander & Catalano v. Cahill*[16] where a law firm challenged some of the new regulations proposed in New York. In that case, the federal appellate court praised the state for its attempt to raise the prestige of the legal profession by regulating tasteless (and obnoxious) attorney advertising but encouraged the regulating bodies to re-consider the First Amendment rights of the lawyers. The Court upheld the 30-day moratorium discussed above as "narrowly tailored to advance important State interests" but struck down some of the other advertising prohibitions such as not allowing law firm nicknames or mottoes that imply an ability to obtain results (i.e., bestlawfirminamerica.com).

And, under the "watch out for layers of regulation" theory, be aware that regardless of any mass disaster contact moratorium your state has enacted (look in your Rule 7.3 or thereabouts), the Federal Aviation folks have a superseding moratorium of contact with victims of airplane disasters.[17]

Of course, paralegals are held to the same regulations as attorneys with regard to solicitation of clients. In discussions with laypeople, it is important to be aware of allowing the layperson to lead the discussion. In other words, the layperson should ask the legal professional (attorney or nonattorney) for a referral to an attorney or firm before the referral is offered. In the ordinary conversation between friends, this isn't an issue. It becomes a legal/ethical issue when, for example, you hand your business card to a stranger who has just been injured in a car accident.

In *Florida Bar v. Went For It, Inc.*, 515 U.S. 619 (1995), the Supreme Court upheld a statute banning contact with victims and families of victims of mass disasters for thirty days. Notice the name of the defendant in the case. Where do you think the name came from?

In April 1994, Lawrence Canter and wife, Martha Siegel (the law firm of Canter & Siegel), sent a posting to over 6,000 "Usenet" newsgroups. The message offered the law firm's services to sanyone who wanted to take part in a U.S. government lottery of "green card" work permits. The subject line was this: "Green Card Lottery 1994 May be the Last One!! Sign up now!!" As many as 6 million people may have received the message. What do you think? Good advertising? Direct e-mail? Solicitation? (Hint: Canter has been called "The Father of Modern Spam." He was also disbarred by the Supreme Court of Tennessee for this and other ethical violations.)

State professional responsibility rules require the legal professional to refrain from actively seeking out people who may have legal claims and to refrain from "convincing" laypeople that they do have a legal claim. The problem that arises, of course, is that laypeople may be irreparably injured if they do not seek legal assistance to pursue their claims or refuse to believe they have a claim. The ethical course is assume that they have access to information through all of our modern technology, to let them make their own decisions about pursuing a claim and refer them to a lawyer only if they ask for assistance. Lawsuits are costly, time consuming, and often very upsetting. Many people will choose not to pursue a legal claim for reasons known only to themselves.

If the purpose of prohibiting in-person solicitation is the presumed inability of the client to say "no," should the rule be applicable to Internet chat room interaction? Why or why not?

Pro bono Work

Working pro bono, that is for free, also makes the legal system more accessible. We discuss pro bono work under Rule #9—the duty to improve the legal system.

RULE #5 WRAP-UP

Access to the judicial system for all Americans is a lofty goal. It is a goal we aspire to and we work toward. Bringing information to people who have legal claims but may not know their rights is part of making legal services available. Even though some advertising is distasteful to us (and recognizing that taste is a difficult if not impossible thing to legislate), advertising is a good thing. It makes it easier for members of the public to find help in legal matters. But, advertising can be both good and bad. Solicitation can also be good and bad. In-person contact for the purpose of getting a paying client may fall under the rules of prohibited solicitation. Informing members of the public of their rights and encouraging them to "sign on" may also be a good thing, such as in the case of *Primus* and the ACLU litigation to end the practice of sterilizing women. However, as good as it is to help people recognize their legal problems and remedies, it is never a good idea for a paralegal to accept anything of value for referring a client to a lawyer. Direct mail falls somewhere in between advertising and solicitation. It, too, can be used for good and for those up to no good.

The Internet has posed some new questions in the world of advertising and solicitation, as have mass disasters. In the final analysis, what we're looking for is informing the public, helping the public gain access to the judicial system when it is needed, and not abusing the First Amendment right to commercial speech.

RULE #5 REVIEW QUESTIONS

1. Is it your duty to give information to the public? Why or why not? In what circumstances would it be improper for you to give information to the public?

2. What is the definition of "advertising"? When did advertising legal services on television become legal?

3. What is "direct mail advertising"? How is it different from plain advertising?

4. What is "solicitation"? When is it good? When is it prohibited?

5. What is a referral fee, and is it legal for you to accept one?

6. What was the point of the case *Florida Bar v. Went For It, Inc.*? What was the defendants' argument?

7. Freedom of speech stems from our Constitution. Do you know where it is in the Constitution? What other freedoms might concern paralegals?

8. Visit some law firm Internet sites. What do they have in common? How are they different from each other?

9. What are some things paralegals can do to help the cause of access to justice?

10. Visit *http://www.martindale.com*. What is there? What is the purpose of the Web site?

[1] 384 U.S. 436, 86 S. Ct. 1602 (1966).

[2] 105 S.Ct. 2265 (1985).

[3] *South Carolina v. Robinson*, 321 S.C. 286, 468 S.E.2d 290 (1996).

[4] 816 P.2d 335 (Idaho 1991).

[5] "The Gingerbread Man's Run is Over!" *Louisiana Bar Journal*, 54(2) (August/September 2006).

[6] In *Saladini v. Righellis*, 426 Mass. 231, 687 N.E.2d 1224, 1997 WL 751609 (Mass. 1997).

[7] *In re Primus*, 438 U.S. 432 (1978).

[8] Florida advisory opinion A-00-1 (August 15, 2000): An attorney may not solicit prospective clients through Internet chat rooms, defined as real-time communications between computer users. For guidance on the issue, the Florida panel looked at opinions from other states and relied upon four in particular: West Virginia L.E.I. 98-03 (October 16, 1998), Michigan Opinion RI-276 (July 11, 1996), Utah 97-10 (October 24, 1997), and Virginia A-0110 (April 14, 1998).

[9] Iowa Ethics Op. 96-1 (1996); Pennsylvania Ethics Op. 96-17 (1996); South Carolina Ethics Op. 94-27 (1995); and Tennessee Ethics Op. 95-A-570 (1995).

[10] See, for example, Florida's Fla. Bar Standing Comm. on Adver. Internet Guidelines, p. 2. If the home page contains no audio, photographs, illustrations, or other information other than as outlined in Rule 4.7, 2(n)(1)-(10) the home page need not be filed for review.

[11] See, for example, Arizona's Comm. on Rules of Professional Conduct of Ariz., Op. No. 97-04 dated April 7, 1997.

[12] *Shapero v. Kentucky Bar Association*, 486 U.S. 466, 475 (1988).

[13] There is an exception in California for Legal Document Assistants. See California Business & Professions Code Sections 6400 through 6415.

[14] NLPA was based in Ohio. The federal court had jurisdiction over NLPA because it was practicing law in Illinois.

[15] *U.S. v. Johnson* 327 F.3d 554 (7th Cir. 2003).

[16] Mem. Decision & Order, 30-pp, pdf., USNDNY, Dkt. 5:07-CV-117 (July 20, 2007).

[17] Aviation Disaster Family Assistance Act (49 U.S.C. §1136), 45 day moratorium.

Represent Each Client with Diligence and Dedication . . . within the Bounds of the Law

DUE PROCESS AS OUR CORNERSTONE

At the foundation of our American system of justice is the concept of "due process." Exactly how much process is due depends in large part on the circumstances. The Sixth Amendment of our Constitution guarantees us the right to counsel when we are charged in a criminal matter. And no doubt we are all familiar with "the *Miranda* warning" given to the accused: You have the right to an attorney, and if you cannot afford one, one will be appointed to you. And we've heard the part about "you have the right to remain silent" from the Fifth Amendment. But the Bill of Rights guarantees the criminal accused more than that: not to be deprived of life, liberty, or property without **due process of law**. And the Sixth Amendment guarantees us an impartial jury of our peers in a speedy and public trial, to be confronted with witnesses, and the right to subpoena witnesses. We are protected against excessive bail under the Eighth Amendment. All of these things are part of the process we are due because we are in America.

Due Process Requirements to the Client

In examining these rights under the microscope of the U.S. Supreme Court, we are reminded again and again that we have the right to the representation of an attorney at every step in the proceedings.[1] And where the attorney's representation is lacking in quality, care, and diligence, the constitutional guarantee of due process is violated.[2] So it's not just an attorney we're guaranteed when accused of a criminal matter—it's a competent, loyal, and diligent attorney. Outside of the criminal justice system context, when we hire an attorney in a civil matter or to simply draft a will, we are entitled to a competent and loyal attorney who will represent us **diligently**. Diligence includes doing the work in a timely manner and keeping the client apprised of progress.

Due Process Requirements to the System

Balanced against the attorney's duties to his or her client of competence, loyalty, and diligence is the attorney's (and paralegal's) duties to "the system of justice." In other words, the system cannot work unless the professionals in the system have respect for the system, unless they deal with the system with honesty and integrity, and unless they do their job diligently "within the bounds of the law."

WHERE IS THE BOUNDARY OF THE LAW?

The "bounds of the law" in many cases will be hard to determine. The rules of professional conduct are broad, are difficult to apply, and change continually. Older case and statutory law says that where the line between the lawful and the unlawful is difficult to find, we should look to whether the attorney is acting in the role of an "adviser" or an "advocate." This makes sense. Advocates, such as when the lawyer represents the client in a criminal matter, must take the facts as they find them. They may interpret the facts but must not try to change them in their own or their client's mind. They should, however, interpret factual situations in their client's favor while working as advocates. Advisors need to view the facts one way, and then another way, and perhaps a third and fourth way in order to give the client all of the possible alternatives.

Take a look at your state's Rule 2.1. It says that the bounds of the law may not always be what they seem. In representing the client, we should look not only to what the law says but to other considerations such as moral, economic, social and political factors.

Frankly, you'll be amazed at some of the things so-called "professionals" do in the diligent representation of their clients. There's a line between "diligent" and downright illegal. Let's see if we can find that line.

Suppressing Evidence

We (legal professionals) are specifically prohibited from suppressing (hiding) evidence that we or our clients have a legal obligation to reveal.[3] This prohibition extends to hiding witnesses as well.[4] When we know our client has suppressed evidence or hidden witnesses, we have an obligation to notify the court. When we don't do that, we become responsible for the acts of the client.[5] The reasoning behind these regulations is that the proper administration of justice and due process requires that the court be made aware of all evidence and witnesses. Without access to the evidence, it cannot make an educated and just decision. As an example, where two parties have signed a contract but only one of them has it, when the two parties get into a legal dispute, the party with the contract must turn a copy over to the other. Otherwise, it will be impossible to prepare for trial or arbitration or, for that matter, any discussion about the contract. We can see that hiding the contract would throw the monkey wrench into the judicial machinery.

It is a commonly held (but wrong) belief that the attorney can hide the weapon used by the client in a crime because the weapon is privileged or confidential. This is a wrong belief because this item is not necessarily protected under attorney/client privilege (depending upon the source of the weapon) and not necessarily "confidential information," because it is an instrument of a crime, not information. Let's take some examples.

When your client says: "I stole this rifle from Walmart," the confession is confidential. (If you don't believe that it is, review Rule #2.) When the client tells you where the dead bodies of his victims are, that information is confidential.[6] However, if you take physical possession of incriminating evidence, that you have it is not confidential or privileged and you have an affirmative duty to give the incriminating evidence to the proper authorities.[7] If the incriminating evidence is removed from its location with your assistance, then the details of where the physical item was found and the original condition of the item (plus any testing you've had done) must be disclosed regardless of your duty of loyalty to the client, confidentiality, and the attorney/client privilege.[8] If you, acting in good faith, change the crime scene in any way, you violate the rules that protect the public's interest in effective and fair prosecution. You have a duty to preserve the evidence in the same form as it was. If you change it (e.g., wipe fingerprints off of the evidence), the prosecution will be deprived of the opportunity to discover the evidence. You, of course, will suffer the consequences.

The client's communication to you telling you where the evidence is protected by the privilege and is confidential information. Observations you make of the evidence as a consequence of confidential communications are protected from disclosure, both because of the communication and because your observations are privileged work product.

Incriminating physical evidence that you get through someone other than your client is not protected by the attorney/client privilege or a duty of confidentiality. You must turn the evidence over to the prosecution, and you may be required to testify about how you came into possession of the evidence.[9] In these situations, the duty of client loyalty gives way to the need of the public to prosecute criminals. In the famous *Belge*[10] case (in which the client told his lawyer where to find the dead body), photographs of the body taken by the lawyer were also protected and not subject to voluntary disclosure. It is only when the lawyer takes possession of incriminating physical evidence from its present location that the duty of voluntary disclosure arises.[11]

WHAT DO YOU THINK?

You are interviewing a client of your criminal defense law firm. He tells you that he has killed his four-year-old son, but he has not been arrested for that crime because no one knows that his son is missing. He was arrested on a burglary charge. What should you do?

Not all attorneys hide evidence to protect the client. Sometimes they have their own self-interest in mind. In one case, an attorney for the executor of an estate received a letter from a relative of the dead person (the decedent) saying that the relative surrendered all interest in the decedent's estate.[12] The attorney hid the letter from the only remaining interested heir and also told that heir that the estate would be contested by the other relative for some time. The attorney did this, of course, so that his legal fees would continue to grow. The California Supreme Court made a finding that the attorney had hidden the letter for his own gain. Not smart—a violation of his duties to the judicial system and definitely grounds for attorney discipline.

Fabricating Evidence

Instead of hiding evidence, what about making up evidence? Back in the early days of photocopy technology, this wasn't so easy. Technology today, however, makes it an easy task to change documents and create them to look authentic. However, if you deliberately fabricate evidence or knowingly allow the client to fabricate evidence for the purpose of putting it before the court, you are guilty of "perpetrating a fraud upon the court" and "obstructing justice."[13] This fabrication can take several forms.

Tampering with Evidence

One of my personal favorites is the case of a defense attorney who enlarged the bullet hole in state's evidence (a leather belt) by forcing a dowel through it, thereby ruining the probative value of the evidence.[14] He was disbarred. (But you have to ask yourself: What was he *thinking*?)

Inducing a Witness to Testify Falsely

*To **suborn**
is to induce a person to
do an illegal act.*

An attorney will be disbarred for obstruction of justice if found guilty of **subornation of perjury** or otherwise tampering with witnesses. Where the attorney makes an agreement to pay or have the client pay a witness for lying under oath, that attorney will most likely be disbarred.[15] Or paying money to police officers to influence their testimony, whether to induce them to testify truthfully or falsely, will also lead to disbarment of lawyers.[16] An attorney may reimburse witnesses for their expenses but must not pay them more than an amount that reimburses them for loss incidental to having been a witness.[17] Whatever amount is paid to the witness must not be such a large amount that it looks like a bribe.

Keep a watch for the Supreme Court's opinion in *Pottawattamie County v. McGhee*, where the prosecutors and police allegedly fabricated evidence against two men in order to get them convicted of the murder of a retired police officer. The two men (McGhee and Harrington) spent 25 years in prison before the fabrication came to light. In their lawsuit against the prosecutors who used the false evidence against them, the men allege that the police first tried to bribe a young man (Hughes) to get him to incriminate these suspects. Hughes wrote several different under-oath statements incriminating various people but did not settle on the "right ones" (the men the police wanted to be prosecuted— McGhee and Harrington) until the police threatened him with responsibility for the murder. Under that pressure, Hughes fabricated a new story framing McGhee and Harrington. Then the police told Hughes' friends that they would go to jail if they did not corroborate Hughes' fabricated story. The Supreme Court will shortly rule on whether the prosecutors are immune from prosecution. If they are not immune, this dynamic story of fabrication will be in the news again soon.

> **WHAT DO YOU THINK?**
>
> If a lawyer offers a lot of money to a witness of facts "if we win," is that inducing that witness to fabricate evidence or just indicating that there will be money from a large judgment with which to pay a larger witness fee? Look at *Florida Bar v. Wohl*, 842 So. 2d 811 (Fla. March 20, 2003).

Allowing a Witness to Testify Falsely

Even where the false testimony isn't the lawyer's idea, the lawyer has an obligation not to allow the client to offer false testimony or false documents. Perjured statements by clients are outside of the attorney/client privilege and are not protected.[18] That the client has said he will lie on the witness stand, for example, is protected by the attorney/client privilege. But if he actually does lie on the witness stand, his earlier statement to you will not be protected, and you will have to admit it to a court. Then you, as the legal professional, have violated this rule by allowing the client to follow through with the lie. If the client tells you he intends to commit perjury, the best course of action is to convince the client to only tell the

truth. Failing that, the attorney must withdraw from the representation "if that will remedy the situation." If it will not, the attorney should make a disclosure to the court. Check to see if your state Rules of Professional Conduct reconcile this action with the duty of confidentiality. It could be that truthfulness to the court is simply more important than the duty of confidentiality in this limited area.

You, as the paralegal, do not have to struggle with this. If a client tells you that he intends to lie or has lied, you need to tell the attorney you work for. That's it. The rest is up to the attorney. Of course, it couldn't hurt to offer your ethical expertise to help deal with the conundrum. The attorney might not know what you now know about Rule #6.

Affidavits. Obviously, lying to the court in an affidavit is a mistake. Where an attorney filed an affidavit for an extension of time that stated that he had the flu and was unable to work and that turned out to be a lie, the attorney was subject to discipline.[19]

Making False Documents

This violates the rule even when the false documents aren't created in the context of representing a client. Where an attorney received loans from a bank via false representation and gave untruthful deposition testimony about the loans, his license to practice law was revoked.[20] Notice that this was not in the context of an attorney representing a

In *Johns v. Smyth*, 176 F. Supp 949 (E.D. Va. 1959), defense counsel did not offer oral testimony nor argue his client's defense before the jury. The attorney later told the court that he had reason to believe that his client's story was untrue and he could not in good conscience argue that it was true. Whereas the court agreed that the attorney could not properly manufacture a defense or "plant the seeds of falsehood" in his client's mind, it could not approve of the attorney's virtual abandonment of an attempt to represent his client simply because the attorney had reason to doubt his client's testimony.

The court acknowledged that it is often difficult to differentiate between the error in judgment of attorneys and their lack of best efforts. Where attorneys would choose for tactical reasons to forego oral argument or to examine their client as a witness, it could not be considered an omission constituting client neglect. In *Johns v. Smyth*, the court did not consider the attorney's acts and omissions as tactical maneuvers, especially in the light of the attorney's later admission that he did not believe in his client's innocence. More modernly, you will find cases in your state that will render guidance in this conundrum. Should the need arise, do the research.

client. This was the attorney acting in his own legal affairs. Even so, if he falsified documents for himself, it is reasonable to assume that he would do the same for a client and the court felt that this sort of person should not practice law.

> **WHAT DO YOU THINK?**
>
> The attorney you work for alters a check after it has been cashed and uses a copy of the altered check as an exhibit filed with the court. What will happen to the attorney when his deceit is discovered? To help you in your research, see *Reznick v. State Bar*, 460 P.2d 969 (Cal. 1969).

THE PRACTICE OF DECEIT

Being deceitful seems to be an everyday event in some form or another. Lying gets us into trouble in all parts of our lives and none of us is immune. When deceit is practiced within the job, however, it becomes a matter for investigation by the employer, a court, the state bar, or other disciplinary authority.

Your state's Rule of Professional Conduct 4.1 says something like this: A lawyer, in representing a client, **may not knowingly make a false statement of material fact or of law to a third person.** Check in your rules under Rule 8. Somewhere near Rule 8.4, it says that it is professional misconduct to engage in conduct involving dishonesty, fraud, deceit, or misrepresentation.

There are many cases that speak of the "materiality" of the deceit. What is "material" is like asking what is a "little lie." Cases about legal practitioners deceiving beneficiaries about the amount of their inheritance; lawyers simulating clients' signatures on settlement checks; or stories of lawyers participating in other obvious connivances aimed at the court, opposing counsel, or their own clients litter the reports. All of these are clear examples of "material" deceit. The kind of deceit that has not been discussed at length by the courts is the potentially immaterial deceit. Here's the rule: When determining the materiality of the deceit, look at the task at hand and not the ultimate outcome of the case. In other words, how material was the deception to accomplishing the task? If the deceptive representation was crucial to the accomplishment of the task, it is a "material fact" for purposes of Rule 4.1.

Let's take an example. Your task is "find the defendant who is evading service of process." It can be a simple (and perhaps fun) matter to call the defendant's employer and say that you are an old girlfriend of the defendant and would like to look him up. "Could I please have his home address?" The task has been accomplished. The cost was a small lie (presuming, of course, that you are not the defendant's old girlfriend).

In this instance, the lie was told clearly within the "representation of the client." Although the misrepresentation was immaterial to the outcome of the case, it was enormous when analyzed in the context of the task at hand (getting the defendant's address). This is where the average legal professional fails in the analysis. We tend to think of "materiality" as going to some ultimate issue in the case and not to the task at hand. Even this "little lie" is material and, as a result, prohibited.

Deceit in Procedure of Discovery

Over the years, some stories of outrageous deceit have circulated in the legal community. One person who works for a large, well-known firm tells a story of a complex leveraged buyout negotiation process that was going on between his firm and another. An associate of his firm, as the story goes, was told to dress up like a messenger and retrieve a package from opposing counsel. The package was to go to the opposing counsel's client, but before it went, the "messenger" was to make a copy of the documents in order to gain an advantage in the negotiations.

It is not difficult to see that this deceptive practice took place during the representation of a client, albeit in a nonlitigation setting, but during representation nonetheless. Even though the deception might not have affected the ultimate outcome of the representation, the goal was to get a copy of documents belonging to someone else, and the deceptive practice was material in accomplishing that goal.

Left a stack of documents somewhere? Of course, we have all mistakenly left papers behind. In a case from California, a lawyer left a stack of documents in a conference room. Opposing counsel picked them up, copied them, and proceeded to use the information. When his actions came to light, this attorney argued that it was his duty under the law to represent his client diligently and taking advantage of the other lawyer's mistake was part of that duty. The California Supreme Court disagreed.[21] The duty to act diligently does not include breaking the law.

A more commonplace instance of deceit in the law office has to do with the in-house postage meter. Interrogatory response deadlines come and go, but if the missed deadline is only a day or so old, it is an easy matter to change the date on the postage meter so that it will appear that the envelope was mailed on the correct day. Again, if the task at hand is mailing in a timely fashion under the rules of discovery, changing the date on the envelope is not "material" to the outcome of most cases, but it is a false statement of material fact regarding the mailing.

Attestation:
An affirmation that the document is true.

Another common example of law office deceit is the law office employee who signs the client's name to discovery document *attestation* or has the client presign forms. It does not seem such a horrible thing if the law firm has the client's permission to sign the document in the client's absence for the sake of expediency. Several courts, however, have strongly disagreed with that position. A better idea is to get opposing counsel's agreement to allow the lawyer to sign for the client as "attorney-in-fact" until such time as the client returns and can sign the document or attestation personally. If the other counsel has knowledge and has agreed to it, it should not be a problem explaining the situation to a judge later. It is not a misrepresentation of material fact if the lawyer signs his/her name in place of the client's name.

> **WHAT DO YOU THINK?**
>
> You are a notary public. The laws that govern you require you to actually witness the signing of any document you will notarize. An attorney in your firm brings you a presigned document and asks you to notarize it. The attorney "swears" that the signature is legitimate. What do you do?

Employees and Deceit

Even lawyers who recognize that a deceptive act is improper if they do it commonly believe that they can shield themselves by getting someone else to do it. Rule 5.3 (on the supervision of nonlawyer employees) makes it clear that the lawyer is on the hook for all activities of employees that would be a violation of professional ethics if engaged in by a lawyer.

Therefore! The paralegal who is instructed to use deceptive practices is guilty, on behalf of the employer, of deceptive practices.

So, what can you do? You want to keep your job. You've been asked to do something illegal such as notarize a presigned document or sign a declaration that is backdated. It is something that the attorney would not do, but thinks it is somehow not improper to ask you to do it. What are your options?

Here's some practical advice: Find your state rule that says the lawyer is responsible for the paralegal's conduct if the lawyer orders or knowingly ratifies it. (It's somewhere in Rule 5.3.) Copy, frame, and hang it on your office wall. It will, no doubt, make the point.

HARASSING JURORS

In the movie based on the John Grisham book *Runaway Jury*, the antagonists plant a person on the jury (John Cusack) so that he can influence the outcome of the trial. The antagonists, however, weren't working for the other side of the case or the lawyer or client on either side. They had their own motives. For a lawyer to be involved (Dustin Hoffman, plaintiff's counsel, was invited to participate in the jury tampering scam but declined) would have been a serious violation of this rule. Of course, members of a jury can be investigated for possible interest in the outcome of the case, unauthorized communications about the case, or other reasons that would cause the members to be disqualified from serving.[22] These investigations, however, must not be "vexatious or harassing," and any improper conduct by or toward a jury member must be reported to the court promptly.[23]

OVERPAYING EXPERT WITNESSES

The rule has always been that expert witnesses may be paid a "reasonable amount" for their services, but not an "excessive amount." How much is reasonable and where the line is to "excessive" remains an unknown. Certainly in high-profile cases, such as O.J. Simpson's criminal trial, the experts were paid exorbitant fees. Perhaps the status of the witness and the defendant, along with the complexity of the expert issue, are factors in the "excessive" determination. It has also traditionally been the rule that witnesses should not be paid a contingency fee because such an arrangement may influence their testimony. In light of the many times an expert is needed in contingency cases, however, this tradition is being eroded.

WHAT DO YOU THINK?

A lawyer offers to act as a witness in exchange for $500,000. Should he be disciplined? To give you a head start, look up *U.S. v. Blaszak*, 349 F.3d 881 (6th Cir. 2003).

FAIRNESS TO OPPOSING COUNSEL

When we are working as advocates for our client, sometimes this is difficult to do, but it is a part of our duty to work diligently, but within the boundaries of the law. Let's go see where that boundary is here.

Check out your state's Rule 3.4 and see if you can find the place where is says that a lawyer should not make any statements of personal opinion about the credibility of a witness or evidence, the justness of the plaintiff's claim, or the guilt of the accused. Found it? Good! Now consider this recent case from North Carolina where, in closing argument, the lawyer stated: "This case is just nonsense!"[24] What do you think? Violation of 3.4?

COMMUNICATION WITH OPPOSING PARTY

Rule 4.2 says that the legal professional must not communicate with an opposing party except through that party's counsel. This is because the legal professional who is speaking directly to the opposing party may be seen to be taking an unfair advantage. Of course, opposing counsel may give permission to an attorney to speak with the client. For example, a lawyer might say to you (the paralegal), "Just call my client and ask him," in some trivial matter. In some instances, the attorney who is also a party to the action may speak directly with the other party. This makes sense. Even though the lawyer-party has an advantage over a nonlawyer party (due to education and experience in the legal system), sometimes they would have to speak to each other during the course of the litigation. There is an argument that the lawyer-party's fundamental rights as a litigant outweigh the state's interest in preventing direct communication with the opposing party. In other states, however, even the lawyer who is *in pro se* (representing himself) may not communicate with the other party if the other party is represented by counsel.[25]

WHAT DO YOU THINK?

You have credible evidence that the defendant corporation is systematically destroying relevant evidence. You want to get information from, at the very least, the corporation's management-level employees, director of corporate security, director of human resources, and chief of uniformed security. Can you have *ex parte* communications with these people? To aid you in your answer, read *Cronin v. Eighth Judicial District Court*, 781 P.2d 1150 (1989).

Rule 4.3 warns the legal professional not to allow an opposing party who is not represented by counsel to believe that the legal professional is disinterested. It makes sense that unrepresented people may assume that a lawyer is simply a disinterested authority on the law. The lawyer should correct that misunderstanding and should not give any legal advice to the unrepresented person other than the advice to obtain legal representation. These rules have few exceptions. The best course for legal professionals is to not communicate with any party to an action who may have a conflicting interest except through that party's attorney. If the party does not have counsel, explain that your job is only to do the best for your client, not to help the adverse party, and that the unrepresented person should seek the assistance of counsel. It is not the unauthorized practice of law to advise an unrepresented person to obtain counsel. Further, it would not be considered giving the opposing party legal advice to suggest some places where that person may be assisted at no cost, such as referring the unrepresented person to a free legal clinic.

COURTESY TO THE COURT

It seems obvious that it is improper to engage in conduct intended to disrupt the court (Rule 3.5). The advocate is supposed to stand firm against abuse by a judge but should not reciprocate, in the manner of two wrongs not making a right and because of the fact that the judge has the power of contempt and the lawyer does not. The best thing the lawyer can do is protect the record for review by a higher court and refrain from belligerence or theatrics. Regardless of who is "right," the judge has the power to hold people in the courtroom in contempt. This can lead to a fine and/or jail time.

GIVE THE COURT ONLY TRUTHFUL STATEMENTS

In addition to courtesy, complete honesty is also a must for the legal professional. Rule 3.3 treats this **duty of candor** toward the tribunal. It is improper to make a falsae statement of fact or law to a tribunal. For example, if a lawyer asks for a continuance for his subpoenaed witness to arrive at the court, and the court later finds out that the witness had not been subpoenaed, the lawyer will land in contempt of court. These contempt citations often include a fine intended to reimburse the court and opposing counsel for wasted time. Think about it logically. If a lawyer lies to the court and that lie causes the opposing counsel to spend time unnecessarily, the opposing party's client should not have to pay for that wasted time.

Rule 3.3 offers one of the most striking questions ever discussed in a classroom setting or strategic trial meeting: What do I do if the client tells me that he's going to commit perjury? The Rule says that the lawyer may refuse to offer evidence that the lawyer reasonably believes is false. The conflict between the legal professional's duty to the client and duty to the public is almost overwhelming. Is there one answer? Does it matter if your client's case is civil or criminal? Consider the situation where the attorney advises his client to lie about the date on which her car accident occurred to avoid a problem with the statute of limitations?[26] Or the attorney who advises his client to "play dumb" and, if questioned about certain past convictions, to deny them.[27]

GIVE THE COURT ALL OF THE LAW

Probably the most overlooked duty is our duty to disclose law that is contrary to our client's position when that law is not disclosed by opposing counsel. Does that mean that we have to do our opponent's job? Yes, that's exactly what Rule 3.3 requires. If we know of controlling law that is directly opposed to our position, the best tactic is to cite it for the court, be up-front, and distinguish it on its facts or another way. Trying to hide the *controlling law* is never a good ploy.

*Controlling law is the law that **controls** the outcome, so it is in effect on that issue at the present time.*

LYING TO THE COURT AND DICTA

The Comments that your state may have adopted along with the Rules of Professional Conduct say (with respect to Rule 3.1) that legal professionals can urge any permissible construction (interpretation) of the law in representing the client. Law schools and paralegal training institutions spend a great deal of time discussing "dicta," or that part of a judicial decision or opinion that is not directly related to the holding of the court. Many instructors admonish that it is wholly improper to use a dictum, to cite from it or quote it. In practice, however, this is not the case. A more realistic rule is that dicta are entitled to consideration as being a persuasive authority, but they are not binding as authority within the meaning of *stare decisis.*

It is conceivable that a dictum that is repeated by the courts over a period of time becomes precedent as strong and persuasive as a rule of law. Further, some courts have held that dicta may be entitled to persuasive consideration because of the prestige of the judge who wrote them,[28] and dicta of the U.S. Supreme Court should be considered very persuasive.[29]

It is certainly permissible to use dicta when drafting a legal brief or other persuasive document. It should be cited or quoted, however, in a fashion that is appropriate and not misleading. It is also inadvisable to cite a passage as the rule of law when in fact it was taken from the dissenting opinion. (Yes. Lawyers have done that.) The basic rule of thumb is, whereas creative construction of the law is permissible, construction of the law must not be fraudulent.

Many laypersons accuse legal professionals of using deceptive devices, loopholes in the law, and confusing legal terms in order to win. What these individuals fail to realize is that the advocate's job is to win. Clients have confidence in and pay that attorney whom they feel is best equipped to win. People who desire to lose certainly do not need to waste their time and money hiring an attorney. Rule 6 instructs all members of the legal profession that it is their ethical duty to win for their client, if at all legally possible. Legal professionals who do not use all of their faculties to do so betray a sacred and long-held trust.

__Stare decisis__ is a Latin phrase. It is the doctrine under which courts adhere to precedent on questions of law in order to insure certainty, consistency, and stability in the administration of justice.

FILE ONLY RIGHTEOUS CLAIMS WITH THE COURT

Whereas there is no definitive regulation that mandates that attorneys take every client who seeks their legal assistance (for instance, where the cause is so repugnant that they could not provide diligent legal assistance), once they have accepted the client, attorneys are compelled to argue any legal points that have merit on behalf of that client. The advocate role requires that the attorney argue for any claim that the attorney does not, after due consideration and investigation, consider to be without merit or frivolous.

Check your Rule 3.1. It says that a lawyer *shall not* bring or defend a *frivolous claim or contention*. This, of course, does not mean that only suits over existing law should be brought or defended against. Were that the case, new law would seldom be forged. What it does mean is that the lawyer must believe that the claim or cause has merit, even if it requires modification or reversal of existing law. Sometimes those are the best cases. The legal practitioner has a duty to use the legal system, not abuse it. This means both the substantive and procedural part of the law.

Abuse of process, the use of the process of the law for improper means, can be brought as a cross-complaint or countersuit in civil cases in many states. If the lawyer is named as a cross-complainant, it may mean that the lawyer must hire independent counsel for representation. In addition, a malicious prosecution suit can be brought after the conclusion of the frivolous suit. Therefore, it is the wise practitioner who considers all of the consequences of that lawsuit on the edge of frivolity.

In awarding sanctions against a lawyer for frivolous or bad faith tactics, the court should not look at one or two things, but the totality of the circumstances.[30] Where the plaintiff's law firm brought a claim that was worth $32 in the superior court by inflating the value with frivolous causes of action, and the suit was brought on a mechanics lien that had expired, the court had no problem finding that it was frivolous and brought for the sole purpose of harassment.[31] The penalties are severe.

> A **frivolous action** is one that is brought primarily for the purpose of harassment or where there is no good faith argument to support the action.

GIFTS TO JUDGES

Check it. Rule 3.5 admonishes that the legal professional should not seek to "influence a judge by any improper means." This includes gifts of money. Some judicial positions are now filled by way of election, however. How much of a campaign contribution can a legal professional make to a judge's campaign? Each professional might want to look this up in his or her state. Under some state's codes of judicial conduct, lawyers may not make any contribution to a judge's campaign fund.

The giving of gifts or loans to members of the judiciary is prohibited to avoid the **appearance of impropriety** (Rule #10) as well as to avoid bias and prejudice. Commonsense exceptions may be where the judge is a family friend, in which case small exchanges of gifts during the holidays are not a violation of the Rule. Another exception may be where a judge has performed a marriage or other special ceremony, in which case a small token of appreciation is warranted.

If you're thinking about making a gift to a judge or other official, bear in mind that the purpose for the prohibition is to ensure impartiality. A gift or loan, therefore, must not be of such importance or size such that it would give rise to the argument that the integrity and impartiality of the judiciary are in question.

U.S. Supreme Court justice Antonio Scalia came under fire in 2004 for going duck hunting with Vice President Dick Cheney shortly before the Supreme Court was to hear a case regarding Cheney's contact with certain Enron executives during the formulation of President Bush's energy policy. A lower court ruled that Cheney had to reveal certain documents. The Supreme Court agreed to hear Cheney's appeal. Surely their friendship would cause Justice Scalia to look at the case differently. Ethics scholar Stephan Gillers said of the hunting trip, "A judge may have a friendship with a lawyer, and that's fine. But if the lawyer has a case before the judge, they don't socialize until it's over. That shows a proper respect for maintaining the public's confidence in the integrity of the process."[32] The code of conduct for federal judges sets guidelines for members of the judiciary, but does not set clear-cut rules. "A judge should . . . act at all times in a manner that promotes public confidence in the integrity and impartiality of the judiciary," it says. "A judge should not allow family, social or other relationships to influence judicial conduct or judgments . . . or permit others to convey the impression that they are in a special position to influence the judge."

Despite what was in the news concerning Vice President Cheney vacationing with Supreme Court justice Scalia, attorneys and their employees must not communicate with the Court during the pendency of a case unless a copy of the communication is promptly given to opposing counsel.[33] This rule applies to communications about the merits of the case and not to clerical issues.[34] Any attempt to solicit information on the merits of a case pending before that court from court personnel is prohibited.[35]

WHAT DO YOU THINK?

Your firm frequently practices law before Judge Scintilla. Scintilla's daughter is interviewing for a job as a paralegal with your firm. Would it be improper to hire her? Why or why not?

OTHERWISE BREAKING THE LAW

It is never proper to encourage or aid a client in a violation of the law (Rules 1.2 and 3.1). The legal professional as advisor can appropriately counsel a client as to the probable outcome of a course of action (Rule 2.1). It is also appropriate to continue to represent the client after he or she has unilaterally taken action that the legal professional has advised against or knows will not be the most beneficial for the client. It is not appropriate, however, for the legal professional to knowingly assist a client in taking illegal action or making frivolous claims. It is misconduct for the professional to encourage the client to commit a criminal act or to advise the client about how to avoid the consequences of a criminal act.

PROSECUTOR'S ROLE TO SEEK JUSTICE

We are supposed to be diligent in the representation of our clients. Unlike other attorneys, the prosecuting attorney's duty is not to win, but to reach a just result.[36] Prosecutors' clients are the public, the state, and the government, so they must be aware that public policy can be aided only by justice. They must utilize their best efforts to see that the guilty are convicted and the innocent do not suffer. While representing the public and the government, prosecutors must often make decisions that would be made by the client if the client were a private attorney. For that reason, prosecutors must always act in the best interests and with zealousness for the client: the public. They should construe all reasonable doubts in favor of the accused.

Prosecutors have the duty to make timely disclosure of any evidence or witnesses known to them that may tend to negate the defendant's guilt or mitigate punishment.[37]

The prosecution must disclose all substantial material evidence favorable to an accused.[38] For example, consider the case where the prosecutor did not disclose that the alleged victim was himself accused of filing false reports until after the preliminary hearings were held. Because the reports were "favorable to an accused" and pertinent to the credibility of a material witness, the prosecutor had a duty to provide the reports to the accused. The role of prosecuting attorneys is more than that of an *advocate;* their duty is not to obtain convictions, but to fully and fairly present to the court the evidence material to the charge on which the defendant stands trial.[39] This responsibility includes a duty to disclose to the defense substantial material evidence favorable to the accused in appropriate cases. This duty also encompasses the prosecuting attorney's duty to refrain from tactics that would be unethical if used by the accused's attorney.

Advocate:
One that argues
for a cause.

Now might be a good time to pick up a copy of *My Cousin Vinny* and watch it. It's a comedic film about an inexperienced lawyer's first look at the criminal justice system. See how many unethical events or actions you can spot in the movie.

RULE #6 WRAP-UP

The cornerstone of America's judicial system is "due process." We are guaranteed certain protections and procedures in the Constitution. Additionally, we are guaranteed the loyalty of the attorney we hire. As a paralegal, you owe each and every client that duty of loyalty, dedication and "diligence." But your diligence must stop before you break the law by such things as hiding or destroying evidence; fabricating evidence; and tampering with evidence, witnesses, or jurors. If you find out that your client will commit perjury or has committed perjury, you have certain obligations to the judicial system. This is true because the system has rights, too. You don't want to use deceit in your paralegal practice, and you don't want to let anyone else make you do something deceitful on behalf of a client. You want to be courteous and professional toward everyone, even when they don't remember that they are supposed to be courteous and professional to you. This courtesy and professionalism extend to the court, as well.

You cannot communicate directly with a represented person on the other side of litigation, and you cannot let that person communicate with you.

Remember that the prosecutor's role in the judicial system is different from the rest of the system. Despite what you may see on the nightly news, the prosecutor's job is to seek justice. If you go to work in the prosecutor's office, I promise you will always have an interesting job.

RULE #6 REVIEW QUESTIONS

1. What is "due process"? Why is it important in our judicial system?
2. What is "suppression of evidence"? Give some examples of how you might suppress evidence.
3. What is "fabricating evidence"? "Tampering with evidence"?
4. What is the difference between inducing a witness to testify falsely and allowing a witness to testify falsely? What is subornation of perjury?
5. If your client tells you that she intends to lie in her interrogatory responses, what should you do, step by step?
6. If your client tells you that she lied in her interrogatory responses, responses that were sent to opposing counsel long ago, what should you do, step by step?
7. If you are asked to lie about who you are in order to get information about one of your cases, what should you do?
8. Why is it important to be courteous to opposing counsel?
9. What is dicta, and can you use it?
10. What is the prosecutor's job? How is it different from defense counsel's job?

[1] *Powell v. Alabama*, 287 U.S. 45, 53 S.Ct. 55 (1932).

[2] *Johns v. Smyth*, 176 F.Supp. 949 (E.D.Va. 1959).

[3] Rule 6.2(a), EC 2-27.

[4] *Id.*

[5] *Id.*

[6] In *People v. Belge*, 50 A.D.2d 1088, 376 N.Y.S.2d 771 (4th Dept. 1975), aff'd, 41 N.Y.2d 960, 390 N.Y.S.2d 867 (1976), a client informed his lawyer of the location of the corpses of young women the client had killed. The court held that the client's interest in confidentiality prevailed over the parents' interest in knowing their fate and the social interest in the proper treatment of the corpses.

[7] *People v. Meredith*, 631 P.2d 46, 175 Cal. Rptr. 612 (Cal. 1981) (defense investigator removed victim's wallet from trash can as a result of client communication; held that prosecution entitled to be shown the location of wallet, which was crucial to homicide prosecution); *State v. Olwell*, 394 P.2d 681, 64 Wash.2d 828 (1964) (counsel required to produce knife obtained from client over objection of attorney/client privilege).

[8] See *People v. Meredith*, supra, and *State v. Olwell*, supra.

[9] *Morrell v. State*, 575 P.2d 1200 (Alaska 1978) (kidnapping plan in defendant's handwriting properly turned over to authorities and lawyer required to answer source questions). *People v. Lee*, 3 Cal.App.3d 514, 83 Cal. Rptr. 715 (1970) (lawyer had no right to withhold shoes of client given by wife independently to lawyer).

[10] See note 6.

[11] See also *State v. Douglass*, 20 W.Va. 770 (1882), where the court held that lawyer's observations of the location of his client's pistol were protected by the attorney/client privilege. N.Y. Ethics Op. 479 (1978).

[12] *Sullins v. State Bar*, 542 P.2d 631 (Cal. 1975).

[13] *Reznick v. State Bar*, 460 P.2d 969 (Cal. 1969).

[14] *State ex rel Nebraska State Bar v. Fisher*, 103 N.W.2d 325 (Neb. 1960).

[15] *In re Wright*, 248 P.2d 1080 (Nev. 1952).

[16] *In re Howard*, 372 N.E.2d 371 (Ill. 1976).

[17] Rule 3.4(b).

[18] *Committee on Prof. Ethics and Conduct of the Iowa State Bar Assn. v. Crary*, 245 N.W.2d 298 (Iowa 1976), see also the lengthy Comments following Model Rule 3.3.

[19] *In re Bishop*, 210 S.E.2d 235 (S.C. 1974).

[20] *Iowa State Bar Assn. v. Hall*, 463 N.W.2d 30 (Iowa 1990).

[21] Rico v. Mitsubishi Motors, 42 Cal. 4th 807 (2007)

[22] Rule 4.4.

[23] *Id.*

[24] *State v. Hamrick*, N.C. App. 2003.

[25] *Runsvold v. Idaho State Bar*, 925 F.2d 1118 (Idaho 1996); Rule 4.2.

[26] *Vaughn v. State Bar*, 2 Cal.Rptr. 11 (1960).

[27] *Smith v. State*, 523 S.W.2d 1 (Tex.App. 1975).

[28] *Hill v. Houpt*, 141 A. 159 (Pa. 1929).

[29] *Fouls v. Maryland Casualty Co.*, 30 F.2d 357 (1929).

[30] *West Coast Devel. v. Read*, 3 Cal.Rptr.2d 709 (1992).

[31] *Id.*

[32] *Los Angeles Times* (January 17, 2004).

[33] *Heavey v. State Bar*, 551 P.2d 1238 (Cal. 1976).

[34] *Stern Bros., Inc. v. McClure*, 236 S.E.2d 222 (W.Va. 1977).

[35] *Matter of J.B.K.*, 931 S.W.2d 581 (Tex.App. 1996).

[36] Rule 3.8; *People v. Zimmer*, 414 N.E.2d 705 (N.Y. 1980).

[37] *People v. Ruthford*, 534 P.2d 1341 (Cal. 1975).

[38] *Currie v. Superior Court*, 281 Cal.Rptr. 250 (1991).

[39] Rule 3.8.

Don't Practice Law without a License

WHAT IS THE UNAUTHORIZED PRACTICE OF LAW?

The unauthorized practice of law (UPL) and its relationship to access to justice are two of the most complex challenges in legal ethics today. As you know, the practice of law has traditionally been restricted to only licensed attorneys. Attorneys must have a certain amount of education and pass a bar exam.[1] Attorneys are regulated by their state bar associations or Supreme Court regulatory branch so the public has some assurance that it will be protected from unqualified, negligent, or dishonest attorneys. Furthermore, it is every legal professional's duty to protect the public from unscrupulous practitioners (see Rule 8.3). So, even though there appears to be an adequate number of honest, hardworking lawyers, the vast majority of the public will not be able to afford to hire a lawyer when the need arises. When we discuss UPL, then, we discuss that delicate balance of **protecting the public** and **access to justice (Rule #5)**. The conflict created by these two concerns makes choices about UPL more difficult than ever before. Therefore, when trying to determine what is UPL, we look at both what will best protect the public from unqualified people making important legal decisions and what will leave room for legal assistance for those presently without representation.

Why Should Only Lawyers Practice Law?

Your state's Rules of Professional Conduct say something like this:

> **Rule 5.5:** A lawyer shall not: (a) practice in a jurisdiction where doing so violates the regulation of the legal profession in that jurisdiction; or (b) assist a person who is not a member of the bar in the performance of activity that constitutes the unauthorized practice of law.

In the 1960s, it was a popular belief that the prohibition against the practice of law by nonlawyers is based in the need of the public for integrity and competence of everyone who renders legal services. Because of the fiduciary character of the lawyer–client relationship and the inherently complex nature of our legal system, it was believed, the public can only be assured of the responsibility and competence required if the practice of law is confined to those who are subject to the requirements and regulations imposed upon members of the legal profession.[2]

Note that your state's Rule 5.5 is twofold: It is improper to practice law without a license, and it is improper to assist another in doing so. For all the discussion, however, the ABA, the state bar associations, and the courts have been reluctant to set a definite standard for what, exactly, constitutes the practice of law. (The ABA actually said in its earlier Model Code that it was "neither necessary nor desirable to attempt the formulation of a single, specific definition of what constitutes the practice of law. It is a matter for determination by the courts of that jurisdiction."[3]) Leaving it to the courts to decide, then, means that what activities constitute the practice of law will be determined jurisdiction by jurisdiction, activity by activity, case by case. As a result, the law on UPL is changing continually and is different in every jurisdiction. As a paralegal, you are responsible for complying with legal authority governing UPL in your own jurisdiction. Do not think that you will find a "bright line" of UPL. You will not. Every instance must be analyzed individually. Here is a good rule of thumb: The practice of law is using your legal knowledge and skill, applying it to a person's specific facts, and communicating advice or conclusions based on that knowledge and facts to that person.

Why Should We Care?

The unauthorized practice of law is one of the greatest concerns to those entering the paralegal field. It is also of concern to lawyers and people who are currently in law school or are awaiting positive bar exam results. It is very easy to "practice law" inadvertently, even innocently. The public interest is at stake, though, as well the legal profession and its reputation, so the courts and bar associations are not forgiving of violators.

We Really Do Know What the Practice of Law Is

Activities to be aware of in UPL fall into four categories: (1) prohibitions on the practice of law by nonlawyers, (2) lawyers aiding UPL, (3) the responsibility of lawyers for their nonlawyer personnel, and

(4) misrepresentations by nonlawyers as to their status. Your state's Rules of Professional Conduct, state and federal laws, a tradition of case-by-case determination, and the various state bar associations' opinions all contribute to the diverse points of view in all four areas. In this chapter, we will address all of these categories in order. Our objective is to define the "practice of law" with sufficient particularity so that the student will be able to avoid all activities that are "unauthorized." The goal is to protect the public while providing access to justice for everyone.

PROHIBITIONS ON THE PRACTICE OF LAW BY NONATTORNEYS

The general rule is that the practice of law is limited to those who are licensed and admitted to the bar after satisfying certain state requirements with regard to education, moral character, and examination: a licensed attorney or lawyer. Not the least of all of the considerations concerning those who are licensed to practice law is that these people are subject to the profession's disciplinary regulations. Those people who have not been qualified as attorneys but who, nevertheless, seek to practice law may be subject to civil penalties or, in some states, criminal penalties.

The activities that constitute the "unauthorized practice of law" are subject to the interpretation of each state. That means that there is no universal standard. Most states provide no definition, but other states have laid the foundation for some common themes on a case-by-case basis. Some of the more common expressions you will see are the following:

1. Is the activity one "traditionally practiced by lawyers"?[4]
2. Is it "commonly understood" to involve the practice of law?[5]
3. Does it "require legal skill or knowledge beyond that of a layperson"?[6]
4. Is it "characterized by the personal relationship between attorney and client"?[7]
5. Is this activity one that "the public interest is best served by limiting performance to those who are attorneys"?[8]

The problem with all of these definitions is that they are rather vague and are based on tradition. In our quickly changing society, maybe "tradition" isn't the best standard.

All states have statutes that limit the practice of law to licensed attorneys. By now, you know where to locate these statutes in your state law. In most states, these statutes say only something not helpful such as "those without a license cannot practice law," and the courts are left with

> You should familiarize yourself with your state's UPL regulations. A Google search of the term "unauthorized practice of law" + [*yourstate*] will lead you to the law in your state. If you can find a case, it will probably give you any statutory law you need in addition to the Rules of Conduct. Go to your state's cache of ethics opinions and read the ones on UPL. If you haven't found those opinions yet, a good place to start looking for them is on the Web site of the disciplinary authority in your state, such as your state bar association.

the task of interpreting those words. The few states that attempt to define the acts that constitute the *practice of law* generally refer to three broad categories of activity:

1. Representing others before judicial or administrative bodies[9]
2. Preparing legal documents that affect the legal rights of others[10]
3. Advising others with regard to their legal rights[11]

1. Representing Others as UPL

In *State ex rel. Stephan v. Williams*,[12] the nonlawyer signed pleadings, made appearances and examined witnesses. That's got to be clearly UPL. Appearing in a state or federal court to represent another person is one of the obvious signs of UPL.

In pro per
is short for in propria persona. That is Latin for "representing yourself."

Even though we might think otherwise, because a husband cannot be *in pro per* for himself and his wife, representing his wife is UPL.[13]

Even attempting to help a client in requesting a continuance in some of the more conservative states is UPL.[14] This may seem like overkill because asking for a continuance doesn't have any substantive law implications, but it is an appearance in court on behalf of another person—and only a licensed attorney may do that.

2. Preparing Legal Documents as UPL

There have been a number of cases on secretarial services preparing legal documents as UPL. Even the early ones held that selling legal documents and preparing them for a fee are not improper so long as the information typed has been written out first by the client, or it is typed at the instruction of the client.[15] However, in *Florida Bar v. Furman*, the Florida court seemingly overturned that decision late in 1984 by convicting Rosemary Furman, the owner-operator of a secretarial service specializing in legal forms, of practicing law without a license based on its opinion that her "relationship" with her client was like that of attorney–client. She was sentenced to 120 days in jail, ninety of which would be waived if she would not violate the court's order and refrain from typing legal forms. The conflict between Ms. Furman and the Florida Bar began in 1979.[16]

Drafting the simplest complaint and uncomplicated petition for dissolution (divorce) without the oversight of an attorney is UPL.[17] In other words, drafting legal documents (number 2 mentioned earlier) is the practice of law unless the drafter is supervised by an attorney.

Obviously, if the paralegal is preparing legal documents at the request of a lawyer, this is not UPL. Preparing legal documents is what paralegals are supposed to do! The courts have created a legal fiction to explain this. They say that when the supervising attorney approves of the work product (such as by signing it), "he adopts [it] as his own."[18] After drafting a document, the paralegal has it reviewed by a lawyer and, if a signature is required, the lawyer signs it. Paralegals cannot sign in the place of a lawyer, but they do "draft" documents.

3. Advising Others and Books and Kits as UPL

If you sat down with your friend, listened to her story of the awful thing that has happened to her, and proceeded to explain her legal rights to her, you would be "practicing law" because you are using your legal knowledge and skill, applying them to her specific facts and giving her advice. That part seems clear. Paralegals, even though they may be very knowledgeable about the law, cannot share that knowledge by helping others with their legal problems—not even your best friend; not even for free; not even if you begin with the disclaimer "I'm not allowed to practice law, but . . . "; and not even if you write it down and give it to her or point out the answer to her in a book. Those are the three elements to look for: using your knowledge of the law, applying it to a particular person's fact pattern, and giving a conclusion or opinion.

Look for *U.S. v. Johnson* on the publisher's Web site. What do you think about the services Mr. Robinson and NLPA provided to Mr. Johnson? Shouldn't the defendant have the right to decide what legal services will serve him best?

In *In re Calzadilla*, 151 B.R. 622 (Fla. 1993), the bankruptcy court ruled that secretarial services may sell printed materials and sample forms and type bankruptcy forms from written information provided by clients, and they may advertise these services. They may not, however, advise how best to fill out the forms or assist in filling out schedules. They may not "correct" what they believe to be errors by the patron. They also may not use the word "paralegal" in their advertising material as that may mislead reasonable laypeople into believing that they are permitted to provide legal assistance.

Although it doesn't seem like writing a book could be UPL because books do not address individuals' fact patterns, some states have put this

In *Statewide Grievance Committee v. Patton*, 683 A.2d 1359 (Conn. 1996), the court shut down an organization called Doc-U-Prep. The defendant in that case gave customers a form to fill out and sent the form to the Doc-U-Prep headquarters in Massachusetts. That organization completed the forms with the information provided and returned the completed documents to the defendant who delivered them to the customers. All of the legal forms were for uncontested matters such as a will, corporation, or name change, but included Chapter 7 bankruptcy, a subject in which many legal technicians practice as Bankruptcy Petition Preparers (BPPs). The court overruled all of the defendants' First Amendment freedom of speech and Fourteenth Amendment equal protection and due process challenges, holding that "prohibiting unsupervised paralegals from work with legal consequences is rationally related to public protection."

to the test.[19] Most courts have applied a "personal relationship between attorney and client" test to books like *How to Avoid Probate* and the *Divorce Yourself Kit*. Surely people need these books and use them successfully every day. Holding that they violate state UPL statutes would mean taking them off the public library shelves and out of the bookstores. The need for access to justice would not be met that way. No litigation to ban these books has been successful.

The consensus of the courts is that such kits are not UPL so long as they are sold to the general public and the seller does not answer questions relating to specific individuals. Companies selling a kit <u>and</u> personal legal services have been shut down by the various law enforcement agencies. For example, in late 1997, a "trust mill" in California was closed after a state bar investigation revealed that nonlawyers were selling living trust "packages" on behalf of a lawyer. The sales agents used a sample living trust that they promised to customize for each purchaser.[20] So, actually meeting with the client creates that "personal relationship" and crosses the line between UPL and access to justice.

However, kits and books that the consumer can purchase and receive no in-person legal advice are not UPL.

WHAT IS NOT UPL

Overlapping Functions—Not UPL

Some activities, while they look like the practice of law by laypeople, are authorized by the law. These activities can be performed by both lawyers and nonlawyers, so they are often referred to as "overlapping functions."

Some of the most obvious rights and activities involving overlapping functions are the following:

1. The right to lay participation in the exercise of certain federally protected rights[21]
2. The right of nonattorneys to representation before federal administrative agencies[22]
3. The right of indigent criminal defendants to representation by law students[23]
4. The right of nonattorneys to self-representation[24]
5. Lay practice before state administrative agencies[25]

"Incidental to"—Not UPL

Some statutes specifically permit certain groups of individuals and certain organizations to practice law because it's just a little bit of law and unavoidable. We call these the "incidental to" businesses:

1. Preparation of instruments by title companies and real estate brokers[26]
2. Estate planning by banks and insurance agencies[27]
3. Debt collection by commercial agencies[28]
4. Tax practice by accountancy agencies[29]

You can see the obvious problem that these "incidental to" businesses face. They are allowed to give some limited legal advice because it is incidental to their ordinary course of business. They must be careful not to cross the line into the blatant practice of law. As no one can tell them exactly where that line is, it's difficult to know what is lawful and what is not. Most of these industries stick to the bits of "practicing law" that they have been doing for many years (the "tradition" standard again) so they avoid trouble. Periodically, however, when they branch out, they are accused of UPL violations. Talk to real estate agents about continuing education. They will tell you that the law of what they can do and what they can't do ebbs and flows with time.

Doing Your Job—Not UPL

Paralegals who are doing their job "prepare legal documents," but it is not UPL because it is done under the supervision of a lawyer. Paralegals perform legal research and share the answers with clients, but this is not UPL because it is done at the behest of a lawyer. South Carolina, in a case heard by its supreme court, set the following standard for permissible paralegal activities:

> Paralegals are routinely employed by licensed attorneys to assist in the preparation of legal documents such as deeds and mortgages. The activities of a paralegal do not constitute the practice of law *as*

long as they are limited to work of a preparatory nature, such as legal research, investigation, or the composition of legal documents, which enable the licensed attorney-employer to carry a given matter to a conclusion through his own examination, approval, or additional effort.[30] [Emphasis added.]

What about Disbarred or Suspended Lawyers?

In *Florida Bar v. Thomson*[31] the Florida Supreme Court held that attorneys suspended from the practice of law may perform law clerk (paralegal) work in an office during their suspension. In describing the duties such a person could perform, the court said:

> [He] limited his functions exclusively to work of a preparatory nature such as research, taking statements of witnesses consistent with initial investigation of a case, assembling information for review, and like work that would enable the attorney-employer to carry a given matter to a conclusion through his own examination, approval, or additional effort. *He adds that all of his activities have been performed under the direct supervision of the attorney-employer, and that he has not held himself out to be an attorney, has not signed any pleadings or letter in behalf of any attorney, has made no court appearances, has had no direct contact with any client or given any legal advice to any client, and has conducted himself in the sole role of research investigator for his employer.* [Emphasis added.]

> We also find the services allegedly performed by Thomson in his capacity as a law clerk or investigator similar to those performed by paraprofessionals or paralegals in this state and elsewhere.

There have been opinions to the contrary based on the theory that such a disbarred or suspended attorney would not be able to refrain from practicing law. Other opinions state that disbarred or suspended attorneys should be separated from the practice of law entirely for the protection of the public. This would be a good time to find out what your state says on this subject. Can a disbarred lawyer work as a paralegal in your state?

Prohibitions under Scrutiny

Prohibitions on the practice of law by nonattorneys are subject to criticism on policy grounds by attorneys and laypeople. These prohibitions have been challenged on First Amendment (free speech), due process (the right to representation), and antitrust (anti-monopolies) theories. They have been called paternalistic and self-serving.[32] Studies show that very few of the UPL prosecutions and civil cases involve actual injury to a member of the public and that, in many instances, lawyer intervention is much more costly for the public and the service provided is substantially slower. In other words, there is a vast segment of society that needs legal assistance but cannot afford a lawyer. When a member of the public gets good assistance from a nonlawyer who is practicing law in violation of the UPL laws, nothing happens. However, when a member of the public is harmed and makes a complaint to the district attorney or the bar, an investigation may or may not be initiated, and the nonlawyer may or may not continue in business, harming other people.

WHAT DO YOU THINK?

Do lawyers fight to keep the practice of law exclusive because they want all of the business for themselves? because they believe that the public is not smart enough to make good choices in representation? or because the public needs to be protected against unqualified legal practitioners?

The ABA has always maintained (1) that the public is best served by maintaining the high standards of quality achieved by self-regulation and (2) that only licensed attorneys should be subject to regulation by the ethical considerations. In other words, the organized bar believes that both the effective administration of the legal system and the interests of the clients as consumers of legal services can be provided for only by licensed attorneys.

What Is the Effect of UPL?

In fact, the public is often harmed by UPL. *In re McCarthy*[33] is a good illustration of the consequences of the potential harm UPL causes to the public in a bankruptcy setting. In that case, Ms. McCarthy hired a nonlawyer who advertised himself as a "bankruptcy specialist" to do her straightforward bankruptcy. He did not fill out the forms properly, though, resulting in a significant financial loss to Ms. McCarthy. The bankruptcy court brought the negligent nonlawyer to the attention of the authorities. However, because she was not represented by a lawyer, Ms. McCarthy had no way to get her money back through a legal malpractice case. Obviously, lawyers and nonlawyers alike can make mistakes that ultimately harm the client. However, lawyers can be sued for malpractice; but nonlawyers, as in Ms. McCarthy's experience, cannot. Where there is a pattern of below-standard legal work, lawyers may be subject to discipline. Again, nonlawyers are exempt from this sort of discipline. The best that Ms. McCarthy could get was the satisfaction that the fellow who had done her bankruptcy improperly would be prohibited from doing bankrupcty work for anyone else.

Exceptions to General UPL Rules

There are, of course, exceptions to the prohibition on the practice of law by nonlawyers and, because determinations in this area have been made on an ad hoc, case-by-case basis, the exceptions vary greatly among the jurisdictions. There are, however, common themes and exceptions established as a matter of constitutional right that are universally recognized by the states. These exceptions permit self-representation, lay participation in certain administrative proceedings, lay participation in the exercise of federally protected rights, and law student practice, especially in the area of indigent representation.

Self-representation. The right of self-representation in federal courts is codified in 28 USC §1654:

> In all courts of the United States the parties may plead and conduct their own cases personally or by counsel as, by the rules of such courts, respectively, are permitted to manage and conduct causes therein.

Although the U.S. Constitution does not specifically guarantee the right of self-representation, the U.S. Supreme Court has interpreted it that way in *Faretta v. California*[34] stemming from the right to a lawyer in criminal matters. The Court reasoned that, as there is the right to have an attorney, there must be an equal right to not have an attorney. Additionally, the Court said, the Sixth Amendment right of self-representation is made applicable to the states via the Fourteenth Amendment.

Law students. In *People v. Perez,*[35] the California Supreme Court held that valuable practical training and increasing the availability of legal services for indigent people were strong-enough reasons to permit "limited practice of law" by law students, providing they are properly supervised. Of course, the states vary immensely as to in what area and under what circumstances law students may practice law. All states that allow law students to represent others, however, include adequate supervision caveats, permit appearances at special administrative hearings and preparation of legal documents, set specifications as to the educational background of the student, and provide for the student's proper introduction to the court.

Using the "access to the courts" theory, the federal government has allowed paralegals and law students to represent others in Medicaid, food stamp, and unemployment compensation matters. Likewise, indigent prisoners have been utilizing nonattorneys since 1969 under the same theory.[36] In the strides made for the use of paralegals in representing indigents, prisoners, and others who may not have adequate representation, the concurring opinion of Justice Douglas has been cited again and again:

> The increasing complexities of our governmental apparatus at both the local and the federal levels have made it difficult for a person to process a claim or even to make a complaint. . . . [I]t is becoming abundantly clear that more and more of the effort in ferreting out the basis of claims and the agencies responsible for them and in preparing the almost endless paperwork for their prosecution is work for laymen. There are not enough lawyers to manage or supervise all of these affairs; and much of the basic work done requires no special legal talent. Yet there is a closed-shop philosophy in the legal profession that cuts down drastically active roles for laymen. That traditional, closed-shop attitude is utterly out of place in the modern world where claims pile high and much of the work of tracing and pursuing them requires the patience and wisdom of a layman rather than the legal skills of a member of the bar. . . . (p. 491)

As it is just a concurring opinion, Justice Douglas's words do not have the force of law, but there is a growing number of people who agree that the closed-shop attitude of only lawyers practicing law is out of place in the modern world. For this reason, as we will see, the shop doors are beginning to open.

Administrative agencies.

Administrative agencies. Many federal agencies permit lay representation. The National Labor Relations Board and other administrative bodies allow any layperson to represent others before them, whereas other agencies, such as the Patent Office and the Interstate Commerce Commission, require specific educational qualifications and the passing of an examination. With regard to state administrative agencies, however, there is a great deal of inconsistency. Some state courts have even ruled that the state legislature has no power to authorize practice before agencies created by the legislature. Others have followed the Florida ruling in *Florida Bar v. Moses*,[37] which held that the legislature and the judiciary have concurrent authority in this area and either may make such rules to assist the public in attaining adequate representation.

The U.S. Supreme Court has held that the states have no authority to regulate lay representation before federal agencies because of the supremacy clause (Article VI) of the Constitution.[38] Likewise, the U.S. Supreme Court has held that the states cannot interfere where lay representation is the only alternative to protect federally guaranteed rights. The Supreme Court also held that nonlawyer inmates are allowed to furnish legal assistance in the preparation of various petitions for postconviction relief to other inmates who are poorly educated and unable to retain counsel.

Some examples, just to name a few, of federal law allowing nonlawyer representation are the following:

Small Business Administration [13 CFR 121.11, 134.16]

National Credit Union Administration [12 CFR 747]

Federal Energy Regulatory Commission [18 CFR 385.2101]

Drug Enforcement Administration [21 CFR 1316.50]

Aid to Families with Dependent Children [45 CFR 205]

Food and Drug Administration [32 CFR 12.40, 12.45]

Comptroller of the Currency [12 CFR 19.3]

Immigration and Naturalization Service [8 CFR 292.1-3]

Environmental Protection Agency [40 CFR 124, 164.30, 22.10]

What Is Definitely Not "Giving Legal Advice"

The Conduit Theory. Working in the field of law requires common sense. A commonsense approach to UPL will prevent you from becoming paralyzed by the fear of violating one of what seems to be an infinite list of rules. In the traditional law office setting, you will often hear a lawyer say to a paralegal, "Call Client X and tell her. . . . " Even if the paralegal is instructed to give Client X what would technically be called "legal advice," that the advice is given by the paralegal does not mean that it is UPL. The paralegal is simply acting as a *conduit of the legal advice* from the lawyer to the client, just as if the lawyer had written the advice in a letter and sent it to the client. The conduit theory, then, covers most instances of the paralegal giving legal advice to the client.

Ordinarily, the paralegal has been instructed in what to say—that's why we can call it the conduit theory. Sometimes, however, the paralegal has been told what to say to one client in one circumstance and would now like to give that same advice to a different client in a similar circumstance. Here the line begins to blur. In certain circumstances, it may be permissible to give the advice to the client, and in others, it may not. In yet other circumstances, it may be acceptable to say, "This is what I think the answer is, but I'm going to check with a lawyer and if the answer isn't right, I'll call you back." In that way, the client has gotten a more immediate answer, the paralegal has been helpful, and the paralegal is going to discuss the question with that conduit-lawyer to verify the answer.[39]

Asking Questions. Paralegals often interview clients. Interviews are usually simply a series of questions: What happened? where? who was there? and what happened next? Although the paralegal is speaking directly with the client, this is not UPL because no legal advice is being given. In fact, you (the paralegal) will probably be thinking about the cause of action and the procedural steps that will be necessary and even what the likely outcome will be, so long as you don't share these thoughts with the client, you are not UPL-ing. Inevitably, you will take the call from the client who is in a panic and demanding to speak to a lawyer who, equally inevitably, is not available. You cannot give the client any legal advice but you can ask questions: "Tell me everything you would say to the lawyer and I'll write it down. Then someone will get back to you." Asking questions and taking down the information will most likely satisfy the panicked client, at least for a while.

Corporations

Corporations present a special problem because they are not "persons" as we traditionally think of them. Therefore, corporations cannot utilize the right of self-representation. Most states agree that a corporation must be represented by a lawyer in a court of law, but nonlawyers can represent them in administrative proceedings.[40] So it is UPL for the nonlawyer president of a corporation to file and answer in a court and prosecute an appeal.[41] This is a good place for you to do some research. Can a corporation send an employee to a small claims court proceeding in your state?

WHAT DO YOU THINK?

In a Florida Bar Advisory Opinion, 627 So.2d 485 (1993), Florida, traditionally very hard on UPL offenders, opined that a nonlawyer property manager could represent the individual or corporate landlord in uncontested residential evictions, so long as the authority was given to the property manager in writing and the action did not involve a judgment for past rent. Isn't the property manager practicing law without a license? Why should (or shouldn't) an exception be made for this instance?

Paralegals working in corporations face interesting UPL problems when they are not working under the supervision of lawyers. With recent corporate cutbacks, it is now commonplace to see a corporate legal department staffed solely with paralegals. When the corporate paralegal is asked for legal advice by someone in the corporation, does she or he commit UPL by responding? The answer is maybe, depending upon the nature of the question. An employee of a corporation doesn't really have a "client" in the typical sense of the word—just other employees. If we liken this paralegal's position to that of the typical personnel manager, who is often called upon to answer legal questions regarding personnel issues, then it is not UPL; the answer to the legal question is incidental to the person's primary job. If the corporate paralegal's primary job is coordinating outside legal counsel, when the paralegal is asked, "What do you advise we do in the *Brown* case?" by a corporate officer, the paralegal's response "Take Mr. Brown's deposition" is not necessarily UPL. Who's the client?

LAWYERS AIDING THE UNAUTHORIZED PRACTICE OF LAW

Attorneys can violate the regulations that prohibit their aiding UPL by improperly supervising their employees and associates, by allowing a nonlawyer to influence their independent professional judgment (dividing fees), or by entering into an improper business relationship with a nonlawyer. We discuss each one in order.

Improper Supervision

Earlier we talked about paralegals preparing legal documents that are then accepted by the lawyer, and so the task of preparing legal documents is not UPL. The theory is that the lawyer will read the document and "adopt it as his own." But what happens when the lawyer is not reading the documents? What if your supervising lawyer signs the documents without reading them? By failing to properly supervise nonlawyer staff members, lawyers break the law by aiding in UPL. The point of having the lawyer do legal work is to ensure that the public gets educated, trained, responsible, and regulated lawyers performing this important work. When the lawyer doesn't do his or her job, and leaves the job to a paralegal who is unsupervised, the public is not getting the protection that the law has designed.

This is also true in the case of contract or independent or freelance paralegals doing work in an area in which the lawyer has no expertise. For example, the real estate lawyer hires a probate paralegal to handle the probates that come into the office. The lawyer hires the paralegal not because there is too much work or he simply doesn't want to perform the probate work, but because he doesn't know how to do probate work. If this is the case, the real estate lawyer cannot supervise that paralegal because she or he has no knowledge of probate law. This improper (or absent) supervision constitutes UPL.

There are many, many cases on lawyers who have been disciplined for failure to properly supervise employees and violating the lawyer's UPL duties. See the publisher's Web site or search these terms in your favorite search engine: UPL + "inadequate supervision" + [*yourstate*].

For an almost amusing case, read *In re Schelly*, 446 N.E.2d 236 (Ill. 1983), in which a lawyer employed a disbarred attorney as a law clerk and even after having been repeatedly disciplined by the bar and the court for allowing this clerk to practice law, the attorney continued to employ the clerk, and the clerk continued to try cases when his supervising attorney instructed him to ask the court for continuances. Finally, the court charged the attorney with aiding his employee in UPL and failure to supervise and convicted him of not restricting or supervising his law clerk.

Improper Division of Fees

We learned in Rule #5 that paralegals must not accept referral fees. That's because the law says, quite simply, that lawyers must not divide fees with nonlawyers. The law has long believed that no one but lawyers should make decisions about legal matters. If nonlawyers are eligible to profit financially from legal matters, their influence will poison the relationship of trust between lawyer and client. So, for this reason, paralegals who refer clients to their employing law firms cannot get "a piece of the action." Furthermore, paralegals cannot have an employment contract that states that the salary will be based on the outcome of the case or the profits of the firm.[42] To pay such a fee would be a violation of UPL standards. This law, however, does not mandate that employees be paid a fixed salary. Bonuses, annual or more frequent, are perfectly permitted, so long as the bonus is not based on a percentage of the law firm profits or a percentage of a particular legal fee.

Improper Business Relationship

Check your state's Rule 5.4. It prohibits lawyers and nonlawyers from being in business together if any part of that business will be the practice of law. Historically, this was to prevent a nonlawyer from having any say about the outcome of a legal matter. An exception is made to this rule for group legal service providers such as NAACP and the ACLU. Another exception is labor unions.

In the everyday practice of law, however, this rule is still in place. For example, consider the case in which a lawyer introduced a person to his clients and told them that this person was an attorney who was licensed in another state and had practiced law in Europe. Thereafter, this person consulted with the clients without the supervision of the lawyer. Notwithstanding the contention that the unlicensed person was only assisting the clients in obtaining counsel in Europe and that he actually rendered no legal assistance, the lawyer was held to have aided the nonlawyer in UPL. Further, the court held that since the two individuals shared fees on a regular basis, theirs was an improper business relationship.[44]

This Rule and the Rules on lawyers and nonlawyers not sharing fees are subject to criticism by those organizations that are trying to make access to the judicial system more affordable. To that end, in 1990, the District of Columbia modified the ABA version of Rule 5.4 to allow partnerships between lawyers and nonlawyers.[45] This arrangement allows the lawyer and paralegal to pool their resources to start a law firm. It also allows the paralegal to work with, not for, the lawyer. This relationship will benefit the public by making the judicial system more attainable.

> In *Atkins v. Tinning*, 865 S.W.2d 533 (Tex. 1993), the court found that such an agreement is illegal for the lawyer only, as the prohibitions on fee splitting apply only to lawyers. The court awarded the nonlawyer his share under the agreement and disciplined the lawyer. Note that illegal referral fees are ordinarily held to be illegal for both parties and will therefore not be enforced by the court.[43]

THE LAWYER'S RESPONSIBILITY FOR NONLAWYER PERSONNEL

We have seen this truism in almost every Rule we have studied: Lawyers are responsible for the conduct of their employees. This is *respondeat superior*, which is Latin for "let the master answer." This rule dates back to 1747 when the Court of Chancery held that the solicitor must answer to his client for the negligence of his clerk as if it were his own act.[46] Similarly, in 1902 an American court held that attorneys would be liable for the intentional criminal acts of their clerks against the attorneys and their clients.[47] This rule means that the lawyer who employs you will be held responsible for any ordinary negligent things that you do on the job. If you mis-calendar a deadline, it is the lawyer who will answer for it in court. You may be fired, but not fined by the court. If your supervising lawyer tells you to do something dishonest, the lawyer will be held responsible to the court system and the state's lawyer disciplinary system. You may be prosecuted if your actions are also criminal. If you violate the rules relating to UPL, your supervising lawyer will suffer the consequences. You are also under the jurisdiction of the court and the court may sanction you, too.[48]

Supervision and Hiring

Because the lawyer is responsible for the acts of his or her paralegal, Rule 5.3 unquestionably makes the employer-attorney responsible for the unethical conduct of the paralegal. That the employer must make reasonable efforts to see that the paralegal's conduct conforms with the ethical obligations of the lawyer is also clearly stated in this Rule.

Exactly what are "reasonable efforts" and what is conforming conduct for the paralegal is a moving target. A simple rule of thumb, however, is this: Paralegals may not do anything that would be unethical if done by a lawyer. Attorneys cannot accomplish an unethical end by having their employees perform the actual unethical act. This is important for you to know and to be able to defend. To that end, read *In re Bishop*, which you can find on the publisher's Web site.

Lawyers who employ paralegals must ensure that the paralegals know their obligations under the duty of confidentiality. You already know your duty, but other paralegals may not, so the law puts the burden on the attorney to provide training in the rules of professional responsibility. You may have an obligation to take continuing education courses because of your state law, membership in a paralegal organization, or your employment contract. As the lawyers who employ you are obligated to ensure that you keep abreast of the laws of ethics as well as other procedural or substantive areas, you might want to make sure that your employer will pay for you to attend continuing education courses and give you time off to attend. Some large law firms bring continuing education into the firm for you. It would be good to know that, too. Do not assume that every lawyer knows about the duties owed to you under Rule 5.3.

The court will sanction the supervising attorney who uses the paralegal improperly, such as the case where the attorney authorized his nonattorney employee to sign the attorney's name to a bankruptcy petition. The court found that there had been no participation by the attorney in the bankruptcy filing. The court sanctioned the attorney the moving party's attorney's fees. Typically the court will cite ABA Opinion 316 (1967) authorizing the use of nonlawyer assistants "so long as it is [the lawyer] who takes the work and vouches for it to the client and becomes responsible to the client."

In *Matter of Martinez*,[49] the court found that the paralegal's failure to identify himself as a nonlawyer, quoting legal fees, and cashing a settlement check payable to the client with no supporting documentation constituted improper conduct. The attorney's failure to identify his assistant as a nonlawyer was the attorney's improper conduct, and all of the improper conduct of the paralegal was *imputed* to the attorney by virtue of the lawyer's duty to supervise his employee to ensure that the conduct of his assistant comported with the attorney's own professional obligations. There are lawyers who believe that something that they are prohibited from doing will be fine if a paralegal does it. To prevent any misunderstanding about this, it may be worth your while to find your state's equivalent of the *Martinez* case, put it in a frame and hang it in your office. If you are ever asked to do something improper, just point to the framed case and explain that the lawyer will bear the worst part of the penalty when the improper conduct is discovered—which it will be.

To **impute** means to attribute fault or responsibility to someone else.

In *Louisiana State Bar Assn. v. Edwins*, 540 So.2d 294 (La. 1989), a disciplinary proceeding, the court found that a paralegal independently operated a branch office for Attorney Edwins. The paralegal (Robertson) told clients he was an attorney, quoted legal fees, prepared pleadings and signed Attorney Edwins's name, and had exclusive control over an account where client settlement checks were deposited. Robertson completed the client's matter without the client ever meeting the attorney. In determining if Edwins knew about Robertson's activities, the court considered Robertson's letterhead: "Now you can have a lawyer too . . . through Prepaid Legal Services, Rob Robertson" (p. 301). Moreover, the client Robertson "helped" had no input as to the settlement and no meaningful explanation of the distribution of the settlement funds. Attorney Edwins was disbarred when the court found that he had improperly "delegated the exercise of his professional judgment" to the legal assistant.

Delegation

A lawyer may delegate work that does not require the exercise of professional judgment to paralegals. Tasks that require giving legal advice (other than conveying information received from the attorney), representing clients in courts, or signing legal documents may not be delegated because these tasks are reserved to attorneys as "the practice of law."[50]

What this means from a practical standpoint is that it is often the paralegal's responsibility to say "no" to a lawyer who tries to delegate an improper task. For example, although it may be acceptable for a lawyer to instruct the paralegal to sign the lawyer's name to an enclosure letter, it is not acceptable to ask the paralegal to sign the lawyer's name to a pleading. As another example, it is an accepted practice to send a paralegal to a deposition to take notes and observe in place of a lawyer, but it would be UPL for the paralegal to ask questions of the deponent or otherwise actively participate in the deposition. Proper delegation enables the legal profession to bring legal services to the public more economically and efficiently. Improper delegation can be UPL.

MISREPRESENTATION

Those states that have taken steps to regulate the activities of paralegals have taken greatest interest in ensuring that paralegals will not be mistaken for attorneys. In order to protect the public from innocent mistakes regarding the identity of paralegals and those tasks they may perform, several states have made regulations pertaining to the image projected by paralegals. For example, states disagree on whether paralegals can be listed on letterhead stationery and in telephone directories. The supervising lawyer will ultimately be responsible for errors. Some states allow paralegal names listed on letterhead stationery so long as it clearly says "paralegal" under the name. The balance we're looking for is giving the public all of the information possible while ensuring that members of the public do not mistake a paralegal for a lawyer.

As a paralegal, you will probably be given your own business card. Under your name, it should say "paralegal" or "legal assistant" or whatever your designation might be. It cannot say nothing at all because anyone looking at a law firm business card will assume that the person listed there is a lawyer. Lawyers do not have to put the word "lawyer" on their business cards (although they usually do), but paralegals must have their nonlawyer status designated in some way.

WHAT DO YOU THINK?

If your business card must say "paralegal" on it, what about the sign on your office door? Will members of the public who see your office door think that you are a lawyer?

ENFORCEMENT OF UPL REGULATIONS

Injunction, criminal prosecution, citation for contempt of court, and writs of quo warranto are the most widely used methods of enforcement of the unauthorized practice regulations. Nearly all jurisdictions have felony or misdemeanor statutes, although it is maintained that injunctive relief is the most effective method for stopping the offender.

With regard to who may initiate the proceeding for an injunction, many states allow suits by the *integrated bar* or other disciplinary authority such as a committee of the Supreme Court of the state. Is there a state bar section or a Supreme Court division? If a judge discovers, as in the *McCarthy* case, that a nonlawyer is assisting a *pro per* litigant, what agency should the judge call? In California, UPL was left to the district attorney's office until recently when the state bar agreed to take up these prosecutions. The district attorney's office is responsible for prosecuting serious felonies—the type that involves death—so the UPL cases, as you can imagine, were not top priority. If

*Have we defined **integrated bar** yet? I don't think so. An integrated bar is a bar association that has mandatory membership of all lawyers. For example, California has an integrated bar, meaning that you can't practice law in California unless you are a member of the California Bar.*

you haven't already, now would be a good time to find out who regulates UPL in your state.

There have been class actions filed by attorneys to stop UPL. But these cases require a showing of irreparable injury or some proof that the attorneys represent the public interest. Suits that have attempted to prevent UPL on the theory that attorneys have the exclusive right to practice law and, therefore, the right to be protected from competition from unlicensed people are steeped in antitrust problems. This theory, furthermore, does not consider that the prohibition on UPL is to protect the public from incompetent representation, not to protect attorneys from competition. These cases, while popular in the 1960s and 1970s, seem to have run their course.

Criminal contempt citations have been called an overreaction to a rivial problem, but they are, nevertheless, common. Criminal contempt is where an act interferes with the orderly administration of justice, or impairs the dignity of the court. If you are practicing law in a court without a license to practice law, your acts could easily be interpreted as interfering with the administration of justice. A direct citation is one that is closely connected to the court or a pending case, and can be issued by the court on its own motion. For those activities that occur without the court's knowledge, an indirect citation may be requested of the court by the state attorney general, a bar association, or an individual attorney.

Quo warranto is Latin for by what authority. The writ asks, "by what authority are you practicing law" and asks for the "cease and desist" remedy.

Quo warranto writs are used to restrain corporations from exceeding their chartered purposes. This action is brought by the attorney general on behalf of the public to prevent corporations from practicing law incident to their primary purpose or business. An example of this is where the attorney general seeks to prevent real estate brokers from giving legal advice or filling out certain real estate documents for their customers as part of their ordinary business.

An Illinois appellate court held that there is no private cause of action for a violation of Illinois' unauthorized practice statute unless the allegations were of negligence or the defendants had actually held themselves out to be attorneys (*Torres v. Fiol*, 441 N.E.2d 1300 [Ill.App. 1982]).

There are other ways to prevent or stop UPL found in tort[51] and in contract,[52] but the truth is that very little is done to prevent "true" UPL (the practice of law by people who have never been trained in law) because, at least in some part, the offense is a crime and the criminal justice system is overwhelmed with crimes considered more important.

> Effective October 1, 2004, practicing law without a license in Florida (including "holding out" oneself as a lawyer) is a third-degree felony punishable by up to five years' imprisonment and a fine of up to $5,000, Fla.Stat. sec. 454.23. Similarly, a disbarred or suspended lawyer who practices law is guilty of a felony, Fla.Stat. 454.31. The Florida Bar supported the new laws, but did not initiate them.

RULE #7 WRAP-UP

So, now we completely understand what the practice of law is, when it's not okay to do it, how we might do it inadvertently, and what the penalties are, right? We now know that the practice of law comes in three colors: representing others, preparing legal documents, and giving legal advice. We looked at a plain and simple, easy-to-apply rule for what is giving legal advice: using your knowledge of the law, applying it to a particular person's facts, and drawing a conclusion or opinion. Letting attorneys not properly supervise you is a good way to violate the "preparing legal documents" rule of UPL. Even though paralegals can "prepare" legal documents, an attorney must review and approve them. And, we now know that there are lots of agencies that allow lay practice so, if you're not interested in the "traditional" paralegal path of working for lawyers, there are other places where your legal skill and knowledge can be put to good use—helping the public. We also took a look at protecting yourself from something that a lawyer might ask you to do that you shouldn't do and what the penalties might be if you do.

RULE #7 REVIEW QUESTIONS

1. What are the two competing concerns for the public that make UPL choices so difficult? How would you resolve these concerns?
2. In your state, where is the law regulating the practice of law by nonlawyers?
3. In one sentence, what is the practice of law?
4. What are the three most commonly used categories of the practice of law?
5. Are books about resolution of legal matters UPL? How about kits such as *Do Your Own Divorce?* What are some reasons for allowing books and kits? What are some arguments against them?
6. What are three activities that people commonly confuse with UPL? Activities that are not UPL but many people think they are?

7. Can disbarred or suspended lawyers practice law in your state? Do you think they should or should not be able to? Why or why not?

8. How is the public harmed by UPL?

9. Name three exceptions to UPL rules.

10. Name three administrative agencies that allow nonlawyers' representation.

11. What is the special UPL problem faced by corporations?

12. What are the three ways that lawyers inadvertently aid nonlawyers in UPL.

13. What does improper or insufficient supervision have to do with UPL?

14. What does improper delegation have to do with UPL?

15. What are the penalties for UPL in your state?

[1] There are a few exceptions to this rule. For example, in Wisconsin anyone who graduates from a law school in that state is admitted to the bar. Also the District of Columbia.

[2] ABA Model Code EC 3-1

[3] ABA Opinion No. 198 (1939).

[4] *State Bar of Arizona v. Arizona Land Title & Trust Co.*, 366 P.2d 1 (Ariz. 1961).

[5] *Id.*

[6] *Baron v. City of Los Angeles*, 469 P.2d 353 (Cal. 1970).

[7] *New York Lawyers Association v. Dacey*, 234 N.E.2d 459 (N.Y. 1967).

[8] *Le Doux v. Credit Research Corp.*, 125 Cal.Rptr. 166 (1975).

[9] *Id.*, note 2.

[10] *Id.*

[11] *Id.*

[12] 793 P.2d 234 (Kan. 1990).

[13] *Blunt v. Northern Oneida County Landfill*, 536 N.Y.S.2d 295 (1988).

[14] *Florida Bar v. Golden*, 563 So.2d 81 (Fla. 1990).

[15] *West Virginia State Bar, et al. v. Early*, 109 S.E.2d 420 (W.Va. 1959), and *Florida Bar v. Brumbaugh*, 355 So.2d 1186 (Fla. 1978).

[16] For other more recent cases in this area, see *Kentucky Bar Assn. v. Legal Alternatives, Inc.*, 792 S.W.2d 368 (1990), and *In re Bachmann*, 113 B.R.769 (1990) on typing services. Also see *In re MidAmerica Living Trust Assn.*, 927 S.W.2d 855 (Mo. 1996); *Florida Bar v. American Senior Citizens Alliance*, 1997 WL 80081 (Fla. 1997); *Oregon State Bar v. People's Paralegal Service*, 1997 WL 404081 (Or.App. 1997).

[17] *U.S. v. Hardy*, 681 F.Supp. 1326 (N.D.Ill. 1988).

[18] *State ex rel Oregon State Bar v. Lenske*, 584 P.2d 759 (Or. 1978), dealing with a disbarred attorney employed as a law clerk.

[19] *New York County Lawyers Assn. v. Dacey*, 234 N.E.2d 459 (N.Y. 1967), in which a nonattorney wrote and published a book that advised readers on probate matters, examining whether the activity is characterized by a personal relationship between lawyer and client.

[20] *Trust Mill Halted*, CALIFORNIA BAR JOURNAL 1 (December 1997).

[21] *NAACP v. Button*, 371 U.S. 415, 83 S.Ct. 328 (1963).

[22] 5 USC §555(b); *Sperry v. Florida*, 373 U.S. 379, 83 S.Ct. 1322 (1963).

[23] *People v. Perez*, 594 P.2d 1 (Cal. 1979); *Argersinger v. Hamlin*, 407 U.S. 25, 92 S.Ct. 2006 (1972).

[24] *Johnson v. Avery, supra*, but see *U.S. v. Stockheimer*, 385 F.Supp. 979 (W.D. Wisc. 1974), in which the district court held that defendants in a criminal action were allowed to use two disbarred attorneys to assist them in their defense under their right to self-representation. The court did not grant immunity to the two attorneys from the unauthorized practice of law.

[25] L. Brickman, *Expansion of the Lawyering Process Through a New Delivery System: The Emergence and State of Legal Paraprofessionalism*, 71 COLUMBIA L. REV. 1153 (1971).

[26] Real estate broker: *Conway-Bogue Realty Insurance Company v. Denver Bar Association*, 312 P.2d 998 (Colo. 1957); title company: *State Bar of New Mexico v. Guardian Abstract & Title Co., Inc.*, 575 P.2d 943 (1978).

27 Jerome Glaser, *Note, Unlawful Practice of Law by Trust Companies and Banks*, 32 So. Cal.R. 425 (1959).

28 *Cohn v. Thompson*, 16 P.2d 364 (Cal.App.Supp. 1932).

29 *Zelkin v. Caruso Discount Corp.*, 9 Cal.Rptr. 220 (1960).

30 *In the Matter of Easler*, 272 S.E.2d 32 (S.C. 1980).

31 310 So.2d 300 (Fla. 1975).

32 Morison, *Defining the Unauthorized Practice of Law*, 4 Nova L.J. 363 (1980).

33 149 B.R. 162 (1992).

34 422 U.S. 806 (1975).

35 594 P.2d 1 (Cal. 1979).

36 *Johnson v. Avery*, 393 U.S. 483, 89 S.Ct. 747 (1969).

37 380 So.2d 412 (Fla. 1980).

38 *Sperry v. Florida*, 373 U.S. 379, 83 S.Ct. 1322 (1963). See, for example, the Indian Child Welfare Act of 1978, 25 USCA §1911(c) that allows for nonattorney representation. Since the act is federal law, the state UPL laws are preempted. See also, 9 Jour. of Para. Ed. & Prac. 1 (April 1993) for a comprehensive article on paralegal representation before the Social Security Administration.

39 For a Kentucky Bar Association opinion on the "conduit" theory, see KBA U-47, which you can find through their web site: http://www.kybar.org/246.

40 In *Eckles v. Atlanta Technology Group, Inc.*, 485 S.E.2d 22 (Georgia 1997), the Georgia Supreme Court held that the corporation does not have the right of self-representation. However, a Georgia appellate court allowed a corporation to be represented by a nonlawyer before the county board of equalization in *Grand Partners Joint Venture I v. Realtax Resource, Inc.*, 1997 Ga.App. Lexis 392 (1997).

41 *Travelers Ins. Co. v. Roof Doctor, Inc.*, 481 S.E.2d 451 (S.C.App. 1997) See also *Albion River Watershed Protection Assn. v. Dept. of Forestry*, 24 Cal.Rptr.2d 341 (1993), holding that unincorporated associations must be represented by a person licensed to practice law.

42 This does not include programs like profit sharing or 401K plans.

43 See *Plumlee v. Paddock*, 832 S.W.2d 757 (Tex. 1992), where the attorney paid an ambulance company a set fee plus a percentage of attorneys' fees for personal injury case referrals. The court found that the contract was an illegal business relationship as to both parties and refused to enforce the agreement.

44 *Bluestein v. State Bar of California*, 529 P.2d 699 (Cal. 1974).

45 D.C. Rule 5.4: A lawyer may practice law in a partnership or other form of organization in which a financial interest is held or managerial authority is exercised by an individual nonlawyer who performs professional services, which assist the organization in providing legal services to clients, but only if:
1. the partnership or organization has as its sole purpose providing legal services to clients;
2. all persons have such managerial authority or holding a financial interest undertake to abide by these Rules of Professional Conduct;
3. the lawyers who have a financial interest or managerial authority in the partnership or organization undertake to be responsible for the nonlawyer participants to the same extent as if nonlawyers participants were lawyers under Rule 5.1;
4. the foregoing conditions are set forth in writing.

46 *Floyd v. Nangle*, 26 Eng.Rep. 1127 (Ch. 1747).

47 *In re McGuinness*, 74 N.Y.S. 1054 (1902).

48 *Columbus Bar Assn. v. Thomas*, 109 Ohio St.3d 89 (2006).

49 754 P.2d 842 (N.W. 1988).

50 Ethical Consideration 3-6 sums up proper delegation:

> A lawyer often delegates tasks to clerks, secretaries, and other laypersons. Such delegation is proper if the lawyer maintains a direct relationship with his client, supervises the delegated work, and has complete professional responsibility for the work product. This delegation enables a lawyer to render legal service more economically and efficiently.

51 Negligence: *Biakanja v. Irving*, 320 P.2d 16 (Cal. 1958).

52 *Divine v. Watauga Hospital*, 137 F.Supp. 628 (N.C. 1956).

Be Loyal to Each and Every Client

Every person involved in the field of law has a duty to use "independent judgment" on behalf of every client. What does that mean? "Independent judgment" means that the duties you owe to other people do not influence your judgment regarding a client. Let's take an example from everyday life: your best friend. Would you represent someone who was suing your best friend? No. Why not? Because your strong feelings of friendship for your friend, and all of the duties and obligations that go along with that friendship, would interfere with your ability to represent the client to the best of your ability. This is logical. Although you might want to do a good job for your client, your feelings for your friend won't let you or, at the very least, will influence you. And your friend will probably try to stop you from representing the client because of all of the "confidential" information you have about him. So, we look at the problem of adverse interests from two directions: you doing your best for your client, and the other person protecting himself or herself from your use of confidential information.

If we set aside the best friend example, we see that professional judgment is often influenced by information received from past or present clients. The essence of this Rule is that a legal professional must not compromise a client's needs and desires by outside influences or other loyalties. The legal professional owes *complete loyalty* to each client, and that loyalty should be demonstrated by (1) direct and personal contact with the client and (2) professional judgment that is not influenced by outside forces. This is a duty that we owe to each and every client: complete, unfettered loyalty. By accepting representation or even accepting an assignment on a client matter, we pledge to do our best for this client and to never use his confidential information against him

The ABA and other law associations and courts have repeatedly said that, in our society, effective use of nonlawyer legal professionals to aid in providing quality legal services at a reduced cost, not to "practice law" or take the place of the attorney, is <u>essential</u>. They also say that a planned, organized paralegal program within a law firm will allow paralegals to fulfill their roles and benefit the public while giving attorneys a way to remain in contact with the client and to exercise their own, independent professional judgment free from outside demands. Well, that's what they say, anyway. The reality where you work may be different. Maybe you work for extremely busy people. Maybe you work for new or unknowledgeable lawyers. It's important for you to know the Rules regarding conflicts (duty of loyalty) that apply to lawyers for two reasons: (1) The duty of loyalty applies to you, and (2) if the lawyer you work for doesn't know the details of these Rules, you'll know, and you can use your knowledge to help the lawyer, the firm, and the client.

We divide the duty of loyalty to every client into four parts:

1. The outside interests of the legal professional that might interfere with his or her professional judgment
2. The interests of multiple clients that the legal professional is attempting to represent
3. The interests of third parties that interfere with the professional judgment of the legal professional or the relationship between legal professional and client
4. Confidential information held by the legal professional that cannot be used adversely to the former client

YOUR OUTSIDE INTERESTS

The most obvious problem in this area arises when legal professionals involve themselves in transactions with their clients. An example is when you sell your house. The couple who makes an offer on the house are your former clients, and you suggest that you can all save some money by drawing up the papers yourself. The couple, even though they no longer have an attorney/client or fiduciary relationship with you, still look at you as one who is acting on their behalf. They trust you. However, like any other seller, you are acting only in your own best interests. What's the end of the story? The sale closes and you move to another town, but the former clients become disenchanted with their purchase of the home and ask the court to set the sale aside. Who prevails? The former clients, of course. You have a higher duty to the purchasers than to people who are strangers to you, even though your earlier client relationship no longer exists.[1] You have this higher duty forever. Does this mean that you can never sell anything to or buy anything from former clients? No. You can avoid violating this Rule by advising the buyers to seek independent counsel. This would provide them with the independent judgment they need. It shields you from the appearance that you are trying to take advantage of them.

Courts look at purchases of property from a client or other business relationships with a client by the client's attorney or staff members very carefully because of the inherent possibility of this sort of conflict. Historically, it has been found that the opportunity for *overreaching* in these business relationships is so significant that it warrants severe disciplinary action. Courts have held that even in instances in which an attorney has acted in good faith and with an honest intent, the mere possibility of fraudulent intent (the appearance of impropriety) is enough reason for reprimanding the attorney. That there is a possibility that you could defraud former clients or take an unfair advantage of them is enough.

Overreaching is outwitting or cheating others.

The NFPA Model Code provides the following:

EC 1-6(a) A paralegal shall act within the bounds of the law, solely for the benefit of the client, and shall be free of compromising influences and loyalties. Neither the paralegal's personal or business interest, nor those of other clients or third persons, should compromise the paralegal's professional judgment and loyalty to the client.

Family and Friends

Have you ever seen *Class Action* with Gene Hackman and Mary Elizabeth Mastroantonio? Mastroantonio is Hackman's daughter in the movie. Hackman has his own law firm. Mastroantonio works for Big Evil Law Firm. They end up on opposite sides of a case. But all is well because they had read Rule 1.8, where it says:

A lawyer related to another lawyer as parent, child, sibling or spouse shall not represent a client in a representation directly adverse to a person who the lawyer knows is represented by the other lawyer except upon consent by the client after consultation regarding the relationship.

Look for the part in the movie where the judge gives them permission (upon proper motion, no doubt) to litigate against each other. Without giving away the movie, let's just say that it does illustrate this conflict of interest very nicely. States differ on this rule, so now would be a good time to see if it is in yours.

Overreaching or Fraud

We often find examples of overreaching in probate cases. The attorney who represents an estate has a duty to get the highest possible price on the sale of every estate asset. How can he do that if he wants to buy the asset for himself? If you are the purchaser, you would naturally want to pay the lowest possible price. Because of the obvious conflict between these two positions, business dealings like this must be scrutinized carefully. In a case in which an attorney purchased an asset from an old and helpless client and misled the probate court in order to prevent disclosure of the transaction, the court found that the attorney should be disbarred. In the court's view, this activity constituted ***moral turpitude***.[2] The same was true in a case in which the attorney made the improper sale of estate property to his wife.[3] There is no reason that the sale would be any less tainted had it been to a member of the lawyer's staff, family, or a close friend.

Turpitude is wickedness.

WHAT DO YOU THINK?

An attorney friend of yours buys and later sells a bar that he knows is in conflict with the best interests of his client. He also tells some untruths in his application for a liquor license. Has he violated his fiduciary duties in this matter? What should the penalty be? What should the penalty be if the wrongdoer is a paralegal? Is there any difference in the fiduciary duty owed by the paralegal to the client? To help you answer these questions, read *People v. Lopez*, 796 P.2d 957 (Colo. 1990).

Transaction in Good Faith

There are cases where the court can find that the good intentions of the attorney may *mitigate* the improper conduct. In one of these cases, the attorney bought stock from a client at less than its value, but the sale was subject to the exclusive right of repurchase for the client, and the sale was made so that the client could pay off gambling debts. Although the court condemned the attorney's conduct, it held that, in this limited instance, he was acting in the best interests of the client.[4]

To *mitigate* means to lessen or minimize the severity.

In another case, the attorney's initial transaction with a client was viewed by the court as being in the client's best interests. Later, however, the client asked the attorney to reconvey the property that had been conveyed to him. The attorney refused on the grounds that he was holding the property as security for his fees. The court held that it would be proper for the attorney to file a lien on property owned by a client but not to unethically retain title to it.[5]

To make sure that the transaction is in good faith, and therefore not in violation of this Rule, you need "good faith full disclosure" of all of the facts and the written consent of the parties. To make sure you are never accused of overreaching, you can stay away from transacting any business with a client or, if you must do business with a client, you can insist the client be represented by an attorney to protect the client's interests.

> **WHAT DO YOU THINK?**
>
> A person who happens to be a client of your law firm owes you money. To ensure you will be paid the money, you file a lien on the client's property. The client agrees that this is the right thing to do. Have you done anything wrong? To aid you in finding an answer, review *Connor v. State Bar*, 791 P.2d 312 (Cal. 1990).

Witness

Here's another very logical application of this Rule: Where you are likely to be a witness in the client's case, you have a conflict of interest and should not be involved with the representation of that client. Check your Rule 3.7. It says that a lawyer "shall not" act as an advocate at a trial in which he will be a witness. There are a few exceptions such as where the lawyer is only to testify about minor, uncontested matters or where the lawsuit is about the lawyer's legal services. This doesn't mean that, if you are going to be a witness in a trial, you cannot participate in all of the pre-trial work. Rule 3.7 is just about working on the trial itself. The entire firm may not be vicariously disqualified, however, just the legal professional with the conflict.[6]

> **WHAT DO YOU THINK?**
>
> Attorney and six nonlawyers file an action against Defendants. Attorney files the lawsuit and acts as attorney of record. Defendants bring a motion to disqualify Attorney on the grounds that he will be a witness. Should he be disqualified? What would you want to know in order to rule on this motion. To help you answer this question, see *Raster v. Ameristar Casinos*, 280 S.W.2d 120 (2009).

Friends

You work for a law firm. Your friend needs a lawyer. What could be more logical than you providing your friend with the best legal advice available (your firm) and you bringing a good client (your friend) to your workplace? How happy for everyone! Well, maybe.

If everything goes well, then it will all be fine. But if something does not go well, you may lose your friendship. For one story about friends turning against each other as a result of one friend representing another friend in a legal matter, see *www.lawyersfromhell.net*.

There is no legal precept that says that we cannot represent our friends and relatives. It just may not be a good idea from a human nature standpoint.

Publicity Rights

Another type of interest a legal professional may seek to acquire from a client is an interest in the publicity rights pertaining to the client's case. Take another look at your Rule 1.8. Does it prohibit you from obtaining any media rights? It probably does because of the belief that this sort of financial interest may influence us to extend or complicate the litigation for publicity sake instead of ending the problem quickly, or otherwise acting in the best interests of the client.

WHAT DO YOU THINK?

Your firm's client has been convicted. While in prison, and while no longer a client of your firm, this person corresponds with you. Can you use those letters to write a book about this former client? Take a look at *Bonin v. Calderon*, 59 F.3d 815 (C.A.9, 1995) for a fascinating case.

Gifts

Look in your state's Rule 1.8. Somewhere in there it says that you should not suggest that a "gift" be made to you, nor should you accept a gift from a client. Small tokens of appreciation, such as gifts costing a few dollars during the holiday season, do not violate this Rule, but exercise of your common sense is required. The essence of this regulation is that we should not suggest to the client that we become the executor of the client's estate for a fee, nor should we suggest anything other than a normal fee or salary for legal assistance. Of course, suggesting to the client that we should inherit property under the client's will should be avoided. If a client insists on such a gift, another law firm or disinterested lawyer must draft the will.

Look at your Rule 1.8. It probably says:

Prior to the conclusion of representation of a client, a lawyer shall not make or negotiate an agreement giving the lawyer literary or media rights to a portrayal or account based in substantial part on information relating to the representation.

PROBLEMS IN REPRESENTING MULTIPLE CLIENTS

Rule #2 (of our Top 10 Rules of Ethics) mandates that we keep the confidences of a client. In certain situations, this is almost impossible, so we cannot be involved in the representation. The areas where this comes up are the following:

1. Seller and purchaser
2. Insured and insurer
3. Husband and wife in matrimonial proceedings
4. Debtor and creditor
5. Representing corporations and their officers, directors, and shareholders
6. Multiple defendants in criminal actions

Seller and Purchaser

If a law firm represents both the seller and the purchaser in a transaction, how can the clients be sure that each is getting the best representation possible? It would be almost like negotiating with yourself! However, it is a fundamental principle of legal ethics that a lawyer may represent adverse parties with conflicting interests *where all parties have given their consent after having full disclosure of all the facts.* It's best to look at that requirement in three separate parts: all parties—give their consent—after full disclosure of all of the facts.

For example, if the parties have already worked out the terms of their business deal and simply need someone to document it, with full disclosure of the possible pitfalls and (written) consent, they can have one lawyer draft the documents for both of them. However, it is important to avoid not only obvious conflicts but also the possibility

---

WHAT DO YOU THINK?

One attorney represents both the borrower and the lender in a loan transaction. The lenders are sophisticated businessmen. They actually hired the attorney and gave him a bonus for negotiating a loan with unsophisticated borrowers. The borrowers also retained him and paid his fees but had no knowledge of his relationship with the lenders. What should be the outcome of this case when there is a disagreement between the lenders and the borrowers later? To aid you in your discussion of possible answers, begin with *In re Greenberg*, 121 A.2d 520 (N.J. 1956).

that a conflict will develop later, such as when a document might be subject to different interpretations—which pretty much covers all legal documents.[7]

Under certain circumstances, disclosure and consent will not be enough. For example, some courts have held that the positions of buyer and seller in real estate transactions are inherently in conflict.[8] Therefore, representation by an attorney who represented both the developers and the town concurrently was improper even though the attorney never actually engaged in any transactions between the two interests. This court suggested that, in addition to full knowledge and consent, the client must have time to reflect upon the choice and not be forced into it by the exigencies of the real estate closing. It found that the last-minute waiver obtained from the parties was only a formality and was not meaningful.[9]

In light of these cases, maybe we need to change our rule. It was *where all parties have given their consent after having full disclosure of all the facts.* If we add the words "written" and "meaningful" to the "consent" part, we may have a more complete understanding of what is required.

Insured and Insurer

ABA Formal Opinion 96-403 Obligations of a Lawyer Representing an Insured Who Objects to a Proposed Settlement Within Policy Limits. You can find this online at *http://www.abanet.org/cpr/ ethicopinions.html.*

If you own a car, you probably have experience with this conflict: You have been involved in an auto accident. Your insurance company hires a law firm to give legal assistance to you, the insured, under a liability policy. In this instance, the law firm's client is you (the insured), not the insurance company.[10] It is possible, even probable, that your interests and the interests of the insurance company will conflict. You think the accident was not your fault. You don't want the accident on your driving record, so you want to litigate fault with the other driver. The insurance company doesn't want to incur the expense of litigation. It doesn't care who is at fault or it thinks you are at fault.

WHAT DO YOU THINK?

Your law firm has been hired by an insurance underwriting company to prepare analyses of prospective life insurance purchasers. Your firm also does estate planning. In this situation, it is natural for members of the law firm, even unknowingly or unintentionally, to steer those estate planning customers toward investing in life insurance policies written by the other client, the insurance company. Is that a bad thing? Check out *Florida Bar v. Goodrich*, 212 So.2d 764 (Fla. 1968) to see what the Florida Bar thought about it.

Because of this inherent conflict, the courts have held that one law firm cannot represent both insurer and the injured party, even if there is complete disclosure and consent. Courts have also held that it must be an exceptional situation where the same firm may ethically represent both parties.[11] Certainly, where liability is an issue, the same firm cannot represent the interests of both the driver of the vehicle and the passenger in claims against the driver of the other vehicle.[12]

Husband and Wife

Representing both husband and wife where they have the same interests is not a problem. For example, where the couple are buying a house or business together, their interests are the same and they do not need separate representation. However, in a situation where they have different interests, such as in a divorce, there is an inherent conflict. These conflicts are not always foreseeable, however. When a law firm is representing the husband and wife in a contract dispute with a third person, and the couple decide to divorce while the contract dispute is still going on, a conflict arises unexpectedly. Here the appropriate thing to do is to drop one of the couple (either the husband or the wife) as a client. It is arguable that the law firm still holds the confidential information of the one it no longer represents, and so it should have to disqualify itself from the entire case. However, most courts have found that it is unfair to summarily dismiss an attorney from all representation on the case, particularly if the attorney has already put in a lot of time and effort.

WHAT DO YOU THINK?

Attorney G represents Defendant. Defendant has been accused of taking part in a bank fraud scheme. Attorney G was paid for his legal services in cash by someone who said he was a family member of Defendant. The government inquired into Attorney G's acceptance of the cash, its origins (like, was it some of the stolen money), and what he did with it. The government then made a motion to disqualify Attorney G on the grounds that he was so busy defending himself against the government inquiry that he could not properly represent Defendant. What do you think about the government's tactics. Should Attorney G be disqualified? To help you with your answer, see *United States v. Urutyan*, 564 F.3d 679 (2009)

Some people believe that one lawyer or one law firm can represent both husband and wife in "uncontested divorces." This would help to keep the cost of the divorce down (as each party doesn't have to pay separate fees) and may lead to a more amicable dissolution of the marriage. Although one lawyer cannot represent both parties, in an uncontested divorce one party can hire an attorney who documents the agreement that the husband and wife have worked out between themselves. Then the attorney files the divorce action on one spouse's behalf, and the case is handled as a "default," meaning that the other spouse doesn't file an answer. The spouse who has not hired a lawyer can still communicate directly with the lawyer to work out any problems along the way.

Many law firms, especially firms that handle marital dissolution, post advice on their Web sites. Using your favorite Internet search engine, run a search using these words: "Can one attorney represent both parties in a divorce?" and see what comes up. If you find a state that permits this, let me know!

Debtor and Creditor

Just like seller and purchaser, a debtor and his creditors have an inherent conflict of interest. Even when in good faith, if we represent both debtor and creditor, we represent adverse interests and violate Rule #8. Likewise, we do not want to loan money to a client because that makes us his creditor. If the client is unable to repay the loan, we owe the client our complete loyalty, but must also collect a debt from him.[13]

Representation of Corporations

The general rule is that the corporate legal professional's duty of loyalty is to the corporation, not to officers, directors, or any group of shareholders.

You need to look at your state's Rule 1.13. It discusses the problem of the attorney representing the corporation against directors and officers, at great length:

(a) A lawyer employed or retained by an organization represents the organization acting through its duly authorized constituents.

(b) If a lawyer for an organization knows that an officer, employee or other person . . . is engaged in action, intends to act or refuses to act in a matter related to the representation that is a violation of a legal obligation to the organization, or a violation of law that reasonably might be imputed to the organization, and is likely to result in substantial injury to the organization, the lawyer shall proceed as is reasonably necessary in the best interest of the organization.

(c) In dealing with an organization's directors, officers, employees, members, shareholders or other constituents, a lawyer shall explain the identity of the client when it is apparent that the organization's interests are adverse to those of the constituents with whom the lawyer is dealing.

(d) A lawyer ... may also represent any of its directors, officers, employees, members, shareholders or other constituents ... [subject to the provisions of Rule 1.7 and] consent shall be given by an appropriate official of the organization other than the individual who is to be represented, or by the shareholders.

The cases in this area have conflicting rulings. In one instance, an attorney who had represented all the family members of a family-owned business was disqualified from representing one group of family members in an action against another.[14] This makes sense because the attorney knew everyone's secrets. In another case, two attorneys who were members of the same firm represented a family-owned corporation at the time the corporation entered into an agreement hiring a founding shareholder as president of the corporation. They had also acted as counsel for that shareholder during his years as president. The court held that it was improper for them to represent both sides in a conflict between the corporation and the former president after the president lost control of the corporation, because of the confidential information they held about him.[15]

On the other hand, where the attorneys in question said they had no confidential information that could be used by them or their client-corporation against the former president, the court held that representing the corporation against the former president was not in conflict.[16]

How do we explain these opposite decisions? The factors considered are the length of time of the representation, the amount of money involved, and declarations by the attorneys regarding the amount of confidential information they have or don't have. The court also takes into consideration the amount of money it would cost the client if he has to hire a new attorney.

Just like most of this area, there are no cases dealing directly with paralegals. The best we can do to make judgment calls for the paralegal profession is to hold the profession to the identical standards as attorneys. Erring on the side of caution, we are sure to take the ethical path. You have the same duties of confidentiality and loyalty. That means you bring the same conflicts of interest with you.

Joint Representation of Criminal Defendants

It seems obvious that you cannot work for one side of a criminal case and then for the other side because of the possibility of disclosing confidential information. Similarly, a legal professional who is part of the defense of a criminal defendant may have information that could be damaging to a codefendant. For this reason, dual representation of defendants may be unethical if there is a possibility of breach of confidentiality.

Rule 44(c) of the Federal Rules of Criminal Procedure provides that when two or more defendants who are jointly charged and are represented by the same retained or assigned counsel, the court shall investigate the representation and advise the defendants of their right to separate counsel.

WHAT DO YOU THINK?

Attorney is hired to represent Defendant 1, accused of robbery. Defendant 2 (also allegedly involved in the robbery) asks Attorney to represent him, as well. Attorney sends his paralegal to interview Defendant 2's wife to discuss the possible representation of Defendant 2. Attorney decides not to represent Defendant 2. When Defendant 2 brings a motion to disqualify Attorney on the basis of a conflict of interest created by Paralegal's interview with Defendant 2's wife, how should the court rule? See, for example, *State ex rel. Youngblood v. Sanders*, 212 W.Va. 885, 575 S.E.2d 864, 869–871 (2002). What other information would you need to rule on this motion?

WHAT OTHERS MAY WANT

Rule #3 contains a discussion about the reasons for prohibiting lawyers and nonlawyers from being in business together, because only lawyers should make legal decisions. Where there is a possibility that someone with a financial interest in the success of a law firm (someone who is not a legal professional) has influence over decisions made about clients and cases, there is a possibility that the client, the public, will be harmed. So we say that the Rule is this: The desires of third persons should not enter into legal decisions.

Champerty

Champerty, as you recall from Rule #5, is the purchasing of a claim. Think about working on the representation of a client. That client was injured, let's say, by a malicious person. You feel righteous indignation and a fierce loyalty to your client. This loyalty enhances your excitement about the case and about seeking justice for your client. Now think about the case again, only this time your client is not the injured person but, instead, a company that purchases claims from people for the purpose of litigating them for profit. How do you feel about the case now?

If this sort of business deal were permitted, do you see how it would stir up more litigation? Moreover, it would stir up litigation that proceeds without that loyalty we have for our clients. Champerty would change our perspective to a simple financial interest and someone other than the injured party would have "say" over the case and would be involved in making decisions about the case with the lawyer.

Look in your state's Rule 1.8. Does it say something like this:

> A lawyer shall not accept compensation for representing a client from one other than the client unless:
>
> (1) the client consents after consultation; (2) there is no interference with the lawyer's independence of professional judgment or with the lawyer–client relationship; and (3) information relating to representation of a client is protected as required by [the duty of confidentiality].

Speaking of a financial interest, isn't a contingency fee agreement something like buying a claim? In a typical personal injury case, the lawyer advances all of the litigation expenses for the client and then gets part of the winnings of the case. Isn't paying the litigation expenses "paying" for the case? Your state law provides for these agreements so that they are not improper. Check in your state's Rules of Professional Conduct in Rule 1.8. Notice that this rule is entitled "Conflicts of Interest" and "Prohibited Transactions." Somewhere in there, your law says something like this:

> (a) A lawyer shall not provide financial assistance to a client in connection with pending or contemplated litigation, except that:
>> (1) a lawyer may advance court costs and expenses of litigation, the repayment of which may be contingent on the outcome of the matter; and
>> (2) a lawyer representing an indigent client may pay court costs and expenses of litigation on behalf of the client.

From the New Jersey Rules of Professional Conduct

In many states, in addition to personal injury cases, the same is true in class action suits where it is typical for the lawyers to advance litigation expenses.[17]

As we know, attorneys cannot escape liability for an improper act by having their employees do something that attorneys themselves may not do, so a paralegal may not give money to a client or a prospective client, no matter how great the person's need might be unless your state allows the exception that applies to your situation.

Pro Bono Organizations

Organizations like the NAACP often hire lawyers to represent indigent people. Even though it is the organization that is paying the lawyer, the lawyer's duty is to the actual client. We see this in the example of insurance companies and insureds, too. If the insurance company must pay attorney's fees for the insured, that attorney's loyalty is to the insured, not the folks paying the bills. The U.S. Supreme Court has held that the Constitution allows for an exception to the Rule against allowing the desires of third parties to influence the lawyers' decisions in order to protect the exercise of constitutional rights. As the indigent people had no other access to justice except with the help of the NAACP, protecting their constitutional rights was a more important interest than strict adherence to this Rule.

RULE #2, THE DUTY TO PRESERVE CONFIDENCES, CREATES CONFLICTS OF INTEREST

Our obligation to preserve client confidences continues after the termination of employment. As we learned in Rule #2, our duty of confidentiality continues with us to the grave. This means that we cannot represent anyone adverse to our former client at any time in the future, even after we change jobs, even after the client dies. It means that it is improper to use the client's confidential information against the client. Look in your Rules of Professional Conduct in Rule 1.8. It probably says something like this:

> A lawyer shall not use information relating to representation of a client to the disadvantage of the client unless the client gives informed consent, ...

And, in 1.9 look for this provision:

> (a) A lawyer who has formerly represented a client in a matter shall not thereafter represent a other person in the same or a substantially related matter in which that person's interests are materially adverse to the interests of the former client unless the former client gives informed consent, confirmed in writing.

From the New York Rules of Professional Conduct

Here's how it comes up: A man was employed by defendant's counsel as a law clerk and later as an associate for three years, but he did not work on defendant's case. He later became a partner in the firm that represented the plaintiff. Think about it: Isn't it possible that he has taken all of the defendant's confidential information with him? Couldn't he use that information to hurt his former client? His former law firm filed a motion to disqualify him from the case on the basis of conflict of interest. The court denied the motion. The issue made it into the reported cases because his earlier employer appealed. The appellate court affirmed and discussed the problems of young associates who are employed by large law firms. It acknowledged that it is common practice for young people to change jobs, and that in the course of employment they have access to confidential information of the firm's clients. The court determined it "absurd," however, to assume that every associate of a large firm would have access to every client file and all confidential information. The court held that if the prior representation was "substantially related" to the present representation, the attorney should be disqualified. A "peripheral" prior representation, on the other hand, would not be a sufficient basis for disqualification.[18]

Where's the line between "substantial" and "peripheral"? Whether there is an actual conflict of interest that adversely affects the attorney's performance is a mixed question of law and fact,[19] so an evidentiary hearing is usually held. In most jurisdictions, the court will not require that the two representations be identical, nor that there is proof that the legal professional actually received confidential information.[20]

A good case for you to read on this issue is *In re Complex Asbestos Litigation* 232 Cal.App.3d 572, 283 Cal.Rptr. 732 (1991), where a paralegal moved from a large firm representing asbestos class action defendants to a small firm that represented class action plaintiffs. As part of his defense for making the move, the paralegal claimed that he had permission from the senior litigation partner at his old job, but as the permission was not in writing, he could not prove it. The court gives us a thorough analysis of the situation, so this case is well worth reading. You will find it on the publisher's Web site.

Presumption of Conflict of Interest

A conflict of interest may be presumed.[21] Once a substantial relationship has been established, the new representation in and of itself violates the attorney's ethical duty to former clients.

Some cases say that knowledge of an organization's internal workings will be enough for a *presumption* of conflict of interest.[22] For example, if you have access to the intimate knowledge of the company's business methods, you will never be permitted to be involved in any legal action against that company. Your prior association does not have to be continuous or lengthy. Even a brief consultation is enough.[23] This is why it is important for you to not only keep track of the names of the clients, you need to keep track of what you did for them. For example, if you did a small research project on the case and you weren't told about

What is a presumption? In everyday language, it is something that we reason is true. However, in law we use it to mean rather the opposite. A presumption is a conclusion derived from a particular set of facts based on law, rather than on probable reasoning.

the case, you don't have much confidential information. If you summarized a few depositions, you still might not have much confidential information. But if you had occasion to root around in the client's files and become intimately acquainted with his financial affairs, for example, then you do have confidential information. Knowing what work you did for each client will save you (and your new firm) from an unnecessary disqualification.

WHAT DO YOU THINK?

Paralegal D was offered a new job in a new city for a salary of $200,000 a year at Law Firm HH&R. She gave notice to her current employer (H&K) and got ready to move. She received a call from HH&R withdrawing their offer of employment. They had received a threat from H&K that it would seek to disqualify H&K from a very large case based on the fact that Paralegal D had worked on the case. D reported that she did some research to find online vendors to help with the case some years ago but had no confidential information regarding the case. Nevertheless, the offer of employment was gone. What can she do?

If you don't believe this is a true story, search "Dillman" and "Holland & Knight" on the Internet.

Who Is Disqualified?

If confidential information has been given to an attorney, the attorney's entire firm will be disqualified on the presumption that every legal professional in the office had access to the confidential information.[24] This rule applies to every nonlawyer employee, as well, as we learned from *In re Asbestos.* Does this make any sense to you? Rule #2 says we must keep client information confidential—forever. So then, why would a court assume that everyone in the firm knows all of the confidential information of everyone in the firm? As illogical as this may sound, there are many cases supporting the "everyone is tainted" theory. On the other hand, exceptions are made where the law firms are very large and the employee had no actual contact with the adverse case. To hold otherwise would effectively keep many people from ever changing jobs. And, as we know, our society is increasingly mobile. Where people used to keep a job for a lifetime, statistics show that Americans on average keep their jobs for four to six years. Assume you will change jobs and plan accordingly. Keep track of who you do work for at each firm that employs you and what you did on each case. When you accept a new job, get all of your known potential conflicts taken care of. (We'll talk about how to do that in the following section.)

Preventing Disqualification

Before 1974, lawyers were prohibited from accepting a client if any one attorney in the law firm was required to decline the employment on conflict bases. The problem with this Rule was most difficult for those attorneys who had worked for the district attorney's office. These people had worked on the prosecution of thousands of cases, effectively eliminating the possibility of ever finding a private criminal defense firm that could hire them without a conflict problem. As a result, it became almost impossible for government agencies to recruit bright young lawyers. In response to this problem, the ABA Ethics Committee issued Formal Opinion No. 342, opining that the prohibition should not apply to the firm of a disqualified lawyer who has been screened from participation in the work and has received no compensation stemming from the conflicting case

Ethical Wall Theory

A few years later, a court ruled against the moving party in a disqualification motion, finding that the attorney with the conflict had been effectively isolated from his firm's handling of the case and that, in fact, the firm had erected a "wall" around him.[25] Approving what used to be called the "Chinese Wall" theory, the court discussed the inherent unfairness of turning one attorney who had worked for a governmental agency (in this case, the FHA) into a "Typhoid Mary." The purpose of the wall was to cut off communication from the "tainted" legal professional to the rest of the firm. This would allow the firm to continue the representation and make everyone more comfortable that no occasion would arise for the tainted lawyer to even accidentally give away confidential information.

The name "Chinese Wall" was taken from an analogy to the Great Wall of China, a man-made wall that was built to protect China from invading Mongols. This expression fell into disfavor when it was misunderstood to imply prejudice against the Chinese people. You may see "ethical wall" instead in recent cases.

Ethical walls have not been accepted by all states in all circumstances. Courts in Alabama, Arizona, California, Florida, Kansas, Nebraska, New York, and Texas have expressly disallowed the use of ethical walls at some time or another;[26] in other states, it is reserved for former government employees. If you are considering changing jobs, you should research your state's law on ethical walls. A good place to start is "ethical wall" + "conflict of interest" + [yourself] in your favorite search engine.

For information on how to build a successful wall, see the "How to" section on the publisher's Web site. To be of any use at all, the wall should be erected as soon as the conflict employee joins the firm. If there is any delay, it may be presumed that the conflict employee has divulged all of the former client's secrets, and the firm will probably be disqualified.

Waiver of Conflict by Client

As discussed above, these Rules exist to protect the former client, so the former client ought to have the right to sign a document that "waives" the conflict. Oddly enough, courts have held otherwise, arguing that because the protection exists for the client, and the attorney holds a fiduciary position with the client, the waiver can never be made effectively.[27] Other courts have held that when written consent is given by all of the parties after full disclosure, the conflicting representation will be permitted.[28]

Check your state's Rules of Professional Conduct as discussed previously to see if this waiver provision exists. Then check your state's case law to see if the courts have carved out any exceptions. In today's society, and depending upon the complexity of the case and the sophistication of the client, a written waiver is still a very good alternative to the ethical wall. Remember that the waiver must be obtained from the former client whose confidences and secrets you hold. The waiver is your further written promise not to disclose those confidences and secrets or to ever use them to the client's detriment, and the client's written acknowledgment of his trust in your promise. Remember, also, as the *In re Asbestos* case illustrates, the waiver must be in writing and signed by a person with the right to do so: either the former client or the former client's legal representative.

Appropriate Action and Possible Penalties

In determining whether a conflict of interest exists between two clients, any doubts should be resolved by giving the client all of the facts, explaining the concerns, and allowing the client an opportunity either to consent to continued representation or to seek new counsel.[29]

After determining that there may be a conflict of interest, ordinarily there are two choices at hand:

1. Inform all of the parties of the presence of a potential conflict; bring the potential problem to the attention of the attorney in charge. If possible, get an informed, meaningful, express written waiver from the other side.
2. Withdraw from employment, or decline the employment. The conflict-employee should still make complete disclosure to prevent a possible future problem. Hiding a conflict is never a good idea.

Once the firm has been tainted by the employment of a legal professional with a conflict of interest, firing that individual will not help the law firm. Just as it will be presumed that legal professionals obtained client confidences during their prior employment, it will be presumed that those confidences were disclosed to others during their new employment. This is why many firms exchange a "client list" with employees directly after having made them an employment offer and they have accepted. If, after examining one another's client list, either the firm or the new hire determines that there may be a conflict problem, the offer or acceptance may be withdrawn. So, this is you. You've found a new job that suits you better than your current job. They like you, too, and they offer you a job. You know if this New Firm is on the opposite side of anything you're doing now or have done in the past. You do not necessarily know about cases between New Firm and Current Firm that you have not directly worked on, but New Firm must know. They know where you work, so, presumably, they ran a conflict check on your current employer to find all of the cases that might cause a conflict. They have your resume, as well, so (assuming your resume is complete) they should know about any conflicts that might arise from all of your former jobs. But no one's conflict check is perfect, so when you get to New Firm on your first day, they might ask you to take a look at the entire client list to sniff out any possible conflicts that they didn't find. If you have left a former employer off of your resume, you may have a hidden conflict. At this point, your job is to alert your supervisor about this conflict. Of course, you don't want to do that because you don't want to have to explain why you left that employer off of your resume. So, you hunker down and hope that the conflict never comes to light. But, if you do that, you will violate this Rule #8. You owe loyalty to each and every client, all of the time and forever. You probably won't divulge any confidences, but that may not matter. The most likely outcome of this scenario is that someone at that old former employer law firm finds out where you are, recognizes the conflict, and voila! Your new employer is now the subject of a disqualification motion.

Law firms that are, either intentionally or inadvertently, involved in a conflict problem may be disqualified by the court, subject to disciplinary proceedings,[30] or lose their fee.[31] The court may reverse an earlier decision[32] or issue an injunction enjoining the communication and use of confidential information.[33] The firm may also be subject to a legal malpractice suit either by the client who was damaged or by the disciplinary authority of the state.[34] Paralegals and other nonlawyers, of course, will not be subject to all of these disciplinary actions. Their employers, however, may be subject to them by means of the *respondeat superior* theory if their employee-paralegal has the conflict of interest. Timely recognition of conflicts and complete disclosure are crucial in this area.

This would be a good time to check out "How to Create a Conflict Check System" on the publisher's Web site.

RULE #8 WRAP-UP

Whew! This is a long Rule with lots of parts! The thrust of the Rule is complete, and undivided loyalty is a duty that each of us owes to each and every client. Because we owe the duty of loyalty, we have to keep things that conflict with that loyalty out of our way. Loyalty issues arise due to our outside interests such as our desire to benefit ourselves at the expense of the client. They arise when we are involved in the representation of multiple clients who have inherent conflicts of interest. They arise when someone other than the client is paying the legal fees. And they arise because we hold confidential information. Sometimes we can just avoid these conflicts by choosing clients carefully and avoiding conflicting interests. If we cannot avoid the conflict, we need to do these things:

1. Make "good faith full disclosure" of all of the facts.
2. Explain the potential conflict problems.
3. Advise the client to get legal advice from someone else.
4. Give the client time to reflect.
5. Then, get the written consent of all parties.

RULE #8 REVIEW QUESTIONS

1. What is "independent judgment"? How might your judgment be compromised?
2. What is your duty of loyalty? How do we demonstrate complete loyalty to the client?
3. Your duty of loyalty is divided into four parts. What are they?
4. What are some "outside interests" you have that could potentially compromise your independent judgment?
5. Name four instances where representation of multiple clients can lead to a division of loyalty.
6. If someone other than "the client" is paying the legal fees, to whom is your duty of loyalty owed. Why is that?
7. If you have the confidential information of Client A and now are chosen for an assignment that is contrary to A's interests, what can you do? List your options in order of the steps you might take.
8. If you have an irreconcilable conflict of interest regarding A, what might happen to your representation?
9. If a partner in your firm has an irreconcilable conflict of interest regarding A, are the consequences going to be different?
10. If it turns out that the partner must be disqualified, who else will likely be disqualified? Why?

[1] *Miller v. Sears,* 636 P.2d 1183 (Alaska 1991).
[2] *Eschwig v. State Bar,* 459 P.2d 904 (Cal. 1969).
[3] *State v. Hartman,* 1194 N.W.2d 653 (Wisc. 1972).
[4] *People ex rel. Kent v. Denious,* 196 P.2d 257 (Colo. 1948).
[5] *In re May,* 538 P.2d 787 (Idaho 1975).
[6] *F.D.I.C. v. U.S. Fire Ins. Co.,* 50 F.3d 1304 (C.A.5 (Tex.), 1995).
[7] *In Re Camp,* 194 A.2d 236 (N.J. 1963).
[8] *In Matter of Dolan,* 384 A.2d 1076 (N.J. 1978).

[9] *In re A and B* appears to be in conflict with *Matter of Dolan.* The *Dolan* court distinguished the cases on their facts, however, by pointing out that it would demand strict adherence to the rule it set forth in *In re A and B.* "A municipal attorney's public obligations are such that he must take particular pains to avoid the shadow of suspicion that inevitably is cast when he begins to entangle himself in a representative capacity in the legal affairs of a developer operating within the municipality" (p. 1079).

[10] *Gibbs v. Lappies,* 828 F.Supp. 6 (D.N.H. 1993).

[11] *Kelly v. Greason,* 244 N.E.2d 456 (N.Y. 1968).

[12] *In re Shaw,* 443 A.2d 670 (N.Y. 1982).

[13] *Matter of Levinsohn,* 367 A.2d 431 (N.J. 1976).

[14] *Brennan's Inc. v. Brennan's Restaurants, Inc.,* 590 F.2d 168 (5th Cir. 1979).

[15] *In re Banks and Thompson,* 584 P.2d 284 (Or. 1978).

[16] *Universal Athletic Sales Co. v. American Gym, Recreational and Athletic Equipment Corp.,* 357 F.Supp. 905 (W.D.Pa. 1973).

[17] *Brame v. Ray Bilis Finance Corp.,* 85 F.R.D. 568 (N.D.N.Y. 1979).

[18] *Silver Chrysler Plymouth v. Chrysler Motor Corp.,* 518 F.2d 751 (2nd Cir. 1975).

[19] *Quince v. State,* 732 So. 2d 1059, 1064 (Fla. 1999).

[20] *Trone v. Smith,* 621 F.2d 994 (9th Cir. 1980); *Burger v. Zant,* 718 F.2d 979 (C.A.11 (Ga.), 1983).

[21] *Cannon v. U.S. Acoustics Corp.,* 398 F.Supp. 209 (N.D.Ill. 1975).

[22] *Brown v. Miller,* 286 F. 994 (D.C. Cir. 1923).

[23] *In re Car Rental Antitrust Litigation,* 470 F.Supp. 495 (N.D.Cal. 1979).

[24] *In re Corrugated Container Antitrust Litigation,* 659 F.2d 1341 (5th Cir. 1981).

[25] *In Kesselhaut v. United States,* 555 F.2d 791 (Ct.Cl. 1977).

[26] See:http://www.hofstra.edu/Academics/Law/law_lawrev_hamilton.cfm.

[27] *In re Boone,* 83 F. 944 (N.D.Cal. 1897).

[28] *Kagel v. First Commonwealth Co., Inc.,* 534 F.2d 194 (9th Cir. 1976).

[29] *Gesellschaft Fur Dratlose Telgraphie MBH v. Brown,* 78 F.2d 410 (D.C. Cir.), *cert. denied,* 296 U.S. 618, 56 S. Ct. 139 (1935).

[30] *Matter of Haft,* 146 N.J. 489 (1996).

[31] *Sweeney v. Athens Reg'l Med. Ctr.,* 917 F.2d 1560, 1573–1574 (11th Cir. 1990).

[32] *U.S. v. Bishop,* 90 F.2d 65 (6th Cir. 1937).

[33] *U.S. v. Mahoney,* 27 F.Supp. 463 (N.D. Cal. 1939).

[34] *Lysick v. Walcom,* 258 Cal.App.2d 136, 65 Cal.Rptr. 406 (1968).

Work to Improve
the Legal System

The legal system, like all other systems, is not perfect. It could be made better. Each legal professional has a duty to assist in improving the legal system. Many lawyers are of the opinion that paralegals can't do much to improve the legal system, but there are others who disagree. This chapter will point out some places where you, as a paralegal, can get involved and make the system better for the paralegal profession as well as the public at large.

The late Professor Roscoe Barrow not only taught the law to his students but gave them a value system as well. He taught that the true ethics in the legal profession were not written by the legislature or the bar associations, "but were founded on the notion that the weak and unprotected people are worthy of as much effort as the powerful." The "Barrow approach" to the law was made tearfully clear to all who ever attended Professor Barrow's annual "Peevyhouse lecture."

Peevyhouse v. Garland Coal and Mining Company[1] is a case involving a dispute as to the proper measure of damages where there has been a failure to complete a contract: diminution-in-value or cost-to-complete. The picture drawn in the case is that of simple landowners who had been outmaneuvered by the oil company's corporate attorneys. The landowners (Mr. and Mrs. Peevyhouse—so we have to imagine this elderly couple on the porch of their small home in the middle of acres of beautiful open space) are convinced by the mining company lawyers that the mining company has big machines that will "roll back" the top layer of the land. Then the big mining machines will extract the coal from under the land. Then the top layer of the land will simply be rolled back into place, and all will be just as it was before. As the story goes, the Peevyhouse couple agree to the contract. The mining company comes in, rolls back the land, takes the ore from the earth, and then goes away. Wait a minute! You said you would put the land back the way it was! Too much trouble, the crafty lawyers now protest. The Peevyhouses take their case to court, but the court agrees with the evil lawyers: The value of the land is so small and the cost of replacing the land is so great that the cost to fix the land overwhelms the value of the land as it originally was—so, no, the mining company doesn't have to honor its word. The word of the lawyers meant nothing. The injustice of the court's ruling is clear after even a cursory reading of the case.

Annually, professors and students from all over the San Francisco Bay Area would attend Professor Barrow's lecture, many of them year after year. At the close of the lecture, Professor Barrow would inevitably single out a student sitting in the front row of the lecture hall. Barrow would point a menacing finger at him and say, "Someday you, yes, you like Michelangelo, will take hammer and chisel in hand and go to that rough marble and carve a law which will accommodate our need for fossil fuel-energy and the eternal need of mankind for the land. Yes, through your creativity, to some future class, I will be able to say that the law is for Peevyhouses."[2] It was an admonition not soon to be forgotten. We can learn from Professor Barrow's lecture that lawyers are evil, that they don't keep their word, or we can learn that the law itself is often unjust. You get to choose.

ASSIST IN CHANGING THE LAW

Changes in human affairs over time will necessitate changes in the law. Check your state's Rules of Professional Conduct 6.3 and 6.4. They encourage the legal professional to be active in law reform and legal services organizations that are part of our changing world. The participation of legal professionals will work for the better of the legal system. An example of this can be found in the history of *Molien v. Kaiser Foundation Hospitals.*[3] In the mid-1970s, Valerie Molien went to Kaiser Hospital for a routine physical examination. The examining physician diagnosed Valerie as having infectious syphilis and advised her to tell her family members about it because they might be infected as well. Valerie's husband underwent the testing, as did other members of her family, and when none of them was determined to have syphilis, family members began to fight. Husband and wife became suspicious of one another and finally divorced. All of the family members suffered severe emotional distress, but Valerie's husband, Steve, was the most severely affected. Eventually it was discovered that the doctor's original diagnosis had been in error. Valerie had never had syphilis.

At that time, California had no cause of action for "negligent infliction of emotional distress." *Dillon v. Legg*[4] was the nearest precedent, a case in which a mother alleged severe emotional distress after having witnessed a car run over her child. In *Dillon*, however, the California Supreme Court relied heavily on the fact that the mother witnessed the accident and suffered actual physical harm. It was questionable whether the California court would stretch the *Dillon* rule to allow Steve some compensation against Kaiser because he had not actually "witnessed" harm to Valerie.

The trial court in *Molien* sustained demurrers to the causes of action, stating that negligent infliction of emotional distress is not actionable in California where the plaintiff had not actually witnessed

To sustain a demurrer has the effect of throwing the case out of court.

the harm to the loved one. On review, however, the California Supreme Court held that modern times demanded that a cause of action may be stated for the negligent infliction of emotional distress and further held that the unqualified requirement of physical harm is no longer justified. The attorney for plaintiff Molien had carved new law in California and championed a good cause for his client. The law should and does change.

Rules of law should be changed if they are not just, understandable, and responsive to the needs of society. Legal professionals should encourage the repeal of outdated laws and work for the simplification of laws and legal documentation. Several years ago, California had an Unfair Competition Law, Business and Professions Code Sec. 17200, which allowed private attorneys to act on behalf of the public to sue businesses that engage in price-fixing, false advertising, or other unfair business practices. One firm abused this law to sue thousands of people, seeking millions of dollars in settlements, even though the firm had no real client or plaintiff who had been harmed. California learned that the law had been badly drafted and needed to be changed. This is a good example of a time and a place where paralegals could use their special expertise to help make the law more fair.

Your state's Rule 6.4 requires that when attorneys are advocating for changes, they must identify for whom they are working: themselves, a client, or the public at large. We can work for changes in the law that will benefit a client, even when we do not believe in the changes themselves. When acting on behalf of the public, we want to be sure that the changes are truly in the public interest.

If you want to know more about this, go to Google or Yahoo and type in "Trevor Law Group."

Simplify, Simplify

One of the most modern changes in the laws has been the "plain language laws." These laws require that certain contracts and other legal documents must be in language that can be read and understood by the layperson without the aid of an attorney-translator. David Mellinkoff, author of books and articles in the area of legal writing, writes, "These laws are not, in my view, a solution, but an index of frustration. As a prod to the profession, they may do some good."[5]

Mellinkoff, in his book *Legal Writing: Sense & Nonsense*,[6] sets forth his seven rules for legal writing that will be comprehensible for the attorney, the court, and the client: Don't use peculiar language (legalese) when laypersons' language is more clear; use precise language when it's more clear; use the rules of English composition and grammar; write clearly whenever possible; write in simple language; plan before you write; and review whatever you've written and take out the unnecessary words. These rules may seem oversimplified and are certainly redundant. They make the point, however, that legal writing need not appear to the layperson to be arcane. Lawyers kept others at bay for many centuries by speaking a language no one else could speak. Not only did a person have to attend a special school to learn the language, but that person had to earn a certificate in order to speak it in public. Recently this prohibition, while not lifted, has been diluted. Many people are learning to speak legalese; the legislature is prohibiting its use in areas where those not versed in it would be disadvantaged.

Federal Rules of Civil Procedure, Rule 8 requires that a pleading contain "a short and plain statement of the grounds for the court's jurisdiction" and "a short and plain statement of the claim showing that the pleader is entitled to relief."[7] However, a court may dismiss a complaint for failure to comply with Rule 8(a) only if the plaintiff can prove no facts that would entitle him to relief.[8] The average person who files documents with a court is held to the same standards as a lawyer in many areas, but pleadings will be read "liberally" so that the meaning and intent can be found.

To write clearly and comprehensibly, arrange your topic points carefully, use the appropriate tone, stay away from sarcasm and pretentiousness, avoid long quotations, and use precedent in your own language rather than in the convoluted prose that the court may have used.

Public Pro Bono Work

It is estimated that over 80% of the need for civil legal assistance is unmet. With this in mind, the ABA, the state bar associations, and the paralegal associations have developed measures to encourage each legal professional to donate a certain amount of time to indigent clients and render legal assistance for little or no fee.

NFPA Model Code EC 1-4(b) states:

> A paralegal shall support bona fide efforts to meet the need for legal services by those unable to pay reasonable or customary fees; for example, participation in pro bono projects and volunteer work.

Check out your state's Rule 6.1. It says something like this:

> Lawyers are strongly encouraged to provide pro bono legal services to benefit poor persons.
>
> (a) Every lawyer should aspire to:
> (1) provide at least 20 hours of pro bono legal services each year to poor persons; and
> (2) contribute financially to organizations that provide legal services to poor persons.
>
> From New York's Rules of Professional Conduct

Notice that there are two ways to fulfill this request: Donate your time or money.

The professional responsibility to provide pro bono legal services as established under this rule is aspirational rather than mandatory in nature. The failure to fulfill one's professional responsibility under this rule will not subject a lawyer to discipline. The professional responsibility to provide pro bono legal service to the poor may be discharged by:

(1) annually providing at least 20 hours of pro bono legal service to the poor; or

(2) making an annual contribution of at least $350 to a legal aid organization.

From Florida's Rules of Professional Conduct

In California, Rule 2-102 ("Legal Service Programs") simply says that the participation in pro bono and public service programs is "encouraged." Section 6210 of the California Business and Professions Code states, however, that the legislature of that state has determined a need for free legal services for indigent persons, especially underserved client groups such as the elderly, the disabled, juveniles, and non-English-speaking persons, and spells out that the state bar is to collect funds for the purpose of funding such programs. In short, the California legislature has taken an active part in increasing public service legal assistance for the needy.

Many law firms have or are developing pro bono branches. Many other law firms require their partners, associates, and paralegals to do a certain minimum number of pro bono hours per year. The growing need for pro bono representation will be an area of great importance to non-lawyer legal professionals in the future because of the comparatively low cost of their use in providing legal assistance to those who may not be able to afford an attorney.

Making pro bono work mandatory looks very much like a violation of the Thirteenth Amendment (prohibiting slavery). However, as everyone is entitled to representation in criminal matters and the public defender's office is subject to conflicts of interest, sometimes courts must appoint lawyers to cases for which they will not get paid very much. In a recent example from Florida, a trial judge tried to appoint one lawyer after another to what would be the defense of an involved RICO (racketeering) case. The first two lawyers appointed both declined the representation. By the third lawyer, in frustration, the court refused to allow him to decline. On appeal, the court agreed that where the appointment will be long and involved and therefore have a severe adverse impact on the lawyer and the lawyer's current clients, the lawyer should be able to motion the court for relief from the appointment.[9] The court remarked that the practice of law is no longer the way Atticus Finch practiced law.[10] You can practically hear the Appellate Court sigh audibly.

As you will learn in Rule #10, pro bono organizations such as Public Counsel (in Los Angeles) are funded, in part, by the interest generated by attorney/client trust accounts. They are also funded, as indicated by Florida's Rule 6.1, by contributions made by individuals and law firms. Public Counsel is the largest provider of free legal services in the universe. The 40 (more or less) attorneys and staff members who work there along with the hundreds of volunteer lawyers, law students, and

---

Law Firm Spotlight

Public Counsel's 2009 Law Firm Pro Bono Award was presented to the law firm of Paul, Hastings, Janofsky & Walker LLP. With great dedication and enthusiasm, their attorneys have represented vulnerable children and youth, homeless families, refugees fleeing torture and death threats, veterans, and nonprofit organizations serving indigent and low-income communities.

---

paralegals from all over Los Angeles County assisted 27,000 low-income men, women, children, and organizations in 2008. The estimated value of their free legal services for that year is $83 million.

Now would be a good time for you to look around for the pro bono organization in your town or city. Look on their Web site; give them a call. Find out what you need to do to help them. Even if you can't donate any of your time now, at least you'll know where to go when you do have time to do it. If you are looking for your first job as a paralegal, and if you're finding it difficult to get your foot in the door, there is free training available to you (in exchange for your donated hours) in a free legal clinic near you.

The Unpopular Client

The question of the unpopular client is one that is the topic of heated discussion in ethics classes. Your state's Rule 6.2 admonishes the lawyer not to "seek to avoid appointment" of representations. If your state adopted the "Comments" along with the Rules, you can see in Rule 6.2's comment that a lawyer is not obligated to accept a client whose character or cause is repugnant; however, the freedom to select clients is tempered by each lawyer's duty to take pro bono cases. The lawyer's obligation to do pro bono work is fulfilled by accepting "a fair share" of "unpopular" matters or clients. By taking on these disfavored clients and causes, the attorney serves the administration of justice.

The questions "Must the female attorney defend the rapist simply because he wants to hire her?" and "Must attorneys take a client whose cause is overly repugnant to them?" are difficult questions to answer questions for lively debate. The ABA's Joint Conference on Professional Responsibility encourages representation of clients with unpopular causes, saying, "One of

---

Law Firm Spotlight

Carlton Fields is a longtime contributor to the pro bono environment of Florida. It has a mandatory pro bono requirement for partners, associates, and paralegals. Take a look at its policy at *http://www. carltonfields.com under "About Us."*

---

the highest services the lawyer can render to society is to appear in court on behalf of clients whose causes are in disfavor with the general public."[11] On the other hand, attorneys must not accept representation of such a person, however, if their distaste for the client or cause is so great that they are unable to render adequate representation. The cases we don't like are the cases that get pushed to the bottom of our To Do list. These cases become neglected cases, and neglected cases lead to malpractice.

All of us should consider how our personal feelings about a client or a cause will affect the quality of our work. Each and every client is entitled to the very best work product and consideration regardless of our personal likes or dislikes. The duties of competency and integrity don't change for different types of cases or clients. If you are interested in researching your state law on this issue, your search terms are "repugnant" along with "Rule 6.2" and [yourstate].

WHAT DO YOU THINK?

If you are assigned to work on a case that repulses you, what are some of your options? How would you approach this with the people you work for and with?

Report Misconduct

We began our discussion with Rule #1 on integrity. This Rule works to improve the legal system by ferreting out those who are not fit or who would harm the public.

Improper Use of the Law

The practice of law is not a vehicle for carrying out personal vendettas. When a paralegal uses his or her knowledge of the law for self-interest and vilification, the paralegal ceases to be a diligent advocate and becomes an impediment to the practice of law. Witness this recent case:

In *Sahyers v. Prugh, Holliday & Karatinos*, 560 F.3d 1241 (11th Cir. 2009), a paralegal sued her former employer for back wages in the form of overtime pay. She instructed her lawyer to not tell the defendants about her claim so they could make no prefiling offer of settlement. After the claim was settled, Sahyers and her lawyer were denied their claim for attorney's fees under the Fair Labor Standards statute. The lower court ruled and the circuit court affirmed that Sahyers and her lawyer exhibited a "lack of collegiality" and "wasted judicial time and resources on unnecessary litigation" by not giving the defendants advance notice of the suit.

The integrated state bar disciplines attorneys, as we know. In some states, it is the court system that disciplines. Discipline is not always meted out in a fair or even manner. In one case about using the law for personal improper purposes, the offending attorney didn't want to pay a personal bill. When a lawsuit was filed against him, he filed repetitive motions and a malicious abuse of process action in response. The discipline: He was suspended from practice for three years. The court said: "Respondent simply avoided paying a just bill, once again using his legal skills to retaliate, harass and damage the plaintiffs. His conduct is beyond a mere violation of the Code; it is willful refusal to admit even the slightest error."[12] Is it fair to discipline this lawyer for using his legal knowledge to his own advantage? And what about a paralegal? If you did the same thing that the lawyer did, what would happen to you?

Criticism of Judicial System

Look at your state's Rules of Professional Conduct in the 8's. Is there something that implies that legal professionals should strive for fairness and competence on the bench and earnestly protest the election or appointment of unsuitable people? Or does it simply say that legal professionals must not tell any lies about candidates for judicial office? If you are going to criticize, which is certainly your right, the criticism should be fair, restrained, and temperate and must not "lessen the public's image of the legal system."[13] To maintain the fair and independent administration of justice, legal professionals are also responsible for defending the judicial system when it is unjustly criticized. If you are working within the system, it only makes sense that you believe in it.

The judicial system may regulate the activities of attorneys more strictly than those of the average person, however. In one case, the attorney was quoted by a newspaper as having said that courts can sometimes be "incompetent and . . . downright crooked." The court found him in violation of the ethical canons.[14] Contrast that court decision with the court's decision in *Yagman*.

In *Standing Committee on Discipline v. Yagman*, 95 D.J. DAR 6873 (9th Cir. 1995), even when attorney Yagman made intemperate critical remarks about a judge being "anti-Semitic," the Ninth Circuit upheld his right to speak. Check it out!

ONE LAST WORD ABOUT INTEGRITY

Rule 8.1 says that legal professionals should be persons of integrity. The more integrity each of us brings to the profession, the better the legal system will be. Regardless of a person's expertise or extraordinary gift for the law, the person will still be held to high standards of moral and ethical conduct, as has been the case historically.

SERVE IN PUBLIC OFFICES

It is desirable for legal professionals to serve as legislators and other public officials because of their unique qualifications and knowledge of the law and high regard for the public welfare.[15] Remember, however, that we must not engage in activities that may result in conflict of interest with our law practice or employment.

Legal professionals campaigning for public offices are still bound by the Rules of Professional Conduct even though they could hold office without license.[16] Publishing statements that are in poor taste but only political rhetoric is not grounds for discipline, but publishing statements that we know to be false probably is. Whether you are pursuing a career in law, business, or politics, you will be held to the same ethical standards. We are protected by the First Amendment's guarantee of free speech so long as such speech does not constitute misconduct under the Rules that govern us. Since the state has a legitimate interest in the conduct of legal professionals, it may restrict the exercise of personal rights guaranteed by the Constitution.

> Did you know that about 37% of Congress is made up of lawyers? Why do you think that is? What is Congress' job in our government?

RULE #9 WRAP-UP

You've heard that quote from Shakespeare: first thing, let's kill all the lawyers. This saying accurately describes how many people feel about the legal profession—and that may include you! But the truth is that many legal professionals are out there trying to make the legal world a better place. Many people, whether through advocacy, changing the law, or teaching, are trying to make the law of America safe for Peevyhouses. Rule 9 creates yet another duty for us: the duty to make the legal system better. And despite a commonly held belief, there is a lot paralegals can do. Get elected to public office! Go to work for a firm that has a pro bono division and work on cases that deserve your hard work and dedication!

RULE #9 REVIEW QUESTIONS

1. What kinds of things can paralegals do to make the law better for the Peevyhouses?

2. How did the lawyer in *Molien v. Kaiser Hospital* change the law?

3. What is pro bono legal work, and how can you do it?

4. What are legal services programs? How are they funded?

5. Could you use your knowledge of law "improperly"? Give one example of what you could do. Why would it be "unethical"? What Rule would you be violating?

6. Attorney Yagman was disciplined for using his First Amendment freedom of speech. What did he say and why might some consider it a violation of his oath?

7. What is the downside of working on a case that is repugnant to you? What are some things you can do if you are assigned to such a case?

8. Is it ethical to criticize the judicial system? If it is, how, when, and where should it be done?

9. Why is holding a public office helping to improve the law? If you were elected to the U.S. Congress, what laws would you seek to change? How would those changes help to improve the legal system?

10. Is there a conflict of interest between holding an elected office and serving as a paralegal? Can you think of any instances where a conflict would arise?

---

[1] 382 P.2d 109 (Okl. 1960).

[2] See David L. Roth, *Tribute*, Comment vol. 1, no. 2 (Spring 1978).

[3] 616 P.2d 813 (Cal. 1980).

[4] 441 P.2d 912 (Cal. 1968).

[5] David Mellinkoff, *The Myth of Precision and the Law Dictionary*, 31 U.C.L.A. L. REV. 423, 425 (1983). See also Steven Stark, *Why Lawyers Can't Write*, 97 NEV. L. REV. 1389 (1984), one of the shortest law review articles in history.

[6] West Publishing Co. (1980). Rules cited with permission.

[7] Fed.R.Civ.P. 8(a)(1), (2).

[8] *Swierkiewicz v. Sorema N.A.*, 122 S.Ct. 992, 998 (2002).

[9] *Hagopian v. Justice Administrative Commission*, __ So.3d ___ (Fla. 2d DCA, No. 2D08-5077, August 12, 2009).

[10] The reference is to a classic novel by Robert Travers (pen name for a judge by the name of John D. Voelker), *To Kill a Mockingbird*.

[11] *Professional Responsibility—Report of the Joint Committee*, 44 ABAJ 1159, 1216 (1958).

[12] *In Matter of Gemmer*, 566 N.E.2d 528 (Ind. 1991).

[13] *Committee on Professional Ethics and Conduct of Iowa State Bar Assn. v. Horak*, 292 N.W.2d 129 (Iowa 1980). See also *Matter of Westfall*, 808 S.W.2d 829 (Mo. 1991) where the attorney made televised statements alleging purposefully dishonest conduct by the court of appeals judge, with reckless disregard for the truth or falsity of the statements. The court found that the attorney violated Rules 8.2(a) and 8.4(a) and (d) ". . . the rule, then, is sensitive to the possibility of its chilling effect and will not be interpreted to silence all lawyer criticism of the judicial system" (p. 836). Also see *In re Disciplinary Action against Graham*, 453 N.W.2d 313 (Minn. 1990).

[14] *Matter of Lacey*, 283 N.W.2d 250 (S.D. 1979).

[15] See your state's Rule 1.11(c).

[16] *State v. Russell*, 610 P.2d 1122, *cert. denied*, 449 U.S. 983, 101 S.Ct. 400 (1980).

Don't Even Think about It

AVOID THE APPEARANCE OF IMPROPRIETY

This is the last chapter of this book. There is an argument to be made that it should have been the first chapter. Maybe we need to begin here: It is not unusual for new paralegal students to be the subjects of unkind remarks such as "Why do you want to work for a lawyer?" "All lawyers are crooks," and "Lawyers are worse than used car salesmen." Newspapers and magazines frequently run "exposes" on attorney malpractice and illegal behavior by attorneys and judges. Because of the frequent emphasis on "dishonesty" in the legal field, many new students wonder if there is, in fact, a code of ethics for those in the legal profession. They are often surprised to hear how carefully attorneys scrutinize their own profession. In recent years, the legal profession has put an increasing amount of emphasis on avoiding even "the appearance" of improper behavior. This standard allows the profession to scrutinize and discipline for activities that do not fit exactly under any of the other nine categories. You will see, then, a potpourri of offenses here.

Because of the continuing concern of both society and the legal profession that the profession is filled with ethical problems, more emphasis is being placed on the *practical aspects* of legal ethics. In the 1970s, the American Bar Association insisted that its accredited law schools make mandatory a class in professional responsibility. It was not until the 1980s that the ABA placed this requirement on its accredited paralegal schools. Unfortunately, however, law school professional responsibility classes, like most law classes, emphasize the *theory* and not the *practical* aspects of the law. Many attorneys who have been disciplined for acts that did not constitute criminal behavior complain that their actions were "innocent," that they had no way of knowing that their acts were unethical. The ABA Model Code's Canon 9 ("avoid the appearance of impropriety") and its Ethical Considerations and

Disciplinary Rules were, over the years, the bases for disciplining those attorneys who did not break the law but committed an act that could have been interpreted by the public as being unethical and is, therefore, a blemish on the legal profession.

Avoiding not just obvious unethical acts but also the acts that may **appear** to be unethical is the topic of this amorphous Rule. As you have seen throughout this text, even an innocent act can take on the appearance of impropriety. Often, it will not be the good intentions of the legal professional (lawyers, paralegals, and others) that are recognized, but the way in which those acts are interpreted by an observer. This interpretation can mean the difference between embarrassing and costly disciplinary defense and someone's good reputation.

Conflict of Interest

Probably the most prevalent use of "avoid the appearance" in case law is in attorney/client conflict of interest problems. In one case where the Second District was feeling its way in conflict of interest and confidentiality problems, the court found that the attorney's actions were a violation of DR 9.101 (b) "[a] lawyer shall not accept private employment in a matter in which he had substantial responsibility while he was a public employee," where the attorney's actions did not violate any specific disciplinary rule.[1] Because this Rule's thrust goes to "appearance" and not actual "impropriety," it is arguable that consent by the former client to the conflict of interest will not (and should not) protect the attorney from discipline.

Judges, too, will be disqualified under the "appearance of impropriety" standard. In 2001, U.S. Court of Appeals disqualified U.S. district judge Thomas Penfield Jackson from further participation in the Microsoft monopoly prosecution for his public comments.[2] Judge Jackson gave media interviews and public speeches in which he made disparaging remarks about Microsoft such as his comment that Bill Gates had Napoleonic complex and that breaking up Microsoft would be like hitting a stubborn mule with a two-by-four.

Exaggeration

Feeling frisky is okay, but not very professional. In one case, the attorney in question scribbled "WRONG" in the margin of a district judge's opinion and then submitted the marked copy as an appendix to his brief to a reviewing court. The higher court found this conduct "indecorous and unprofessional."[3] Perhaps the higher court would have found this conduct amusing on another day, but the risk is too high.

WHAT DO YOU THINK?

The defendant is accused of impersonating the elected prosecutor to try to persuade the Red Cross to give him money for Hurricane Katrina victims. Other charges against him were based on theft. As the Prosecutor would be called as a witness, a special prosecutor was to be appointed to the case. Before the appointment could be made, however, the impersonation count was dropped. Should the court proceed with the appointment of a special prosecutor? This case was decided under the "appearance of impropriety" standard. Take a look: *Jones v. Indiana*, 901 N.E.2d 655 (2009).

To exaggerate to make a point is human nature. In the legal setting, however, it may give the appearance of impropriety. An attorney from Alaska was disciplined for saying that a claim brought against the attorney by a former client would waive "all" attorney/client privilege. In reality, this sort of claim only waives the privilege to the extent necessary for the attorney to defend himself. Although this statement was made in a letter to a lawyer, who probably knew that the statement was simply an exaggeration, the court found the exaggeration lacking in good judgment and cause for discipline.[4]

PROTECTING THE PUBLIC TRUST

The use and distribution of cocaine and marijuana have been held to be sufficient reason to discipline an attorney under the old Canon 9 "appearance of impropriety" standard, even though there was no proof that the commission of the crime was related to his professional capacity. The Alaska Supreme Court held that by committing a crime related to the use of drugs, Attorney Preston had harmed the public trust in the legal profession.[5]

Appearing in court intoxicated shows disrespect for the judicial system, in spite of the court's acknowledgment of California's strong inclination toward assisting, not punishing, those with alcohol dependency problems. Lying to the judge about the consumption of alcohol, however, was found by the court to be an unforgivable aggravating factor.[6] The attorney's behavior surely lowers the public's esteem for and trust in the legal profession.

In another case, offering to exchange legal services for sexual favors and having an affair with a client's wife were cause for disbarment under this Rule.[7] We learned this in Rule #1—Have Integrity. Remember: Close personal relationships with clients can cause conflict-of-interest problems for you at a later time.

> In *U.S. v. Blitstein*, 626 F.2d 774, *cert. denied*, 449 U.S. 1102, 101 S.Ct. 898 (1980), a small quantity of cocaine had been found in the possession of a young actor while he was visiting Denver on his way to Los Angeles to complete the filming of a television series. On the advice of his business attorney in Los Angeles, he hired Blitstein to represent him in Denver, expecting that charges would be brought against him. Thereafter, Blitstein and his paralegal (Pease) flew to California to meet with the actor, pretended to do extraordinary investigation on his case, intimidated him with stories of what the Denver police would do to him, and coerced large sums of money from him. In fact, neither Blitstein nor Pease had contacted the police with regard to a warrant for the actor's arrest, and there was no warrant. Both Blitstein and Pease were indicted for extortion. The Tenth Circuit Court of Appeals found Blitstein guilty, but the disposition of the court against Pease is not on the record. Since Pease's acts were of a criminal nature, Blitstein was not responsible for her under the doctrine of *respondeat superior.*

CLIENT MONEY AND TRUST ACCOUNTS

All of the states are in agreement with respect to the handling of client money and property. The Rules state that all money given to an attorney (other than fees and advances for costs) must be held by the attorney in a bank account that is separate from the attorney's business and personal accounts. This is ordinarily called a **Client Trust Account**. We talked about this briefly under Rule #4 on fair fees.

This is how it works: Each law firm usually has one bank account where all client money is held in trust, as opposed to a different bank account for each client. The money that clients give to the law firm as security that the bills will be paid (usually called a *retainer*) has not been earned by the law firm until the work is actually done or the hours are actually billed to and approved by the client. This money, then, still belongs to the client but is being held by the lawyer. This money is put into an account that is usually called a Client Trust Account, but some states call it a Lawyer's Trust Account or "Attorney's Trust Account." Monthly accountings must be made on those accounts, just as monthly statements are kept on personal checking and savings accounts. In many states, the interest that accrues on Client Trust Accounts is collected by the bank and given to the bar association (or some other designated organization or committee). This money is typically called IOLTA money: Interest On Lawyer Trust Accounts.[8] (It shouldn't be called a "Lawyer Trust Account." It should be called the Client's Trust Account.

The money belongs to the client, after all.) IOLTA monies are used to fund the legal service and pro bono organizations in each state. Although this money is crucial to the funding of legal services projects and pro bono organizations, there is an argument to be made that if the client has to have a great deal of money sitting in an account somewhere that the client can't use for something else, the client should be making interest on that money. This argument was made successfully in Florida,[9] but not in Washington.[10] Because these rulings were conflicting, the U.S. Supreme Court took up the issue. That Court said (in 2003) that IOLTA constitutes "taking" money but the government has the right to take money for the public good. This was excellent news for legal services and pro bono organizations and the thousands of people they serve each year. You can listen to the oral argument before the U.S. Supreme Court, you know, in this and other cases, by going to http://www.oyez.org. You are looking for *Brown v. Legal Foundation of Washington* (2003).

WHAT DO YOU THINK?

A group of attorneys in conjunction with the Florida Bar petitioned the Supreme Court of Florida to amend regulations with regard to Client Trust Accounts to allow attorneys to place client monies in interest-bearing accounts. The court's primary concern was that the monies be readily available for proper disbursement to clients and, secondarily, that the interest collected on such accounts be used for a community purpose, rather than a selfish purpose of the attorney. In approving the proposal and modifying the state's regulations in that area, the court praised the attorneys who initiated the action for upholding their affirmative duties to improve the law.[11] Rule #9: Work to Improve the Law. Did these lawyers do a good thing? Is it more ethical to do a good thing for your client or a good thing for the public?

Securities, promissory notes, stocks and bonds, and other property of the client must be labeled properly so that they are not mixed up together (commingled) with other clients' property. All of this stuff must be held in a safe place, such as an office safe or a bank. The attorney must promptly give client property and money over to the client upon request.

To comply with these trust account rules does not appear difficult, but lack of compliance is the source of many disciplinary actions. Probably because most attorneys don't care for administrative matters, labeling client property and maintaining proper accountings have become tasks popularly delegated to paralegals, office managers, and other nonlawyers. Remember, however, the lawyer will be held responsible for any misappropriation or misuse of funds. Delegation of these clerical and accounting tasks is the right thing to do, but supervision is mandatory.

The number of cases of attorney discipline for "commingling clients' funds" with the personal or business accounts of the attorney is staggering. **Commingling** occurs whenever the client's money is intermingled with the money of the attorney so that its separate identity is lost. If client money is placed in the position of being available for use by the attorney, remember, it will also be subject to claims against the attorney. By allowing client money to be subject to the personal or business debts of the attorney, the attorney violates an important duty that is owed to the client.

Attorneys have been disbarred for conversion of client funds by means of a fraudulent scheme.[12] Attorneys have been suspended from practice for commingling accounts and overdrawing their Client Trust Account.[13] In one case, a client gave money to his attorney to hold for him in an escrow account. The attorney put the money in his personal bank account until the check cleared and then transferred the money, minus his attorney's fees, into his Client Trust Account. The court found him in violation of a Rule regarding the *appearance of impropriety* for improperly handling client money and for failing to examine his monthly bank statements.[14]

Addition and subtraction are important skills for legal professionals. Courts discipline attorneys for letting the trust account funds fall below the amount they were responsible for holding for their clients.[15] When the Client Trust Account balance goes below $0, the bank will report the responsible lawyer to the disciplinary authority.

Law Firm Spotlight

Weil, Gotshal & Manges was the recipient of the ABA's pro bono award for 2009. WG&M has committed itself to setting a national example of law firm excellence in providing pro bono legal services. In 2004, the firm developed an innovative pro bono policy—every lawyer in the firm should perform 50 hours of pro bono work, every partner and counsel should take or supervise at least one pro bono matter, and every new lawyer should work on at least one pro bono matter. By implementing this policy, the firm nearly tripled its pro bono hours. A true leader in using technology to make the legal system better, WG&M is a beta subscriber to Pro Bono Net's interactive Pro Bono Manager. This fully integrated online portal serves as a repository of all materials relevant to the firm's pro bono practice. The repository makes all of the information accessible to all of their offices allowing them to do more, for more people, efficiently. It is no wonder that this firm received the Law Technology News Award for Most Innovative Use of Technology for a Pro Bono Project.

The disciplinary authority has an excellent chance of winning any case against an attorney that deals with the Client Trust Account because (1) banks regularly report any improper use of trust money or instances where the trust balance goes below zero; and (2) there is a paper trail provided by the bank records.

WHAT DO YOU THINK?

In *Clinard v. Blackwood,* 46 S.W.3d 177 (Tenn. 2001), Attorney represented the Blackwoods while a partner at LawFirm. After he moved to a different firm, his previous firm undertook representation of the Clinards in a case against the Blackwoods. When Attorney returned to LawFirm, it used screening procedures to prevent Attorney from sharing information about the Blackwoods' case with other lawyers. The Blackwoods' motion to disqualify LawFirm was denied by the trial court, reversed by the appellate court. The state supreme court disqualified LawFirm in spite of the appropriate screening procedures on the grounds that permitting the representation would give the public the **perception** that confiding in an attorney is sometimes a mistake because the attorney could suddenly switch sides. What do you think? Is that a valid argument in the twenty-first century? Is the public more savvy than that?

If you're wondering why this is so difficult for lawyers to understand, you are not alone. The simple fact is that lawyers are not trained to be bookkeepers. There are no "office management" classes in law school. The lawyer who strikes out on his or her own has to practice law, be the billing partner, and the office manager, and the bookkeeper all during the same 24-hour day. What's one easy solution? Hire a paralegal, of course!

COURTESY TO OPPOSING COUNSEL

Take a look at the titles of all of the Rules of Professional Conduct in the 3's—the rules that apply when we are advocates. Bring only meritorious claims; move the litigation along; be truthful with the court; be fair to opposing parties and their lawyers; and so on. This part of the rules of ethics does not come naturally to many people. It is, nevertheless, the rule, and arguably a better way to practice law. Remember this: The client is the litigant, not you. The client may have bad feelings toward the person on the other side of the matter, but you should not. Legal professionals should not allow the client's feelings to influence

If you haven't done this yet, Google "Attorney Kenneth Heller" and read some of the articles about his unprofessional behavior. He's another example of when you just have to wonder "what was he thinking?"

their attitude toward the opposing counsel.[16] No matter how tough litigation gets, a legal professional must always maintain his or her professionalism. Those who fail to offer the ordinary civilities of litigation, such as continuances, will be sanctioned.[17] And don't forget about Attorney Kenneth Heller who was disbarred in New York in 2009 for a history of incivilities to judges, lawyers, and clients.[18]

Personal attacks on opposing counsel are not permitted under any circumstances, regardless of what you may have seen on television. A criminal defense attorney was held in direct criminal contempt for making personal attacks against a prosecutor, accusing the prosecutor of "lying and cheating," even though the trial judge had not cautioned or warned counsel that his conduct could result in contempt, because his conduct was facially contemptuous. There were nine pages of trial transcript that showed repeated personal attacks against the prosecutor such as, "Let's see if we can cheat some more today . . . cheat, cheat, cheat."[19]

Some other specific instances of conduct that have been grounds for disciplinary action include calling opposing counsel "a sneak and a snitch" in open court;[20] accusing opposing counsel of bribing a witness and threatening physical violence;[21] and accusing opposing counsel of "playing dirty pool," using "smear tactics," "sandbagging witnesses," and a myriad of other colloquialisms.[22]

It is important for all legal professionals to maintain composure at all times during communications with opposing counsel and others in the judicial system. Personal attacks, rude comments, snide remarks, or statements made in anger will rarely, if ever, serve to help a situation and will more often than not exacerbate problems. Sometimes being calm can be of invaluable assistance to the people around you.

RELATIONSHIP WITH THE BENCH

Rule #10 is also responsible for the proposition that legal professionals must not state or imply that they are able by improper means to influence another member of the bar or judiciary. This means that it is improper to tell a member of the public that one has a special relationship with a judge that would influence the outcome of a case.

It is also a violation of the Rules for attorneys to accept employment that is offered to them because of their relationship with a member of the bench.

As we discussed under Rule #6 (Diligence and Dedication), it is improper to try to mislead the court. In a recent case from Florida, a lawyer filed a request for attorney's fees some of which the court denied because the time allegedly spent by "paralegals" was actually spent by the litigants themselves.[23] The court noted, "The inherent possibility for mischief in deeming the client a paralegal of the representing attorney is apparent enough to cast a dense shadow over even the mere theoretical prospect of the argument they make."

RULE #10 WRAP-UP

It is a proven fact that the public confidence in the legal profession has been "eroded" by acts that are misinterpreted by the public as being unethical acts. For that reason, it is a requirement that we keep clients informed about the progress of their matter and explain those actions we take that may be misunderstood. Rule #10, avoiding even the appearance of impropriety, also instructs legal professionals that where ethical guidance is unclear or nonexistent, they should steer their conduct in the direction that would promote the most public confidence in the profession.

The legal profession's primary task is to aid in providing quality legal assistance to the public at a reasonable cost. With this in mind, when a question arises to which there is no clear answer, take the path toward enhancing the public's confidence in the profession. In the areas where the law is clear, such as the integrity of the Client Trust Account, no excuses will be accepted.

When dealing with ethical principles, we cannot paint with broad strokes. The lines are fine and must be so marked. Guideposts can be established, but in the final analysis, we will all follow our own personal moral code.

RULE #10 REVIEW QUESTIONS

1. How does the concept of "protecting the public's trust" overlap with conflicts of interest?
2. What does the idea of being polite to the judge have to do with protecting the public's trust?
3. Is the phrase "appearance of impropriety" too vague? Can you define it?
4. What goes into a Client Trust Account?
5. What items that belong to the client should be kept in a safe or safe deposit box? Why?
6. Why are attorneys so often disciplined for trust account violations?
7. What can paralegals do to prevent trust account violations?
8. Do you agree that there should be a rule about being "courteous"? Isn't courtesy optional under the First Amendment?
9. What do you think is a proper penalty for trying to mislead the court?
10. Do you think that most or many lawyers are dishonest? Do you think that the public has this perception? What can paralegals do to correct that image?

1 *Armstrong v. McAlprin*, 606 F.2d 28 (2d Cir. 1979).

2 *United States v. Microsoft*, 253 F.3d 34 (D.C. Cir. 2001).

3 *Allen v. Seidman*, 881 F.2d 375 (7th Cir. 1989).

4 *Disciplinary Matter Involving Frost*, 863 P.2d 843 (Alaska 1993).

5 *Matter of Preston*, 616 P.2d 1 (Alaska 1980).

6 *Ridge v. State Bar*, 766 P.2d 569 (Cal. 1989).

7 *Grievance Committee v. Broder*, 152 A. 292 (Conn. 1930), a case still cited in the eastern states.

8 There are and have been cases contesting this practice. Some people believe that the client is entitled to the interest that his money makes while it is sitting in the attorney's trust account.

9 *Phillips v. Washington Legal Foundation*, 524 U.S. 156, 118 S.Ct. 1925 (1998).

10 *Brown v. Legal Foundation of Washington*, 538 U.S. 216 (2003).

11 *In re Interest on Trust Accounts*, 356 So.2d 799 (Fla. 1978).

12 *People v. Margolin*, 820 P.2d 347 (Colo. 1991).

13 *In re Grant*, 433 N.E.2d 259 (Ill. 1982). A strong dissent recommended disbarment.

14 *In re Hines*, 482 A.2d 378 (D.C.App. 1984).

15 *In re Feder*, 442 N.E.2d 912 (Ill. 1982). See also, *Black v. State Bar*, 368 P.2d 118 (Cal. 1962); *Cutler v. State Bar*, 455 P.2d 108 (Cal. 1969); and *Vaughn v. State Bar*, 494 P.2d 1257 (Cal. 1972).

16 See Rule 3.4, Fairness to Opposing Counsel.

17 See *Bates v. State Bar*, 275 Cal.Rptr. 381 (1990), and *Laguna Auto Body v. Farmers Ins. Exchange*, 282 Cal.Rptr. 530 (1991). In *Laguna Auto Body*, the court used the terminating sanction against counsel who abused the system.

18 *Emanuel v Sheridan Transp. Corp.*, 2009 NY Slip Op 00458 [58 AD3d 583] (2009).

19 *Arrant v. State*, 537 So.2d 150 (Fla.App. 1989).

20 *In re Elam*, 211 S.W.2d 710, *cert. denied*, 335 U.S. 872, 69 S.Ct. 161 (1948).

21 *Leimer v. Hulse*, 178 S.W.2d 336, *rein. denied*, 323 U.S. 744, 65 S.Ct. 60 (1944).

22 *State v. Turner*, 538 P.2d 966 (Kan. 1975).

23 *Lewis v. Nical of Palm Beach, Inc.*, 815 So.2d 647, 652 (Fla. 4th 2009).

APPENDIX A

ABA Model Rules and Corresponding California Rules

ABA Model	Topic	California Rule
1.1	Competence	3-110
1.2(d)	Involvement in violation of the law	3-210
1.3	Diligence	3-110
1.4	Communication	3-500, 3-510
1.5	Financial Arrangements Among Lawyers	2-200
1.6	Confidentiality	3-100; B&P Code 6068
1.7	Conflicts: Current Clients	3-310
1.8	Gifts from Client	4-400
1.8(h)	Limiting Liability to Client	3-400
1.8(a)	Paying client expenses	4-210
1.8(j)	Intimate Relations with client	3-120
1.9	Duties to Former Clients	3-310(E)
no rule	Intimate Relations with Other Party's Lawyer	3-320
1.10	Impute Conflicts of Interest	no CA rule
1.11	Conflicts: Government Employees	no CA rule
1.12	Former Judge	no CA rule
1.13	Organization as Client	3-600
1.14	Client with Diminished Capacity	no CA rule
1.15	Safekeeping Property	4-100
1.16	Declining/Terminating Representations	3-700
1.17	Sale of Law Practice	2-300
1.18	Duties to Prospective Client	no CA rule
2.1	Lawyer as Advisor	no CA rule
2.4	Lawyer as Third Party Neutral	no CA Rule
3.1	Meritorious Claims	3-200
3.2	Expediting Litigation	B&P Code 6128
3.3	Candor Toward Tribunal	5-200; B&P 6068(d); 6128(a)
3.4	Fairness to Opposing Counsel and Party	5-200; 5-220; 5-310
3.5	Impartiality and Decorum of the Tribunal	5-300; 5-320
3.6	Trial Publicity	5-120
3.7	Lawyer as Witness	5-210

(continued)

ABA Model	Topic	California Rule
3.8	Special Responsibility of Prosecutor	5-110
3.9	Advocate in Nonadjudicative Proceedings	no CA Rule
3.10	Threatening Criminal Charges	5-100
4.1	Truthfulness in Statements to Others	B&P Code 6068; 6128
4.2	Communication with a Person Represented by Counsel	2-100
4.3	Dealing with Unrepresented Person	no CA Rule
5.1	Responsibilities of Partners, etc.	3-110?
5.2	Responsibilities of Subordinate Lawyer	no CA Rule
5.3	Responsibilities Regarding Nonlawyer Assistants	3-110
5.4	Avoid Interference with a Lawyer's Professional Independence	1-310; 1-320; 1-600
	Employing Disbarred lawyers	1-311
5.5	Multijurisdictional Practice as UPL	1-300
5.6	Restrictions on a Lawyer's Right to Practice	1-500
6.1	Voluntary Pro Bono	no CA Rule
6.2	Accepting Appointments	B&P Code 6068(h); 3-700
6.3	Membership in Legal Services Org.	no CA Rule
6.4	Law Reform Activities	no CA Rule
7.1–7.5	Advertising	1-400; B&P Code 6155, 6157-6159.2
7.2	Advertising	no CA Rule
7.3	Solicitation	1-400
7.4	Fields of Practice	1-400
7.5	Firm Names and Letterheads	1-400
8.1	False Statement Re Application for Admission to Practice	1-200
8.2	Judicial and Legal Officials	B&P Code 6068
8.3	Reporting Professional Misconduct	1-500; B&P 6068
8.4	Misconduct	1-120

APPENDIX B

State Rules Numbering System

State	Numbering system	Website where you can find state rules of professional conduct	
Alabama	Same numbering	http://www.alabar.org/ogc/	
Alaska	Same numbering	http://www.state.ak.us/courts/prof.htm	
Arizona	Same numbering	http://www.myazbar.org/Ethics/rules.cfm	
Arkansas	Same numbering	http://courts.state.ar.us/rules/ current_ark_prof_conduct/index.cfm	
California	**Completely different!**	http://www.calbar.ca.gov	
Colorado	Same numbering	http://www.cobar.org/index.cfm/ID/384/ CETH/Colorado-Rules-of-Professional-Conduct/	
Connecticut	Same numbering	http://www.law.cornell.edu/ethics/ct/code/ CT_CODE.HTM	
D.C.	Same numbering	http://www.dcbar.org/for_lawyers/ethics/ legal_ethics/rules_of_professional_conduct/ amended_rules/index.cfm#board	
Delaware	Same numbering	http://courts.state.de.us/Rules/ ?FinalDLRPCclean.pdf	
Florida	*Similar numbering*	http://www.floridabar.org/divexe/rrtfb.nsf/ FV?Openview&Start=1&Expand=4#4	add 4- before rule number; Rule 1.1 looks like this "Rule 4-1.1"
Georgia	Same numbering	http://www.gabar.org/handbook/rules_index/	
Hawaii	Same numbering	http://www.state.hi.us/jud/ctrules/hrpcond.pdf	
Idaho	Same numbering	http://www2.state.id.us/isb/rules/irpc.htm	
Illinois	Same numbering	http://www.iardc.org/rulesprofconduct.html	
Indiana	Same numbering	http://www.in.gov/judiciary/rules/prof_conduct/ index.html	
Iowa	*Similar numbering*	http://www.iowacourts.gov/Professional_ Regulation/Rules_of_Professional_Conduct/	Chapter 32
Kansas	Same numbering	http://www.kscourts.org/rules/Rule-List.asp? r1=Rules+Relating+to+Discipline+of+ Attorneys	
Kentucky	Same numbering	http://www.kybar.org/Default.aspx?tabid=237	additional supreme Court Rule number

(continued)

State	Numbering system	Website where you can find state rules of professional conduct	
Louisiana	Same numbering	http://www.ladb.org/Publications/rules_of_prof_conduct.pdf	
Maine	Same numbering	http://www.maine.gov/tools/whatsnew/attach.php?id=68628&an=1	as of August 2009
Maryland	Same numbering	http://www.law.cornell.edu/ethics/md/code/MD_CODE.HTM	
Massachus	Same numbering	http://www.mass.gov/obcbbo/rpcnet.htm	
Michigan	Same numbering	http://courtofappeals.mijud.net/rules/documents/5MichiganRulesOfProfessionalConduct.pdf	
Minnesota	Same numbering	http://www.mncourts.gov/lprb/05mrpc.html	
Mississippi	Same numbering	http://www.mssc.state.ms.us/rules/msrulesofcourt/rules_of_professional_conduct.pdf	
Missouri	*Similar numbering*	http://www.courts.mo.gov/	put 4- in front
Montana	Same numbering	http://www.montanacourts.org/supreme/rules/rules_of_professional_conduct.pdf	
Nebraska	*Similar numbering*	http://www.supremecourt.ne.gov/rules/pdf/Ch3Art5.pdf	put 3-50 in front Rule 1.1 becomes Rule 3-501.1
Nevada	Same numbering	http://www.leg.state.nv.us/CourtRules/RPC.html	
New Hampshire	Same numbering	http://www.courts.state.nh.us/rules/pcon/index.htm	
New Jersey	Same numbering	http://www.judiciary.state.nj.us/rules/apprpc.htm	
New Mexico	*Similar numbering*	in the process of being revised	put 16- in front, take out "point"; Insert 0 in the middle of two digit numbers. Number 1.1 turns into 16-101 Number 3.1 turns into 15-301. Rule 1.15, however, turns into 16-115.
New York	Same numbering	http://www.nysba.org/Content/NavigationMenu/ForAttorneys/ProfessionalStandardsforAttorneys/Professional_Standar.htm	as of April 1, 2009
North Carolina	Same numbering	http://www.ncbar.com/rules/rpcsearch.asp	
North Dakota	Same numbering	http://www.court.state.nd.us/rules/conduct/frameset.htm	
Ohio	Same numbering	http://www.law.cornell.edu/ethics/oh/code/OH_CODE.HTM	
Oklahoma	Same numbering	http://www.okbar.org/ethics/ORPC.htm	

State	Numbering system	Website where you can find state rules of professional conduct	
Oregon	Same numbering	http://www.osbar.org/_docs/rulesregs/orpc.pdf	
Pennsylvania	Same numbering	http://www.padisciplinaryboard.org/documents/Pa RPC.pdf	
Rhode Island	Same numbering	http://www.courts.state.ri.us/supreme/disciplinary/rulesofprofessionalconduct.htm	
South Carolina	Same numbering	http://www.scbar.org/member_resources/rules_of_conduct/	
South Dakota	Same numbering	http://www.sdbar.org/Rules/Rules/PC_Rules.htm	
Tennessee	Same numbering	http://www.tba.org/ethics/TRPC_2008.pdf	
Texas	*Similar numbering*	http://www.txethics.org/reference_rules.asp?view=conduct	add a zero in two digit numbers; Rule 1.1 becomes Rule 1.01 but Rule 1.18 stays Rule 1.18
Utah	Same numbering	http://www.utcourts.gov/resources/rules/ucja/index.htm# Chapter 13	
Vermont	Same numbering	http://www.vermontjudiciary.org/	
Virginia	Same numbering	http://www.vsb.org/docs/rules-pc_2007-08pg.pdf	
Washington	Same numbering	http://www.courts.wa.gov/	
West Virginia	Same numbering	http://www.wvbar.org/	
Wisconsin	Same numbering	Add Supreme Court Rule 20: SCR20:1.15 == http://www.wicourts.gov/supreme/sc_rules.jsp	
Wyoming	Same numbering	http://courts.state.wy.us/CourtRules_Entities.aspx?RulesPage=AttorneysConduct.xml	

INDEX

CASE INDEX